Selling Suffrage

Popular Cultures, Everyday Lives

SELLING
SUFFRAGE

CONSUMER CULTURE
&VOTES FOR WOMEN

MARGARET FINNEGAN

COLUMBIA UNIVERSITY PRESS NEW YORK

Columbia University Press
Publishers Since 1893
New York Chichester, West Sussex
Copyright © 1999 Columbia University Press
All rights reserved

Library of Congress Cataloging-in-Publication Data
Finnegan, Margaret Mary, 1965–
Selling suffrage : consumer culture and votes for women /
Margaret Finnegan.
p.   cm. — (Popular cultures, everyday lives)
Includes bibliographical references and index.
ISBN 0–231–10738–2. — ISBN 0–231–10739–0
1. Women—Suffrage—United States—History. 2. Women's rights—
United States—History. 3. Political culture—United States—History. 4. Popular
culture—United States—History. 5. Advertising—Social aspects—United States—
History.   I. Title.   II. Series.
JK1896.F56   1999
324.6'23'0973—dc21   98-7438

Casebound editions of Columbia University Press books are printed
on permanent and durable acid-free paper.
Printed in the United States of America
c 10 9 8 7 6 5 4 3 2 1
p 10 9 8 7 6 5 4 3 2 1

To Steve

Contents

Acknowledgments

I gratefully thank all of the individuals who took time out of their busy schedules to read and comment upon different parts and drafts of this work. Eric Monkkonen, Cecile Whiting, George Lipsitz, and two anonymous readers for Columbia University Press provided valuable advice on improving the dissertation upon which this manuscript is based. Regina Morantz-Sanchez and Lisa Jacobson generously commented on both the dissertation and the revised manuscript. Their help, friendship, and intellectual engagement contributed to any strengths this work may possess. Earlier drafts of this work also benefited from the cogent criticisms of Sue Gonda, Jim Pearson, Allison Sneider, and Barbara Wallace. Likewise, Sarah Stage, George Lipsitz, Paula Baker, and Michael McGerr pushed me to clarify my thoughts and arguments by critiquing conference papers I delivered before the Western Association of Women Historians, the Organization of American Historians, and the American Historical Association.

Other individuals and institutions also deserve a word of appreciation. A conversation with Ellen DuBois led me to the Alice Paul Papers at the Huntington Library. Paul's papers are a gold mine for anyone interested in what the material culture of the suffrage movement meant to suffragists. Paul's papers, in turn, led me to the Huntington's Susan B. Anthony Ephemera Collection, a treasure trove of suffrage memorabilia and clippings. I am particularly grateful to Cathy Cherbosque for allowing me such wonderful access to the collection. Financial support from UCLA allowed me to carry out important parts of the research and to finish the dissertation in a timely manner.

My good friend Margo McBain helped me in countless ways. Barbara Goldman and Bridget Gallitin provided timely help in tracking down several of the photographs included in this book. I am grateful to my mother, Janice Pumpelly, for a lifetime of encouragement and love. Finally, I could not have finished this manuscript without the unwavering support of Stephen Finnegan. He read every chapter and listened to all of my ideas, and he never stopped doubting the value of my professional endeavors, even when their rewards seemed unclear. I dedicate this book to him.

List of Illustrations

Selling Suffrage

Introduction

I first learned about the American woman suffrage movement by watching Saturday morning cartoons in the mid-1970s. Interspersed between the weekly fare of smart-alecky animals, death-defying superheroes, and sugar-coated cereal commercials, the American Broadcasting Company used to show a series of short, animated, educational spots entitled *Schoolhouse Rock* (still on the air today). Along with segments on grammar and mathematics, the series included several pieces on American history, one of which summarized the fight for the Nineteenth Amendment, which gave women the right to vote. With a catchy tune and a hip-looking heroine, "Sufferin' Thru Suffrage" revealed that women themselves demanded the ballot, that they took to the streets on behalf of their principles, and that, ultimately, democracy triumphed.[1]

Since I began this project, that cartoon's images and musical refrains have randomly intruded on my consciousness. Initially, I linked the memory to my "sufferin' thru" the researching and writing of the dissertation that was to become this book. Upon further reflection, I realized that my recollection also revealed a lot about the dialogical nature of historical practice. This Saturday morning entertainment highlights for me the engagement between my own past and present, and between past and present interpretations of the woman suffrage movement. It reminds me that history always reflects conversations between interpreter and interpreted, and between bygone events and current circumstances. Some scholars bemoan the lack of concrete affirmations and fixed representations that such an open-ended model of historical practice suggests, but these continuous dialogues make the study of history dynamic and exciting.[2] They provoke new questions about old, familiar subjects, and uncover fresh, meaningful perspectives for understanding

American life. With regard to this study, for example, topical inspiration stemmed as much from wanting to understand the historical roots of contemporary equations between women's liberation and consumerism ("You've Come a Long Way, Baby") as from a deep-felt interest in the seventy-year struggle to enfranchise women.

Interest in these issues helped me conceptualize an area of historical inquiry, but my specific research goals were shaped by a diverse body of sources connecting consumer capitalism and the twentieth-century, nonradical woman suffrage movement. Suffrage organization records, suffrage and commercial newspapers and magazines, and the papers, memoirs, and memorabilia of suffragists reveal a long-ignored facet of the movement and its political culture: the larger cultural context in which suffragists practiced the art of politics. These sources highlight the adaptation of a group of activist women to an increasingly urban, commercial, consumer-capitalist environment. In many ways, this adaptation translated into full-scale appropriation. Particularly during the 1910s, suffragists incorporated modern methods of advertising, publicity, mass merchandising, and mass entertainment into their fight for voting rights. They adopted commercial standards of design and display. They equated consumer rights with consumer desire. But suffragists also added their own slant to capitalism's consumerist thrust by reworking its basic assumptions to fit their ideology. When industries tried to sell goods by extolling women's public presence, suffragists turned this approbation into a justification for expanding the boundaries of women's space. When advertisers celebrated modern notions of personality, suffragists followed suit, creating idealized performing selves— walking, talking representations of glorified womanhood—epitomizing the worthy woman voter. And when department stores, manufacturers, and a changing society made consumption central to middle-class women's lives, suffragists turned their roles as shoppers into arguments for granting women the ballot. Blending political aspirations with everyday duties, suffragists redefined both "voter" and "shopper," making both terms synonymous with responsible, rational, and empowering action.

By acknowledging the overlapping boundaries between commercial and political culture, suffragists contributed to a growing public dialogue about American politics in an age of mass culture and consumerism. Could mass culture aid the democratic process? Might it foster rational discourse about issues of national importance, such as suffrage? Did consumerism prepare women for voting, or did it prove their disqualification for this sacred right? Would consumerism and the technologies of mass entertainment level the playing field between elites and nonelites, men and women, public actors and spectators? In the late nineteenth and early twentieth centuries, the answers to these questions were far from certain, and many suffragists expressed a vested interest in them. In some cases, suffragists linked these questions to early feminist demands, including voting rights and greater public freedom and responsibility for women. Just as often, however, such questions became springboards for debating the mutually constitutive aspects of consumer and political culture, and consumer and political identity. Suffragists were not the sole participants in this debate. They responded to, and crossed paths with, retailers, advertisers, manufacturers, writers, cartoonists, antisuffragists, voters, and other progressive reformers.

Nor did all suffragists voice the same opinions. In answering critics and promoting votes for women, suffragists—sometimes even the same ones—came to different conclusions about how membership in a consumer society affected politics and political life. Some suffragists emphasized the promotional side of consumerism. Emulating popular commercial strategies, they strove to sell the movement like a modern commodity. Often disdaining political opinion as a product of emotional and spectatorial manipulation, these reformers attempted to sway minds through the colorful methods of advertising and merchandising. Other suffragists protested against unregulated consumer industries. For them, consumer identity *was* political identity. They believed only politicized—voting—women shoppers could protect families against unfair and unethical business practices. Both positions—a focus on which simplifies the multiplicity of consumer-centered perspectives suffragists held—confirmed the assumption that consumer experiences would affect voting behavior.

In what ways and to what extent did suffragists and others expect consumerism to wield such influence? Teasing out the answers to such questions requires an exploration not just of the progressive-era suffrage movement but also of the long history of women's struggle for voting rights. That exploration will take us from the cerebral to the spectacular, from the politics of character to the politics of personality, from the justification of woman suffrage to the business of woman suffragists, and from the desire for liberty to the manipulation of desire.

Despite a wealth of source material, historians have largely ignored the connections between consumerism and the woman suffrage movement. In many cases, researchers of women's political history have actually divorced the suffrage movement from its cultural context. Narrow definitions of political discourse have prompted scholars to concentrate on changes in ideology, conflicting strands of radicalism and conservatism, and the difficulties of instigating and sustaining mass movements. These arguments stress traditional historical texts—letters, political writings, memoirs—that clarify change over time, the evolution of ideas, and differences in opinion, providing insight into women's struggle for voting rights and into the competing organizational structures established by suffragists of different perspectives, regions, and time frames. They also demonstrate that women have a political history and that political history must use gender as an analytical tool.[3]

Historians generally agree on the movement's basic outlines. Although eighteenth-century women like Mary Wollstonecraft and Abigail Adams demanded greater rights for women, most historians trace the roots of the woman suffrage movement to the radical abolitionism of the 1830s and 1840s. As Ellen DuBois argues, by providing a language of political action and collective political experience, abolitionists gave American women of all classes the necessary tools for debating their own political status.[4] The first organized demand for female enfranchisement occurred at the famous Seneca Falls convention of 1848, where Elizabeth Cady Stanton and other woman's rights leaders met to discuss the status of American women. With the American Declaration of Independence as their guide, they proclaimed: "We hold these truths to be self-evident: that all men *and women* are created equal; that they are endowed by their Creator with certain inalienable rights; that among these are life, liberty, and the pursuit of happiness; that to secure these rights governments are instituted, deriving their just powers from the consent of the governed" (italics added).[5]

Faith in natural rights united suffragists in their radical charge against tradition, but Reconstruction politics tore the movement apart. Disagreement over support for the Fifteenth Amendment, which enfranchised black men but not women, divided suffrage supporters. Refusing to endorse the amendment, Susan B. Anthony and Elizabeth Cady Stanton became estranged from their former abolitionist colleagues. Tensions grew worse when they formed the National Woman Suffrage Association in 1869, which excluded men from membership and backed numerous, sometimes controversial, woman's rights causes. Dismayed by the actions of Anthony and Stanton, Lucy Stone and her husband Henry B. Blackwell became the leading forces in the moderate American Woman Suffrage Association (also formed in 1869), a mixed-sex, primarily middle-class organization that limited its efforts strictly to suffrage.[6] Although the two groups merged in 1890 to form the country's most influential suffrage group, the National American Woman Suffrage Association (NAWSA), conflict and disorganization continued.[7]

By this time, suffrage arguments had expanded beyond natural rights. Most scholars have emphasized the growing conservatism of the suffrage movement during this time. White, middle-class suffragists who saw the vote as both a right and a potential tool for reforming society lauded enfranchisement as a way of protecting and expanding the domestic sphere. They contended that voting women could outlaw alcohol and other vices that seemed to threaten both the social order and the economic and physical security of women and children.[8] Believing that enfranchised white women would defend white supremacy and middle-class hegemony, some suffragists made the movement an instrument for preserving dominant class and racial privileges.[9] Still others continued to see suffrage as part of a bold effort to reconceptualize women's roles.[10] These different viewpoints converged and disengaged in surprising and complicated ways, as exemplified by the shifting ideology of Elizabeth Cady Stanton. Few suffragists more eloquently stated the natural rights claims of women than she. Yet, as Ellen DuBois notes, ongoing frustration over the movement's failures narrowed her once-radical vision. Eventually Stanton embraced racist and elitist arguments emphasizing why white, middle-class, and elite women deserved the vote more than black men and immigrants of both sexes.[11]

Different ideological and tactical perspectives kept the late nineteenth-century suffrage movement divided. Not until twentieth-century suffragists accepted their own heterogeneity were they able to create an accessible and successful mass movement. According to Steven Buechler and Nancy Cott, by the time the Nineteenth Amendment passed in 1920, the suffrage movement represented so many things to so many people that a powerful, newly emergent alliance among elite, middle-class, and working-class women guaranteed its triumph over fractious internal discord, dissension over gender roles, and even a world war.[12]

Suffragists disagreed not only on why women needed the vote, but also on how to win it. Some—particularly those in the South—advocated state referenda. Others pushed for a constitutional amendment. In theory, the NAWSA had always favored a federal suffrage amendment, but it did not actively pursue one until 1916, after the brilliant Carrie Chapman Catt became the Association's president. By that time, a new group of radicals committed to a national suffrage bill had challenged NAWSA leadership. Led primarily by followers of Harriot Stanton Blatch's Women's Political Union (WPU) and Alice Paul's Congressional Union (CU), these women (along with several successful western state campaigns in the early 1910s) helped awaken the movement from the self-proclaimed "doldrums" of roughly 1896 to 1910.[13] Infusing the cause with a well-needed dose of spectacle, drama, and cross-class appeal, radicals made woman suffrage a topic of national interest. They inaugurated woman suffrage parades, mass meetings, and entertainments; they aggressively lobbied state and federal legislatures, vocally criticized government, and refused to defer to either authority or tradition.[14]

Recently, historians have looked extensively at radical suffragists, somewhat skewing the record in favor of their activities.[15] Most American suffragists disdained radicalism and supported nonradical groups like the NAWSA, which had more than two million members by 1920. In order to distinguish themselves from their bolder colleagues, these women often described their brand of suffragism as conservative. In evaluating competing suffrage campaigns, historians have followed suit. But the conservative label is misleading. Even after its well-studied break with the CU in 1913, supporters of NAWSA remained politically and ideologically diverse. They ranged from socialists and Greenwich Village freethinkers to staunch Republicans and Dixiecrats. Although they often sided with the Association only grudgingly, most suffragists approved of its two-pronged emphasis on discreet political lobbying and well-publicized—albeit "respectable"—promotionalism.[16] For these reasons, women who allied with the NAWSA will be termed nonradical or mainstream in this study.

Among other points of contention, mainstream suffragists believed radicals used inappropriate and overly sensational political methods. Conflict between the two camps came to a head during World War I. By this time, Paul and Blatch had combined forces to form the National Woman's Party (NWP). Seeking to dramatically highlight the disjunction between fighting for democracy abroad and denying it to women at home, radicals picketed the White House with banners reading: "MR. PRESIDENT, how long must women wait for liberty?" They soon captured the attention of newsreel cameras, journalists, unamused politicians, and violent crowds. In response, nonradicals tried desperately to distinguish themselves from women in the NWP. NAWSA officer Maud Park begged newspaper editors to explain the differences between radical and nonradical suffragists. She even asked them to "leave out the words 'suffrage' and 'suffragists' in all accounts of activities of the Woman's Party."[17] Most of all, nonradicals distanced themselves from their rivals by emphasizing war work. Hopeful that a strong display of patriotism would prove their worthiness to vote and obligate presidential and congressional support for the movement, nonradicals vigorously defended and served American militarism. They funded foreign hospitals, aided servicemen, and freed up industrial and agricultural production for military needs by teaching thriftiness and home-production methods to women.

Although mainstream suffragists eschewed the radical label, they did not feel bound to traditional methods of political campaigning. Despite their protests to the contrary, they found inspiration in militants' embrace of political spectacle. Like their rivals, nonradical suffragists organized parades, pageants, mass meetings, and public performances. They likewise founded woman suffrage retail shops, produced suffrage movies, actively pushed in-house publications, and promoted woman suffrage fashions and mass-produced commodities. Not the staid, drab activists they are often characterized as, mainstream suffragists were inspired political beings who looked to the world around them for fresh tools of public persuasion. Their willingness to mix new and old campaign tactics not only made them savvy but also put them at the forefront of an emerging, commercialized style of politics.

Scholars have not adequately measured this aspect of the nonradical movement. According to Steven Buechler, for example, the use of these tactics during the 1910s reflected the now well-financed movement's new commitment to reaching a broad base of cross-class supporters.[18] This may be true, but it suggests only part of the story. Cultural expression is a complicated affair. Ideology and social conventions have a strong hold on behavior. During the 1910s, Americans remained ambivalent about women's relationship to the world outside the home. Shopping, employment, and voluntarism made women's physical presence a reality of urban, outdoor life. Yet middle-class individuals in particular placed limits on "respectable" women's access to public space. These sanctions constrained the middle-class and elite white women who constituted an important segment of the mainstream movement. One look at their initially wary regard for political spectacle makes this fact perfectly clear.

Explaining why these women adopted spectacular methods of public protest requires a new approach to women's political history—one that pays close attention to the color and complexity of American culture and its various discursive outlets. As cultural theorists remind us, discourse includes far more than linguistic communication. It signifies the full spectrum of verbal and nonverbal ways individuals and societies debate social norms and cultural power. From the movement's beginning, suffragists expressed their demands in material fashion. Whether disrupting civic celebrations or wearing yellow badges, suffragists gave tangible form to their beliefs. Furthermore, they gave these acts ideological significance by associating the movement with the principles of sisterhood, equality, democracy, and feminine virtue. In so doing, suffragists created a diverse, sustainable political culture with a distinct performative dimension.

As the movement's cultural expressions and meanings changed over time, they revealed critical subtexts that seldom found voice in argument and debate. Exploring this occluded dimension of the movement helps reveal the rationale behind the increasingly bold and dramatic nature of twentieth-century, nonradical suffragists' political culture. Women in the mainstream movement explained highly theatrical and public political experiences in ways that made sense to their understanding of social reality. Significantly, by the 1910s, the culture of consumer capitalism was essential to that understanding.

Consumer capitalism refers to a mode of capitalist organization based on the sale of primarily mass-produced and mass-marketed goods. Its culture, variously labeled consumer culture, commercial culture, and the culture of abundance, reflects the competing values, worldviews, and social structures of that system. According to William Leach, during the late nineteenth and early twentieth centuries, the principal characteristics of this culture included "acquisition and consumption as the means of achieving happiness; the cult of the new; the democratization of desire (the belief that individuals had the right to desire the same goods); and money value as the predominant measure of all value in society."[19] Advertisers, marketers, consumer manufacturers, and large-scale retailers have held enormous sway in consumer culture. They have encouraged individuals to see commodities as central to the construction of personal identity, and they have influenced perceptions of public space by using architecture, billboards, signage, and window displays to equate looking with desire and progress with consumerism.

The roots of this culture are in the consumer revolution of eighteenth-century England. As new industrial technologies made goods like china and toys available to unprecedented numbers of buyers, a new middle class centered around conspicuous consumption, and social emulation emerged. The explosion in consumer goods also affected workers' living standards. Inexpensive calicos, fashion dolls, and the like gave even individuals on the margins of society a taste of ownership.[20] In the United States, the culture of consumer capitalism did not begin to assume its modern shape until after the Civil War, when large-scale industrialization, urbanization, immigration, and capital development changed the social and economic face of the nation. Mass production required mass consumption, and new urban institutions such as department stores proved quick to market the fruits of industrial labor and to tempt buyers with increasingly elaborate displays and sales methods. Using what Leach calls a "commercial aesthetic" of color, light, and spectacle, retailers organized design, abundance, and fantasy into a strikingly vibrant, visual celebration of commodities. Beginning in the 1880s, this aesthetic began to transform the urban landscape. Electric signs, enormous billboards, window displays, and giant commercial buildings made city space a giant, theatricalized venue for promoting the sale of material goods.[21]

Debates over the nature of modern identity accompanied these developments. Distraught by what some saw as an epidemic of spiritual and emotional ennui, religious and medical thinkers urged Americans to experience life more vigorously. They encouraged individuals to participate in wilderness adventures, military service, and other activities that challenged the oppressive staleness of an overcivilized society. Advertisers and merchandisers tapped into this emotional trend by promoting commercial goods as the key to more dynamic and charismatic identities. True vitality, they suggested, came from self-fulfillment. And fulfilling selfhood was just a mouth wash or a hair tonic away. As these commercial and noncommercial calls for self-actualization became more prominent, concepts of inherent character gave way to faith in personality- and commodity-defined lifestyles.[22]

Although influenced by such changes, American consumers were not hapless victims. Other forces—such as religion, ethnicity, class, gender, education, and tradition—structured their systems of belief, influencing how they negotiated commercial culture's boundaries and messages.[23] American women carved out a special place in this environment. As Mary Ryan notes, by the early nineteenth century shopping had become an important responsibility for middle-class, urban women.[24] Reliant on the marketplace for daily needs and badges of middle-class respectability, these women developed an almost symbiotic relationship with the entrepreneurs they kept in business. As a modern consumer economy took shape later in the century, the ties between women shoppers and businesses became even closer. Targeting middle-class women with the time and resources to shop, department stores and other sales-oriented businesses worked hard to coax these prized customers into their tantalizing new world. Using artful displays and drawings to wear down buyer resistance and abundant assurances of women's worth to validate consumption, these establishments tightened the links between women and shopping.[25]

However, advertisers, retailers, marketers, and other institutions dedicated to an expanded consumer marketplace maintained a Janus-faced relationship with buyers. Although they flattered women shoppers in public, they degraded and insulted them in professional and managerial forums. In part, this stemmed from professional ambivalence about the growing social and economic importance of their work. Cultural valorization of Jeffersonian, independent producer-citizens and a long-standing American suspicion of luxury stood in contrast to the inducements and goals of retailers, manufacturers, and advertisers. Promoters of consumerism made sense of this contradiction by faulting shoppers. They described their clientele as irrational, narcissistic, easily swayed, impulsive, and pathological. Thus, women who succumbed to the lures of advertising and merchandising had only themselves to blame. Writers, physicians, and psychiatrists echoed this representation, agreeing that irresponsible consumerism could reveal the erratic and inferior nature of women.[26]

For their part, women shoppers lived up to both images of consumer identity. As Elaine Abelson's work on late-nineteenth and early twentieth-century women shoplifters shows, this new sales environment prompted some women to behave irrationally and impulsively. When caught stealing, they appropriated the same discourse of female fallibility highlighted by cynical consumer capitalists and their support staffs.[27] They complained of feeling overwhelmed by desire and of lacking self-control; they took refuge in medical diagnoses of kleptomania. Other women applauded the valorization of shopping. Women in the domestic science movement (which applied scientific management ideology and techniques to homemaking) saw household spending as a carefully honed skill that required good judgment and scientific-mindedness. Members of the National Consumers' League urged buyers to uphold high ethical standards that recognized the links between middle-class consumption and the conditions of industrial production.

Suffragists thus had numerous images and experiences to draw from when they contemplated the connections between consumer and political identity. At different times and under different circumstances, they expressed affinity with all of these viewpoints. Consequently, suffragists' engagement with consumerism sent contrary messages. Supporters of the movement lauded a responsible approach to shopping and defended votes for women as a means of consumer protection. They also identified the woman citizen as a consumer of good politics who had learned the responsibilities of voting by learning to shop wisely. In making consumer identity central to political behavior, these reformers offered a powerful model of what votes for women might mean and how women's special talents and duties might positively contribute to the nation. At the same time, however, suffragists perfected a campaign strategy as purveyors of commercial entertainment that appealed to voters as emotional and manipulable. Following the lead of mass culture businesses, suffragists extended assumptions about easily led women buyers to voters of both sexes. Hoping to undercut opposition through emotional stimulation, they used what one suffragist called "color and dash" to sell their cause. They mastered modern means of advertising, publicity, mass production, commercial entertainment, commercial design, retailing, and publishing. They put up billboards and colorful posters; they created artful window displays; they wore sandwich boards, badges, pins, and mass-produced suffrage fashion accessories; they produced movies, pageants, and plays; they "performed" in vaudeville; they hawked suffrage wares through special stores and catalogs. Campaigns of this nature bloomed first and most spectacularly in large urban centers. Consequently, I look closely at places like New York and Chicago. But small towns and rural areas were not immune to the social, visual, and spatial changes wrought by consumer culture, and nonradical suffragists from less metropolitan locations also experimented with the images and strategies of the new commercial world.

In some instances, the cultural orientation of these tactics proved subtle, for consumerism did not replace the foundations of traditional American political culture; it simply inscribed them with new meanings. Actions originated by suffragists since the movement's inception—like the appropriation of public space and the sale of suffrage newspapers—assumed new significance. Likewise, tactics long embraced by political parties and labor unions—like parades and mass meetings—but newly adopted by twentieth-century suffragists were colored by the language and methods of consumerism.

By being among the first political players to fully and eagerly incorporate the methods and technologies of mass culture into their campaigns, suffragists contributed to the commercialized political sphere that now dominates American culture. They helped shape contemporary equations between political campaigning and political salesmanship by recognizing the importance of image management, consumption, and mass, multimedia exposure. In doing so, nonradical suffragists brought their struggle out of fringe politics and into the mainstream of American debate and political consideration. We may worriedly ponder the long-term consequences of the commercialization of politics, but that suffragists made the necessary transition is a credit to both their success and their creative, multifaceted use of consumer ideology and commercial methods of public persuasion.

It is also a credit to the expanding place of consumerism in American society. By the time the Nineteenth Amendment passed, consumer culture had produced a powerful and unquestioned vocabulary for making sense of social reality and values. When suffragists compared good voters to comparison shoppers, defined commodity-enhanced lifestyles as a right, spoke in tribute to fashion and mass consumerism, and emulated the graphic, material, and visual cues of modern department stores, advertisers, merchandisers, and magazine publishers, they expressed themselves in a verbal and nonverbal code that defined consumer-centered and -directed activity as a perfectly natural and unquestionably valid activity that made consumer culture not merely tangential to political self-definition but central to its expression and makeup.

Chapter 1 sheds light on these issues by exploring the evolving connections between ideas about consumption and woman suffrage. It shows how nineteenth-century suffragists' contrary perspectives on consumerism changed over time and became uniformly more positive during the 1900s. Drawing from a diverse array of movements and philosophies, twentieth-century suffragists sketched out numerous ways they expected women's experiences as shoppers to influence their roles as voters.

Chapter 2 examines suffragists' uses of public space and shows how consumer culture provided a new language for appropriating the physical landscape and a new set of methods for reaching distinct publics.

Many incursions into public space involved carefully controlled performances by woman suffragists. Chapter 3 shows how suffragists tapped into commercial and psychological dictates about the malleability of modern identity in order to represent themselves in appealing— yet carefully stage-managed—ways.

Chapter 4 suggests that woman suffrage merchandise delivered powerful messages about the character of movement supporters. These commodities likewise offered suffragists, and the commercial businesses who saw movement activists and their institutions as potential customers, an important way to raise money.

Following the business history of *The Woman's Journal,* the longest-running women's newspaper in U.S. history, the fifth chapter explores how one group of suffragists consistently tried to combine reform and capitalist enterprise. Their different approaches to creating a financially self-sufficient publication demonstrate not only suffragists' diverse ideas about the sources of commercial success, but their unequivocal acceptance of consumer capitalism as a lens through which to view their world.

Chapter 6 questions the ultimate impact of consumerism on the movement and briefly suggests some of the ways consumer culture affected women's politics in the 1920s.

Selling suffrage, succumbing to the commercialization of politics, changed the dynamics of the woman suffrage movement and opened the door to a new era of political salesmanship. Before that process could begin, new ideas about consumer identity had to take root. Let's begin by addressing their development.

Chapter 1

Consumer Culture and Woman Suffrage Ideology

As the daughter of Ohio congressman Ezra B. Taylor, Harriet Taylor Upton grew up around the boisterous spectacle of nineteenth-century partisan politics. And she loved it. Like her father, she had an unquenchable passion for Republican Party affairs. Denied the vote because of her sex, Upton found nonelectoral ways of participating in this very public world. For a while, she worked as her father's secretary. After women got the vote, she became vice-chairman of the Republican National Committee. The honor of such an esteemed position paid tribute to Upton's enthusiastic partisanship and also to her other political passion: female enfranchisement. She worked tirelessly for NAWSA. For fifteen years—during some of the most difficult and unproductive times in the movement's history—she faithfully served as the Associa-tion's treasurer. She virtually ran the NAWSA office until it relocated from her home city of Warren, Ohio to New York in 1910, and, as the longstanding president of the Ohio Woman Suffrage Association, Upton led the drive to let Ohio women vote.[1]

These accomplishments gave Upton some authority to predict how woman suffrage would affect partisan politics. Like other suffragists, she guessed that political parties would recognize women as a powerful voting bloc and cater to their assumed, gender-specific interests. During the inflationary period following World War I, one interest in particular captured Upton's imagination. Speaking for a nation of shoppers and progressives fed up with the increasingly high cost of food and other goods, Upton declared that women wanted lower prices. Moreover, she added, they would vote en masse for the party that legislated more affordable consumer products. By respecting and addressing the consumer demands of women, concluded Upton, that organization would become the "successful party of the near future."[2]

The future would prove Upton wrong. Woman suffrage did not inaugurate lower prices for consumers. Worse, women voters did not prove an influential—or even noteworthy—voting bloc. Political parties had little to fear from enfranchised women, and once politicians realized this, women—and so-called women's issues—became further marginalized from political power.[3] But Upton's comments remain significant, for they hint at the ideological associations between consumer culture and the suffrage movement.

Those associations had a long history that reflected transformations in both American values and suffrage ideology. As early as the 1850s, suffragists expressed concern over the morality of consumption. Drawing from republican and evangelical Protestant critiques of luxury and aristocratic emulation, they condemned alcohol and debated the virtues of fashion. As the suffrage movement changed, so did these concerns. After the Civil War, the movement eschewed radicalism and became increasingly conservative and expedient. Thus suffragists also rejected the radical reform context that had energized political and religious critiques of unrestrained consumerism. As a consequence, suffragists became less certain about the ideological moorings that had guided their critical responses to consumer capitalism's evolution.

This development dovetailed with the growth and politicization of a consumer consciousness. Urban women had long identified consumerism as an important part of daily life, but during the late nineteenth century it became increasingly naturalized, and even glorified. Progressive-era suffragists participated in that naturalization. They accepted commodity consumption as a given and made consumer issues central to prosuffrage arguments. Placing their cause firmly within progressive reform agendas, suffragists contended that women shoppers/voters would vanquish unwholesome forms of commercial amusement, protect the food and milk supplies, and attack the high cost of living. Moreover, argued suffragists, women deserved the vote because shoppers paid taxes, because the new rules of industrial society demanded new definitions of public and private space, and because women consumers had lifestyle entitlements and familial responsibilities that an activist government needed to protect.

By the time women received the constitutional right to vote in 1920, these arguments had transformed household shopping responsibilities into an ideology of consumer rights and obligations. That ideology, in turn, profoundly influenced how progressive-era suffragists conceptualized both the state and women's citizenship. Pressing their expediency claims further, suffragists argued that penny-pinching women citizens would make government earn its keep, that comparison-shopping female voters would wisely choose among political products, and that only enfranchised women/consumers could rein in greedy businesses. With private shopping skills transformed into public assets, the new voters would make government sensitive to American concerns. Indeed, depicting the vote as a form of political currency, suffragists promised to make government the ultimate service provider—one might even say the ultimate retailer. Like the perfect department store, suffragists' ideal state would be efficient, carefully managed, abundantly stocked (with potential services), and responsive to both investors (taxpayers) and customers (voters).

As these beliefs suggest, suffragists had not abandoned a critical stance toward consumerism; rather, that stance had evolved from a fear of uncontrollable desires to a defense of government-regulated and -protected consumption.

Mid-nineteenth-century suffragists would have found Upton's comments about lower prices surprising. Single issues rarely caused voters to switch willy-nilly between parties. Party identification was a cultural, family affair—as Upton's lifelong experience suggests.[4] More important, early suffragists would have rejected the progressive-era proposition that consumerism contributed to a woman's right to vote. Until Reconstruction, suffrage ideology rested upon the same natural rights arguments that gave men the franchise. Echoing the Declaration of Independence, the 1848 Seneca Falls "Declaration of the Rights of Women" contended that "all men and women are created equal." As citizens, as taxpayers, and as human beings, suffragists demanded the same inalienable rights as men, including the ballot.[5]

This did not mean early suffragists disregarded questions of commodity consumption. Women from across the suffrage spectrum wrote and spoke about topics such as luxury, fashion, and that most worrisome of consumer pleasures, alcohol. But they considered these issues from different, and sometimes contradictory, perspectives. Ideas about gentility and refinement shaped some suffragists' attitudes about consumption. As historians note, mid-nineteenth-century middle-class

Americans obsessively pursued "genteel" lifestyles. Karen Halttunen argues that rigid standards of etiquette, behavior, dress, housekeeping, and personal interaction allowed an increasingly self-conscious middle class to distinguish itself from its supposed social inferiors. Commercial goods, especially apparel and home furnishings, were visible evidence of gentility and became markers of respectable living.[6]

The ideology of gentility, however, ran counter to old republican and evangelical Protestant critiques of luxury or anything that smacked of unnecessary consumption. Adherents of republican philosophy interpreted middle-class gentility as a form of aristocratic emulation. Since Americans in the early republic considered European aristocracy antithetical to liberty and virtue, such critics insisted that genteel lifestyles led straight to dependency, social corruption, and political enslavement. Evangelical Protestants highlighted similar fears, but emphasized that gentility and luxury tempted individuals away from God and salvation. Halttunen argues that these criticisms complicated the pursuit of gentility in the 1830s and 1840s but began to fade in the 1850s, as middle-class Americans became more secure in their class status and more cognizant of their cultural power.[7]

The embracing of fashion by many early suffragists suggests that the ideal of gentility had indeed naturalized consumer luxury into an accepted part of middle-class life. As the historian William Leach points out, many early feminists adopted fashionable dress. Reformer Thomas W. Higginson spoke entirely within the genteel tradition when he connected trends in apparel to the noble pursuit of "beauty." Those who scorn "the utmost extremes of dress, the love of colors, of fabrics, of jewels, of 'featherses,' " [sic] noted Higginson, should remember that such measures are "after all an effort after the beautiful."[8] As such, they deserved respect and appreciation, even when they caused more eyestrain than eye-catching delight. Many suffragists agreed. Accounts of woman suffrage conventions repeatedly describe women "elaborately gowned in the height of the fashion,"[9] and some suffragists obsessively followed the latest styles. Leach calls popular woman's rights lecturer Anna Dickinson a "fashion plate" with a passion for "silk, satin, diamonds, and gorgeous colors." She became so renown as a consumer of fashion that the great jeweler Charles Tiffany personally offered to guide her through his famous New York store.[10]

Other motivations also prompted suffragists to promote extravagant modes of dress. As Leach notes, some woman's rights supporters saw the fashion industry as a means of economic independence. Feminist-minded women edited the popular fashion magazines *Demorest's Monthly* and *Harper's Bazaar*.[11] Oregon suffrage leader Abigail Scott Duniway owned a millinery shop before she started her suffrage newspaper, *The New Northwest*.[12] Writers for *The Woman's Journal* encouraged financially strapped rural women to make money by opening "calico dress depots" that sold dresses in the latest styles.[13]

However, not all suffragists admired fashion or genteel ideology. The radical reform tradition undergirding the early suffrage movement could be unrelentingly critical of refined living. Radical reformers sought to transform social relations. They viewed suffrage—along with temperance, dress reform, abolition, health reform, antiprostitution, worker's rights, and other movements—as natural, interrelated steps toward the uplift of humanity.[14] If the consumption of proper goods could contribute to that development, so much the better. Thus abolitionists and suffragists hosted annual fairs that sold everything from livestock to linens.[15] However, radicals also argued that consumer practices that brought out people's baser qualities needed alteration, and often drew from the same republican and religious refutations of luxury and aristocracy that colored the pursuit of gentility.

This opposition led many suffragists to doubt the moral value of some types of commodity consumption. While their genteel-minded sisters embraced fashion, these reformers questioned its consequences. They decried the health risks associated with tight corsets and long dresses that dragged dirt and mud into the home. They debated the impact of fashion on women's intellect and virtue. In one of her regularly published letters to *The Woman's Journal*, New York suffragist Celia Burleigh warned against the imprisoning nature of the dresses, silks, and muslins found at Stewart's reopened, expanded, luxurious department store. "A woman who engineers" long and elaborate dresses, warned Burleigh, "must give her mind" to her clothing. "Encourage your wives and daughters to be fashionable, all ye who have a horror of strong-mindedness. To be at the same time worshippers at the shrine of fashion, and priestesses at the altar of humanity, is impossible; the two things are incompatible, and in so far as you make them the one, they cannot perfectly be the other."[16]

Class conflict intensified contempt for fashion. Middle-class reformers used republican rebukes of luxury and dissipation to heap scorn upon wealthy women. Radical Gerrit Smith concluded that love of dress turned elite women into a "pitiable and painful spectacle." Echoing critics who described mawkish emulation of the rich as a dangerous form of self-enslavement, Smith insisted that "jewels and gewgaws" corrupted the "lady." "The high callings of [woman's] nature, and the grave and solemn purposes of human existence," wrote Smith, "are, in her case, all sunk in the low and petty ambition to be a pretty doll, an attractive plaything, the bewitching idol of a bewitched man."[17] The Reverend Olympia Brown agreed. What happened to the "delicate moral sense of woman?" asked Brown in 1860, noting that she "spends money in ruthless extravagance, lavishing untold sums upon her own fine clothes when there are so many suffering human beings around her, when she might every day meet young ladies whom with a little of her superfluity she could relieve from want and prepare to gain an honest livelihood for themselves."[18] As Brown suggests, fashion victimized both rich and poor: love of dress led to such self-absorption that wealthy women forgot the duties of noblesse oblige.

The radical reform emphasis on uplifting humanity translated into different problems for working women. Like Smith and Brown, some wage earners agreed that fashion fed class distinctions. Dress marked not only class status but also respectability. For women of limited means, maintaining an estimable reputation in this environment meant forgoing humanistic pursuits in order to refashion and update their apparel. One working woman complained that she could not afford to dress like the well-to-do women with whom she attended church. In order to look presentable, however, she spent her evenings trimming hats or making dresses, rather than reading or learning about the "general topics and questions of the day." "If there could only be a reform in women's dress for church," she lamented. "If women who can dress expensively would set the fashion of dressing neatly and inexpensively for church, and leave costly silks, velvets, and the colors of the rainbow, for the opera, ballroom and promenade, then women who cannot dress expensively and fashionably would be left free to attend church as they ought."[19] For other working women, however, fashion presented a more basic problem: it complicated the search for self-sufficiency. Smith complained that long, cumbersome dresses "harmonized" with biased and unfair labor practices that excluded women "from most kinds of labor, and confine[d them] to those few and poorly paid occupations, in which women crowd and starve each other."[20]

Fashion faultfinders found camaraderie and an ideological base in the dress reform movement. In the early 1850s, several editors and woman's rights advocates advised women to adopt less confining and physically debilitating attire. Numerous reformers responded to this call, but no one captured more attention than Amelia Bloomer, the editor of a small New York State temperance and woman's rights newspaper. In 1851, Bloomer found her friend Elizabeth Smith Miller (daughter of fashion foil Gerrit Smith) outfitted in a "reform dress" made up of a shirtwaist and a pair of blowzy "Turkish Pantaloons" covered with a knee-length skirt. Bloomer immediately copied the suit for her own use. Right away, the New York press derisively labeled the new garb the "Bloomer costume" or "Bloomer dress." But not everyone mocked the bold New Yorker. Hundreds of women wrote Bloomer and asked for patterns and information about her experimental garment, and "thousands" subscribed to Bloomer's paper, *The Lily*.[21] Some of the nation's most influential women reformers—including suffragists Lucy Stone, Elizabeth Cady Stanton, and Susan B. Anthony—embraced the clothing. Women across the North met for dress reform conventions, where they praised the new style and declared their movement "an important auxiliary in the regeneration of woman."[22]

Nonetheless, most Americans rejected this apparel as bizarre and unladylike. Women in "Bloomer costumes" received jeers and taunts. Lucy Stone complained that whenever she wore the outfit to a new city "a horde of boys" would follow her and "destroy all comfort." When the wind blew the skirt up around her pantaloons, people would laugh and stare. Even some reform-minded friends refused to accompany her when she appeared in the new style. Pressures such as these convinced Stone to give up "Bloomers" within a few years. Other reformers— many of whom feared that negative publicity surrounding the fashion alternative threatened the reputation of the woman's rights movement—followed suit.[23]

Because suffragists held such deep and contradictory beliefs about fashion, disagreements over the subject occasionally threatened the unity of the movement. In September 1852, fashion naysayers prevented writer Elizabeth Oakes Smith from becoming president of a local suffrage organization because she wore a "décolleté gown" to a woman's rights convention.[24] More stylish forces prevailed after the famous former slave Sojourner Truth criticized attendees of an 1870 suffrage convention for outfitting themselves in the latest apparel. "What kind of reformers be you," asked Truth, "with goose wings on your heads, as if you were going to fly, and dressed in such ridiculous fashion, talking about reform and women's rights? 'Pears to me you had better reform yourselves first." Editors at the *Woman's Journal* quickly rebuked Truth. Insisting that dress at the event appeared "moderate, neat, simple, and in very good taste," the editors suggested that it was Truth who had committed the faux pas. "Considerations of beauty, grace and taste in dress do not seem to us unworthy a woman—a true woman, or a woman 'reformer'," noted one editorial, "and we should condemn the angularities, the ungracefulness and the absolute deformity of a dress like Sojourner Truth's as severely as she would 'panniers,' 'Grecian bend-backs', etc."[25]

The line between advocate and critic of fashion was not always clear, however. Distinctions between utility and luxury, simplicity and extravagance, and beauty and deformity could be as individual as the people involved in the dispute. Having once fought for simplified female attire, Lucy Stone, for example, would seem a natural ally of Truth. But as proprietor of the *Woman's Journal,* she turned fiercely on the ex-slave; not only did her paper renounce Truth's opinion, but it also personally and cruelly attacked her appearance. The editorial's ferociousness suggests that race could complicate conflicts over fashion. Work by Richard Bushman supports this conclusion. In his study of mid-nineteenth-century gentility, Bushman found that white Americans routinely chastised and caricatured African Americans who attempted to adopt popular markers of refinement.[26] But Truth committed an even greater sin by rebuking white culture. From the perspective of the editorial writer, this was unacceptable; apparently, only white women could challenge white standards of beauty and distinction.

If disagreements over fashion pulled suffragists apart, however, other consumer-centered subjects brought them together. Almost all early suffragists supported temperance, which radical reformers had embraced since the 1830s. As several historians have noted, local and state schisms over drinking often stemmed from middle-class desires to police working-class leisure.[27] Women's historian Ruth Bordin shows that although such claims are persuasive, they simplify the temperance movement's complexity. Temperance advocates were not merely interested in social control; they saw excessive drinking as a real problem with real consequences. Since drinking and treating others to drinks filled important roles in working-class culture, alcohol abuse proved especially prevalent among male workers. With few legal rights and limited economic opportunities, women had reason to fear drunken fathers and husbands. The middle-class women who supported temperance therefore defined alcohol as a threat to all women and children. At worst, it could lead men to abandon or physically mistreat and sexually dishonor their families.[28] At minimum, money spent on alcohol contributed to a family's degradation, rather than its economic, moral, and cultural salvation.[29]

A story told by a Vermont suffragist and temperance supporter in 1852 bitterly described how alcohol abuse destroyed one family. The husband recklessly spent all his money on drink. His wife "struggled bravely" to provide and care for her children, but to no avail. To quench his thirst, the husband sacrificed his family's well-being and dignity. Shortly before her youngest child's birth—the time when a woman most needed the comfort of a mate—he "pawned the clothing which she had provided for herself and her babes, sold her only bed, and drove her into the street to seek charity aid."[30] The storyteller never mentioned the family's class standing. To her, it remained irrelevant: alcohol could impoverish any family. Uncontrolled access to this most corrupting substance made a mockery of domestic ideology, genteel living, and human progress. It could reduce a man to a dehumanized state, and sink any woman or child into disgrace and poverty.

Although critics of fashion and alcohol approached their subjects from different perspectives, their common fear of unrestrained commodity consumption bound them to republican ideology and its conspiratorial fear of suppressed liberty. Supporters of both dress reform and temperance worried that spending run amok, whether by women on apparel or men on drink, reduced individuals to a pathetic state of dependency in which commodities became unhealthy signifiers of identity. Slavery to "gewgaws and jewels" defined fashionable women just like slavery to drink defined imbibers of alcohol. Critics of fashion and alcohol also shared a puritanical suspicion of amusement. They agreed that easily accessible commercial temptations rewarded personal weakness with selfish, blinding pleasure. Indulging in such corrupting diversions harmed both the individual and the community, for they corroded cherished social bonds, like those of the family, and indispensable social responsibilities, like guardianship of the poor.

In this respect, debates over women's dress and men's drinking were specific responses to concerns about social relations in the emerging commercial nation. Numerous monographs discuss the dramatic changes occurring in the mid-nineteenth-century northern cities where most radical reform activity occurred and where most genteel-minded Americans lived. The decline of artisanal capitalism, the beginnings of industrialization, the growth of cities, and transportation and commercial revolutions that made urbanites less reliant on home production transformed the lives of middle-class women and men. As historian Mary Ryan notes, by the mid-nineteenth century, urban, middle-class women had become experienced shoppers.[31] Far from seeing commodities as harbingers of corruption, many recognized real benefits of consumerism, including more leisure time due to less household production, more variety due to consumer choice, and more public interaction due to encounters with the marketplace. As consumer capitalism grew in the late nineteenth and twentieth centuries and middle-class women spent even more time shopping, this enthusiastic embrace of consumerism became widespread.[32]

Some Americans worried about these developments. After all, traditional Calvinist wisdom held that idle hands were the devil's workshop. Leisure freed those hands, and sometimes the market seemed to offer easy substitutes for hard work and responsibility. Could character blossom in such a flaccid environment? Could virtue grow when a consumer ethic of immediate gratification and worldly abundance replaced a producer ethic of self-restraint, discipline, and sacrifice? The eagerness with which many middle-class women transformed *leisure* into *work* through reform and charitable activity, the insistent conjoining of consumerism and human uplift, and the drive to root out possibly degrading forms of consumption reveal that the growth of consumer capitalism raised new questions about the coexistence of materialism and morality.

After the Civil War, however, suffragists began to evaluate consumerism in new ways. This change stemmed partly from the decline in radical reform sentiment. As the history of the suffrage movement demonstrates, the Civil War, Reconstruction, and the growing conservatism and xenophobia of the late nineteenth century took their toll on radical efforts to re-envision the world. Once a cross-class, multiracial struggle focused on the natural rights of all people, the post-Civil War movement became factionalized by internal disputes over race, reform, and political methods. In one of the suffrage movement's most shameful chapters, former radical abolitionists Stanton and Anthony joined forces with rabid racist George Train to denounce the Fifteenth Amendment's enfranchisement of black men and its denial of voting rights to women. In blatant antidemocratic style, some late nineteenth-

and twentieth-century suffragists followed this racist precedent by depicting the vote as a tool of white, middle-class domination and by proposing that only educated men and women of acceptable (signifying Northern European) race, ethnicity, and class receive the franchise.[33]

As radical reformism declined, suffragists became more accommodating of consumer capitalism. In some respects, this may have been inevitable. Since the 1830s, the pursuit of gentility had pounded away at old suspicions of luxury and aristocratic emulation. By the 1850s, radical reformers had become the chief articulators of once widely held republican and religious critiques of nonutilitarian consumption—and even within the boundaries of this narrow and often ridiculed group, little agreement existed over the morality of spending. Once suffragists relinquished radicalism, their last defense against the rationalization and naturalization of a middle-class consumer, commodity-centered identity lost its ideological potency. This did not signal the end of historic criticisms of commodity-enhanced, genteel lifestyles; nor did it prevent new rebukes against extravagance. As we will see, old fears of consumerism found new outlets of expression. But suffragists would never again doubt the inherent value of mass consumption, and they would never again question consumerism's potential contributions to middle-class uplift and social progress.

By the 1870s, suffragists not only accepted consumer comfort—and even luxury—as positive additions to women's lives, they even wrote about consumerism's utopian possibilities. According to architectural historian Dolores Hayden, feminist writer Melusina Fay Peirce believed commodity abundance would spawn buyer cooperatives that would simplify housekeeping and give women more time to pursue personal enrichment.[34] The author of a short story in the *Woman's Journal* predicted how such changes could occur. In the tale, a rural housewife proves her economic worth when she goes to work at a neighboring farm and leaves her kin to fend for themselves. Once the woman's family realizes the monetary value of her domestic labor, she convinces them to buy the proper tools for her work: a "Universal Clothing Wringer" and a "Doty's Washer." Best of all, these items promise to free up time for welcome personal improvements.[35] Consumer goods had gone from barriers to human progress to harbingers of individual growth.

The death of organized dress reform agitation also demonstrated that suffrage supporters no longer doubted consumer capitalism's moral worth. Among suffragists, this acceptance expressed itself in the near-universal toleration of fashion. Leach notes that, except for occasional critiques of "selfish fashionable women," suffrage supporters from the mid-1870s onward seldom questioned the relationship of women's virtue, liberty, and dress.[36] Even Susan B. Anthony—the last suffrage leader to relinquish "Bloomers"—succumbed to the self-satisfaction of her class. By the century's end, Anthony admitted that "every woman, like every man, should be permitted to wear exactly what she chooses."[37] She herself had become "extremely particular" about dress. Finding it "poor economy" to "wear cheap material," Anthony's hand-picked biographer noted that she "always buys the best fabrics, linings and trimmings, and employs a competent dressmaker." Although she wore only "black silk or satin in public," at home she outfitted herself in festive maroon or soft cardinal.[38]

Suffragists' accommodation of consumerism gave a new context and flavor to some familiar suffrage arguments. Recalling one of the most sacred mottos of the American Revolution, early suffragists insisted that "taxation without representation is tyranny."[39] Identifying women consumers as an important segment of the taxpaying public, suffragists in the 1900s complained that shoppers contributed to government coffers but received no political voice. "It would be impossible," noted NAWSA leader Carrie Chapman Catt, "to maintain that immense machinery of government that we do, were it not for money" raised by taxation. Women shoppers paid the bulk of this money via an indirect tax "upon nearly every article of furnishing for the home, upon nearly every utensil used in the home; upon nearly every article of clothing worn by occupants of the home; upon nearly every article of food consumed in the home, and even upon nearly every dose of medicine taken in the home." Indeed, without women consumers, "government would find its chief source of support gone." As long as shoppers picked up the bill, concluded Catt, they had every right to declare their political opinions via the ballot.[40]

Suffragists' accommodation of consumerism also dovetailed with a new brand of suffrage advocacy. With the natural rights foundations of the movement compromised by setbacks during the Civil War and Reconstruction eras, late nineteenth-century suffragists began to emphasize the political expediency of votes for women. Expediency arguments worked in two ways: they offered quick excuses for why men should grant women the franchise, and they presented woman suffrage as a simple solution to social problems. Political corruption? War?

Unfair pricing? Whatever the social ill, suffragists identified votes for women as the remedy.

This logic contained a consumeristic streak. As Frederic Jameson notes, consumer capitalistic societies demonstrate the remarkable ability to redefine abstract principles and ideals as tangible things.[41] Suffragists did so by making the right to vote synonymous with physical possession of a ballot. They then recast the ballot as a household appliance—something neatly stocked in any housewife's pantry. By the 1900s, suffragists had begun comparing the ballot to vacuums, telephones, and sewing machines. Like these items, it was a handy household helper. A suffrage leaflet printed by the New York Woman Suffrage Party concluded that the ballot and the sewing machine both acted as "labor-saving machine[s] for the home." Just as women with sewing machines could sew more quickly than those without, so women with the vote could quickly—and literally—"clean up the city."[42] And as the clearly ridiculous remarks of the puckish character Mad Hatter in the play *A Suffrage Rummage Sale* indicate, denying women suffrage was like denying housewives vacuums—adding to women's daily grind by making them "go on toiling and moiling—scrubbing and sweeping—in the good old-fashioned way."[43]

Expediency arguments also transformed the ballot into a form of political currency. One illustrated suffrage flyer (most likely from the 1910s) showed "the vote" hanging like dollar bills out of a woman's purse as she listened to two politicians hawking "proposed legislation for the home" (see fig. 1.1). "Rival candidates for office are competitors for the woman's vote just as much as rival grocers are for her patronage," noted the flyer.

> Do you not think it would be a good thing for the home and for the state if, wherever there was an election, we had two men competing with each other to see which could get into his platform the best proposals for legislation benefiting the homes and the children in order to appeal to the experts on homes and children—the women—with something in exchange for their votes?[44]

In effect, politicians became merchants, legislation became a commodity, and women voters became comparison shoppers. Given this construction of government and citizenship, it is not surprising that supporters of women's enfranchisement went to the one place where women had best honed their shopping skills: the department store. In 1920, the New York

City League of Women Voters helped Gimbel's department store run a voter education booth. Volunteers taught shoppers to mark ballots and provided detailed records of political candidates. With this material at

FIGURE 1.1 *"A Fair Exchange."*
Advocates of consumer citizenship encouraged women to see voting as an extension of their shopping responsibilities.
Courtesy NAWSA Papers, Library of Congress.

hand, recently enfranchised New York women could shop for future representatives while browsing for household products.[45]

Whatever their metaphoric underpinnings, however, expedient suffrage arguments ultimately centered around the promotion of an activist, citizen-centered state. In this respect, they reflected an increasingly important strand of American political ideology. In the mid-nineteenth century, radical reformers and conservative benevolent workers agreed that moral suasion offered the best hope for reforming society. When suffragists turned toward expediency, they rejected moral suasion in favor of active politicking. And behind that commitment lay the belief that an expanded government should serve—and service—the political and social needs of citizens living in a complex, urban, industrial society.[46]

Reformulated ideas about temperance and woman suffrage demonstrate this ideological sea change. As early as the 1870s, some suffragists complained that disfranchisement denied women the political power needed to control the sale of alcohol. Miriam M. Cole, for example, praised the women who took axes to whiskey barrels, prayed in saloons, and evangelized in city streets during the temperance crusades of the early 1870s, but she lamented that such good deeds "could not make one law black or white." If women had the vote, she argued, they could "change the present temperance laws and make them worth the paper on which they are printed." The ballot, concluded Cole, was the "only ax to lay at the root of the tree" of drink.[47]

Such opinions became more commonplace during the late 1870s. In 1876, Frances Willard convinced the once staunchly antisuffrage Women's Christian Temperance Union (WCTU) to call for the ballot as a means of "Home Protection." As Ruth Bordin notes, Willard's election as WCTU president in 1879 signaled the triumph of the group's woman suffrage forces. And in 1881, after Willard announced her "do-everything" policy (which encouraged WCTU members to support any cause that helped restrict and reduce the use of alcohol), woman suffrage and temperance became permanently linked in organization and popular imagination.[48] However, natural rights were second to expediency. Writing in 1888, Willard claimed that "while fully convinced that the ballot is the right of every woman in the nation, just as much as it is the right of every man," the WCTU "does not base its line of argument upon this fact, but upon the practical value that woman's vote will have in helping the nation to put away the liquor traffic."[49]

Willard's privileging of expediency demonstrates the growing belief that moral suasion could never match the effectiveness of an activist, reformist state. The growth of new liberal philosophy in the early twentieth century gave further credence to this belief. Although competing strands of thought undermined the inherent consistency of this philosophy, a commitment to individualism, educated citizenship, activist government, and "positive freedom" united its different adherents. For our purposes, the new liberal belief in positive freedom is especially important. Historian Edward A. Stettner defines it as the "freedom to develop one's abilities free of severe economic coercions." Philosopher John Dewey saw it as the right to self-realization: the right to reach one's maximum human potential no matter where one fell on the economic or social ladder. For Dewey and other new liberals, self-realization represented a modern, holistic understanding of liberal self-interest. While some nineteenth-century liberals flattened self-interest into private economic gain, progressive theorists suggested that self-interest signified the entire spectrum of individual needs and social obligations that contributed to personal fulfillment.[50]

Although early twentieth-century reformers may not have appreciated the nuances of liberal philosophy, its emphasis on activist government, positive freedom, and self-fulfillment via civic-mindedness tied together some of the main beliefs of progressivism. Progressives of all stripes defended their calls for government regulation and activism by extolling the promises of liberal individuality. Calls for safe and clean foodstuffs, garbage collection, stricter labor laws, and work site inspections all came down to the individual's right to achieve a satisfying and healthy life in an urban, industrial environment.

The new liberal's self-actualized person remarkably resembles the radical reformer's uplifted soul. Both constructions of identity promote the optimistic faith that human beings can, and generally wish to, transcend their baser natures in order to become more highly evolved, content, and socially conscious citizens. Likewise, both new liberals and radical reformers believed that men and women sometimes needed help finding the road to happiness. The combination of this belief and the liberal faith in activist government led to the ironic assumption that in order for government to help people reach their maximum potential, it needed to keep them from indulging their more abject desires. Well-intentioned reformers could advocate uplift, but without the coercive pressure of government to regulate the marketplace, positive change would be piecemeal at best.

Progressive-era suffragists—along with many other reformers—used this logic to justify demands for government control of "commercial vice." Depicting the ballot as an antidote to unwholesome commercial goods and pastimes, suffragists asserted that enfranchised women would shut down indecent dance halls, pool rooms, and theaters by making politicians responsive to women's interests. They would squelch "immoral" motion pictures, the "unlawful sale of 'dope'," and smoke shops that sold tobacco to young boys.[51] A class dynamic undergirded these promises. Dance halls, pool rooms, and theaters primarily served working-class audiences. When suffragists promoted the regulation of such businesses they advanced the white middle-class position that workers and immigrants found self-improvement unpalatable, and that only a government prodded by well-intentioned reformers could protect people from their baser tastes.[52]

More than anything else, progressive-era debates over commercial leisure—and even alcohol—illustrate that older suspicions of consumerism had not disappeared, though they had become detached from their historic political and religious moorings. Once-general concerns about the effect of luxury and aristocratic emulation on public and national virtue had narrowed into focused critiques of how already socially suspect groups—like workers and immigrants—spent their time and money. The lasting power of these criticisms, however, came not from their top-down, middle-class moralisms but from their ability to express fears plaguing large segments of society, from middle-class reformers to working-class parents.[53]

Especially in the 1910s, when the suffrage movement regained its cross-class character, suffragists proved adept at teasing out these shared anxieties. Suffragists realized, for example, that many people besides middle-class whites worried about working-class leisure. One NAWSA flyer warned the "Working Man" that urban amusements placed his "boys and girls . . . in danger of going wrong." Once working-class mothers had the vote, concluded the notice, they could help their menfolk fight the corrupting vices of modern life. This appeal reflected more than ethnocentric assumptions about the universality of white middle-class values; it reflected the continued ambivalence with which Americans of diverse backgrounds viewed mass culture. Within immigrant communities, the growth of mass culture created generational tensions between youngsters (who placed mass culture at the center of a growing and dynamic heterosocial youth culture) and parents (who feared that both mass and youth cultures eroded traditional beliefs and respect for family hierarchy).[54] When suffragists promised to rein in mass culture industries, they hit a chord very likely appreciated by their intended listeners.

As these criticisms of commercial amusements and products suggest, ideas about consumerism still existed within a moral framework. But the growing class divide among Americans, the increasing heterogeneity of the twentieth-century suffrage movement, and the still-uneasy appreciation of the maturing consumer society made that framework muddled and contradictory. Popular stereotypes of women consumers also complicated these ideas. Republican and evangelical fears of consumerism had evolved into not only middle-class anxiety about working-class leisure, but also contempt for women shoppers. Historic critiques of luxury had always contained a misogynistic streak. Succumbing to luxury meant succumbing to temptation—losing control and acting irrationally. It meant sacrificing one's liberty, for to make an idol of luxury was to become a slave to materialism and self-indulgence. Weakness, irrationality, dependency:

FIGURE 1.2 *"An Unexpected Effect."*
Negative ideas about women consumers threatened positive constructions of
women voters.
Harper's Weekly 56 (May 18, 1912): 20.

these were the hallmarks of age-old Western connotations of woman-hood. A person corrupted by luxury became emasculated; became woman. By the end of the nineteenth century, these gendered connotations had attached themselves to the emerging image of the urban woman consumer. Elaine Abelson demonstrates that late nineteenth-century popular culture drew from this historic construct by depicting women shoppers as irrational, impulsive, weak-willed, childlike, narcissistic, even pathologically unstable.[55]

Representations of spendthrift women challenged the fuzzy moralizing with which suffragists considered consumer issues by suggesting that irrational women shoppers lacked the integrity to judge competing standards of consumption. More important, these stereotypes implied that women lacked the qualifications for political participation. The maligned woman consumer represented a republican government's worst citizen; irrational, weak-willed, and easily led buyers might prove easily swayed voters. A 1912 *Harper's Weekly* cartoon made this exact suggestion. A two-paneled drawing shows what happens when women marching in a suffrage parade spy a bargain sale. In the first panel, a line of women wearing lettered sandwich boards spell out the words VOTES FOR WOMEN. In the second panel, the marchers carrying the letters W, O and S desert the parade in favor of the nearby store. As they gaze into the shop-front window, the brusque-looking parade marshal turns in horror to find that the women's absence turns VOTES FOR WOMEN into VOTE FOR MEN (fig. 1.2).[56] An illustrated drawing entitled "Campaign Literature" used similar stereotypes of consumers to poke fun at woman suffrage. In this case, the "campaign literature" studied by a group of women riding to a suffrage parade turns out to be nothing more than frivolous fashion magazines (fig. 1.3).[57] As both cartoons imply, women's innate interest in shopping demonstrated their natural irrationality and frivolity and undermined their ability to seriously participate in political life.

Late nineteenth- and early twentieth-century suffragists deflected these stereotypes by constructing their own ideal of women shoppers, which drew from numerous sources and reflected the growing versatility of mainstream suffrage ideology. Using the same notions of middle-class refinement that allowed earlier suffragists to define fashion as an expression of beauty and gentility, some Americans not only depicted comfortable, commodity-centered lifestyles as legitimate markers of class identity, but also argued that women's rationality, economy, and

CAMPAIGN LITERATURE

FIGURE 1.3 *"Campaign Literature."*
Reproduced by permission of the Susan B. Anthony Ephemera Collection,
Huntington Library, San Marino, California.

good judgment made such standards of living possible.[58] As early as 1880, suffragist Thomas Higginson pressed this point by concluding that "the women of the middle classes are notoriously better [money] managers than the men."[59]

With the growth of the domestic science movement in the 1890s, suffragists found greater intellectual support for this position. Inspired by new theories about the "scientific management" of industrial labor, domestic scientists sought to professionalize housework by turning women into household efficiency experts.[60] Domestic scientists recognized shopping as an important part of the scientifically minded housewife's work and encouraged women to see themselves as skilled household purchasing agents. Twentieth-century suffragists took this ideal for granted. "As a rule," argued *Woman's Journal* editor Henry Blackwell, women were "economists."[61] They knew how to turn pennies into dollars, added progressives and suffragists George Creel and Judge Ben Lindsey.[62] Suffrage supporters used such evidence to suggest that women would make sensible voters. As Nathaniel C. Fowler explained, "He who believes that woman is unfit, incompetent to manage her own and others' affairs, incapable of weighing values, should be confronted with the indisputable fact that woman is the majority buyer of the world." In this capacity she regularly discriminated "between material quality and lack of it"; she made "a dollar bring a dollar's worth." If this same woman was "incompetent to cast a ballot," asked Fowler, "would it not be fair to refuse suffrage to men who do not know any better than to pay two dollars for a dollar shirt or fifty cents for a pair of twenty-five-cent stockings?"[63]

Blackwell went even further. He argued that women's skill at "saving and utilizing" their "family incomes" did more than demonstrate their capability for good voting; it highlighted the value of their enfranchisement. "In the extension of votes to qualified women lies our chief hope of greater public economy," he wrote.

> Let women, as voters, do for the public what they are doing in their daily lives. What is a city, or State, or nation, but an aggregation of homes? Why not have in our public housekeeping the help of the faithful housekeepers, the careful wives and mothers, to limit reckless expenditure, to apply wisely the public income, to provide schoolhouses for all our children, to pay better salaries to our teachers, and by friendly reciprocity to maintain domestic and international peace.[64]

Blackwell's comparison between private homes and more traditionally understood civic spaces connected the expediency claims of woman
suffragists to the progressive-era municipal housekeeping movement.
This movement's advocates spoke in gendered metaphors that compared problem-ridden cities to problem-ridden families. The downfall
of both institutions, they claimed, stemmed from a lack of maternal
influence. By making their private housekeeping skills public, women
would bring order to modern cities, just like they brought order to
modern homes.[65] Other suffrage supporters also included smart shopping in the municipal housekeeper's reform repertoire. Creel and
Lindsey argued that in woman-enfranchised states, women had already
politicized their consumer skills. In Denver, female voters helped lower
utility costs by supporting municipal ownership of the water company.
And throughout Colorado, where women had been given the vote in
1893, enfranchised women had demanded inquiries into local telephone, gas, and streetcar charges.[66]

Suffragists also rejected assumptions about private consumers' inherent narcissism and self-centeredness. Instead, they recognized shopping
as a potential tool of social uplift. Although utopian projections of radical reformers and writers like Melusina Fay Peirce echoed through such
claims, this understanding of consumption also drew from ideas about
the publicization of women's private virtues and contemporary liberal
fantasies about the merger of self-interest and civic-mindedness.
Inspiration for this belief came most directly from the Consumers'
League, which sprang to life after a series of meetings between female
reformers and garment workers in New York City in the late 1880s.
In 1891, the New York women followed the lead of a London consumers'
group and formed the Consumers' League of the City of New York.
Women across the nation followed suit. In 1898, several local Consumers'
Leagues united to form the National Consumers' League (NCL).[67] The
League's guiding principle was that consumption and industrial production were inextricably linked. As a consequence, argued NCL supporters, consumers held direct responsibility for industrial conditions. As an
article entitled "The Morals of Shopping" by the NCL's first president,
John Graham Brooks, concludes, "the buyer at the store is, in the very act
of buying, a creator. The shoddy buyer is a shoddy maker. In a very real
sense, to buy a harmful thing is to help make that thing. . . . To buy products made by laborers working in unwholesome surroundings is to help
perpetuate those evil conditions."[68]

Historian Kathryn Kish Sklar's research on the NCL demonstrates the complicated ways it used "gender-specific justifications" to support legislation "designed to benefit working women."[69] Florence Kelley, who became general secretary of the NCL in 1899, consistently worked to improve the lives of working-class families. Under her guidance, the NCL adopted "consumers' labels" (modeled after "union labels") that helped buyers shop conscientiously. When they purchased goods bearing the consumers' label, they could rest assured that the manufacturer worked with trade unions and acceded to other NCL-demanded labor standards.[70] By insisting that shoppers use their buying power proactively, NCL members acknowledged consumer capitalism as a fundamental and legitimate pillar of middle-class life. Moreover, reformers in the NCL implied that consumerism's main contribution to human uplift came not—as some feminists suggested in the 1870s—from easing the life of the shopper (if anything, NCL supporters had to work harder than other buyers in order to shop responsibly) but from the politicization of consumer identity.

Suffragists ardently supported the NCL. They wrote about it in suffrage newspapers, asked NCL leaders to speak at their conventions, and embraced its objectives, as when the National Woman Suffrage Association of Massachusetts lobbied Boston retailers to shorten summer store hours so that women workers could have more leisure time.[71] Membership lists of suffrage groups and the NCL overlapped. In some cases, suffragists and League advocates worked in common cause. Shortly before the Nineteenth Amendment's ratification, the NCL and the League of Women Voters (the newborn progeny of NAWSA) jointly investigated the causes of, and possible solutions to, the inflationary prices of the post–World War I period.[72]

The close ties between the NCL and the suffrage community help explain why many consumer-centered suffrage expediency arguments echoed the League's insistence upon the politicization of consumer identity. Suffragists often stressed that enfranchised women of all classes could protect the children of working-class consumers. In her 1911 play *Something to Vote For*, for example, Charlotte Perkins Gilman argued that the vote would help middle-class shoppers protect their working-class neighbors. The play tells the story of an elite women's club that gathers to debate one of the quintessential subjects of progressive reform interest: the adulteration of the milk supply. The call for "pure milk" brought together trustbusters, maternal feminists, supporters of pure food and drug legislation, and advocates of consumer and industrial worker rights, all of whom agreed that bacteria-tainted dairy products posed significant health risks to urban shoppers. Gilman's play begins with the club members blithely dismissing warnings about impure milk. Satisfied with their interactions in the marketplace, few of the women believe the local milk trust would ever sell an inferior product. When an impoverished immigrant widow reveals how germ-ridden milk peddled to poor families by the trust killed her only son, the women awaken to their selfishness and begin to understand the social responsibility they owe their politically impotent sisters. Later, when the club women realize they could be the next victims of commercial deceit, they conclude that safe consumerism and votes for women go hand-in-hand. As the club president boldly informs her followers:

> Rich or poor, we are all helpless together unless we wake up to the danger [of contaminated milk] and protect ourselves. That's what the ballot is for, ladies—to protect our homes! To protect our children! To protect the children of the poor! I'm willing to vote now! I'm glad to vote now! I've got something to vote for! Friends, sisters, all who are in favor of woman suffrage and pure milk say Aye![73]

This rousing justification of suffrage—like those on behalf of pure meat, fruit, vegetables, water, clothing, sweatshop and bakery inspections, municipal trash collection, street cleaning, sewage disposal, industrial pollution regulations, and clean, safe streetcars—signifies an optimistic response to widespread feelings of consumer powerlessness.[74] Suffragists complained that these feelings stemmed from the dramatic changes wrought by large-scale industrialization and urbanization. As Massachusetts suffragist Susan W. Fitzgerald explained, "modern economic conditions" that turned home producers into consumers made the housewife dangerously dependent upon outside forces. "Take the simple matter of furnishing wholesome food for her family," she noted.

> In the old days she raised it herself, she and her family knew that it was pure, clean, wholesome, and such as she could afford to give her children. None of this is true to-day. We know not whence comes our food. We have a very fair idea, though, that much of it comes to us impure, unclean, and unwholesome, and yet the mother of a family is obliged to buy that food, taking the risk of

giving to her children food that may bring to them sickness and disease.[75]

Consumers faced similar threats wherever they turned. Fitzgerald insisted that a mother took her children's "lives in her hands" whenever she bought mass-produced clothing. As she told a government suffrage panel,

> any of you who have looked into the matter of the manufacture of garments knows that clothes are made in factories and finished largely in sweat shops, that those sweat shops are often rooms where exist infectious diseases, tuberculosis, scarlet fever, diphtheria—heaven knows what. . . . We know that every year, at the same time that the winter clothing is taken from the shops and factories and scattered through the length and breadth of the land and put on sale in the retail stores, there is an outbreak of infectious diseases which can only be attributed to the shipment of dry goods, of clothing, of garments, from the centers of manufacture into the little towns.[76]

By blurring the idealized nineteenth-century boundaries between public and private spheres, argued suffragists, these economic changes not only denied women control over their presupposed area of influence, but also denied them their right—as women—to defend and serve their families. Since the ideal of republican motherhood was created in the late eighteenth and early nineteenth centuries, politicians and political thinkers had recognized women's primary civic obligation as familial. Mainstream, progressive-era suffragists extolled that principle, placed it within a contemporary context, and used it to demand an equitable and uncontaminated marketplace for women citizens/shoppers. New York Consumers' League President Maud Nathan told woman suffragists that as "spenders of all family incomes," women "have the right to the assurance that what they buy is free from adulteration, and has been produced under clean, wholesome, and humane conditions."[77] That right, in turn, justified another: the right to vote. Only the ballots of women shoppers could make the marketplace responsive to consumers' needs and protective of housewives' familial obligations. Laura Gregg explained that without women voters, politicians would never recognize the political dimensions of consumer problems like adulterated milk. In order to make government act upon such issues, she concluded, women "should have the *right* to register their opinions in regard to these conditions which affect the health and safety of their children, where those opinions will count, and that is—the ballot box" (italics added).[78]

When a troubling and sustained bout of inflation in the early 1900s further threatened middle-class comfort, the coalescence of political and consumer rights segued into the even bolder claim that shoppers had the right to a certain commodity-enhanced lifestyle.[79] In 1907, Henry Blackwell complained that inflation made middle-class women reduce their "daily outlays," and thus consumer pleasures, "in order to make both ends meet." Like other progressives, Blackwell blamed skyrocketing prices on profit-hungry corporations. He speculated that since "improved processes, labor-saving machinery, larger ships, additional railroads and greater tillage produce more corn, wheat, flax, cotton, sugar, lumber and textile fabrics" were increasing the availability of goods, only the sinister motives of business could explain the hardships facing consumers. Suffrage, he insisted, would help women pressure government into regulating that "corrupt conspiracy of corporations and individuals" who "impoverish" shoppers and make families forego their expected degree of material "comfort and refinement."[80]

Using their votes this way would not only help families, argued Blackwell and other suffragists; it would also safeguard the nation. Suffragists warned that without female enfranchisement, the inequitable balance of power between citizens and businessmen— which stood as one of the central tropes of all progressive reform efforts—would become even more lopsided. Henry Blackwell contended that the political interests of consumers had already become secondary "to those of organized monopolies."[81] Echoing James Madison's important essay on the value of political factions, suffragists argued that big business disregarded the citizens' well-being because it did not need to compete politically with the one group whose interests most naturally weighed against its own: consumers.[82] Since most consumers were women, and most women could not vote, industrial giants—who had already eliminated economic competition via monopolization, collusion, and unfair government influence—had gained the sort of unchecked power so feared by the founders. Blackwell's daughter, Alice Stone Blackwell, explained the practical results of such hegemony: "Under laws in which the housekeeping sex have had no voice," she argued, "speculation in foodstuffs has been allowed to run riot, and the price of living has soared to such a height that the whole country is seething with protest."[83]

Votes for women, promised suffragists, would rein in corporate power. "The new women voters will be thrown into direct fundamental opposition" to the "ruthless methods of commercialism," concluded Theresa Billington Greig. "Hereafter, the individual purchasers

FIGURE I.4   *"Prices Are Soaring."*
Suffragists used illustrations like this to convince voters that woman suffrage
would help consumers.
Courtesy NAWSA Papers, Library of Congress.

for the household, the collective purchasers of the State, will begin to look upon shopping with the eyes of law-makers."[84] With the "woman's" vote a reality, equilibrium would return to American politics. Consumer-citizens would achieve as much influence as monopolistic businesses.

Suffragists made similar claims during World War I. Unlike radical suffragists, women in the mainstream movement used the war to highlight American women's patriotism and to prove their vote-worthiness. Consequently, when Food Administration Agency director Herbert Hoover called on consumers to support the war effort through increased thrift, many suffragists supported him enthusiastically. NAWSA even started a Suffrage Thrift Division. The chair of the division, Mrs. Walter McNab Miller, rejected the familiar idea of "conspicuous consumption" in favor of "conspicuous thrift." Traveling the country on behalf of the Association's program of "cooperation and self denial," she encouraged women to serve the nation by eliminating waste.[85] The Thrift Division urged women to adopt Hoover's "Do My Bit Pledge," which promoted "wheatless" meals; limited consumption of meat, butter, sugar, tea, and coffee; and "the necessity of economy" in homes and restaurants.[86] The group taught women how to grow, can, and preserve their own staples.[87] It even asked towns to take themselves "off the market" by raising, distributing, and conserving enough food for their own inhabitants.[88]

Clearly, wartime suffragists extolled a much more Spartan lifestyle than the commodity-centered one defended by Blackwell. Different circumstances could lead to different conclusions about the morality of spending. But the inextricable connections both Miller and Blackwell made between consumer and political identity, and between women's familial responsibilities and their civic gifts, demonstrates how central ideas about consumerism had become to concepts of women's citizenship. This construction of female citizen-consumers also shows how much suffragists had reformulated their ideas about consumption and women's rights.

Despite competing ideas about gentility and radical reformism, most early suffragists had always recognized a political dimension to commodity consumption. Even as they became more accommodating of consumer capitalism in the 1870s and 1880s, they continued to contemplate it within a moral framework. Nevertheless, that framework was changing. The political and religious criticisms of luxury and aristocratic emulation had narrowed into specific attacks on society's most vulnerable and socially suspect members: women, immigrants, and industrial workers. These changes occurred while other influences were permeating the movement. Expediency, liberalism, progressivism, municipal housekeeping, and the growth of a consumer consciousness gave suffragists a new context for considering the links between their identities as citizens and as shoppers. Convinced that women consumers possessed important and valued qualities, such as rationality, efficiency, and accountability, suffragists constructed a model of women voters that countered stereotypes of spendthrift women and contributed to the vision of an activist state—one that would help individuals achieve their full human potential by regulating both the marketplace and commercial pleasure.

With woman suffrage ideology thus committed to a consumerist vision of women's citizenship and American lifestyles, an important part of twentieth-century women's political culture—and American political culture—was established. As we shall see, however, this occurred not only in rhetoric and ideas, but also in physical space and the cultural geography of the city.

Chapter 2

"So Much Color and Dash"
Woman Suffragists, Public Space, and Commercial Culture

In 1917, Minnesota suffragists turned a storefront on the most fashionable street in Minneapolis's busy shopping district into a fully stocked "suffrage headquarters" including a reading room, an information bureau, a reception center, and an area for selling suffrage merchandise. Suffragists ranked these worthwhile features second, however, to the headquarters' most prized attribute: its large, prominent display window, which, through "the art of window dressing" and the ingenious application of "color and dash," offered a visual spectacle of suffrage advocacy. According to one account, the window attracted so much attention that a local professor recommended it to his business classes as an example of "fine advertising."[1]

Minnesota women were not the first suffragists to use commercial sites and display methods to such effect. In the successful California campaign of 1911, Palo Alto women asked merchants on their city's main street to take turns displaying a bulletin board of weekly suffrage activities.[2] In 1915, New York City women used so many shop windows "for advertising and propaganda" that the number was "beyond counting."[3] During the last decade of the movement, suffragists appealed to outdoor audiences in other ways emulative of commercial businesses. They constructed huge billboards on busy city streets; they plastered their organization names across urban skyscrapers; they rented advertising space on streetcars; and they paraded up and down crowded sidewalks wearing sandwich boards and selling suffrage newspapers.

Through these and other methods—including more traditional means of public protest like parades, mass outdoor meetings, and soapbox speeches—progressive-era suffragists laid claim to public space. In doing so, they tightened the historical bond between themselves and an earlier generation of suffragists who viewed the physical space of cities, civic celebrations, and political events as critical arenas for promoting women's rights. These pioneers circulated petitions, lobbied state legislatures, worked the public lecture circuit, and brashly disrupted public cere-monies. Early suffragists' incursions into public space—and the vocabu-lary of liberal individualism they used to justify them—reflected the importance of political ritual and civic participation to nineteenth-century meanings of citizenship.[4] But many suffragists also rearranged the visual appearance of heretofore male-defined public spaces in order to inscribe citizenship with more female-friendly connotations. Preparations for suffrage events turned unlikely locations—like fairgrounds and public halls—into refined and homelike oases in which woman suffrage became a topic of genteel and respectable discussion.

Twentieth-century suffragists likewise appropriated public space. They incorporated themselves into traditionally male-centered rituals of active citizenship, and they redefined the sexual hierarchy of streets, plazas, theaters, and convention halls through calls to motherhood, domestic duty, and feminine grace. But changing definitions of the "pub-lic" required that suffragists defend their tactics in new ways. Following the lead of journalists, reformers, and social scientists, women in the twentieth-century movement identified and sought to influence two significant, yet distinct, publics. To reach well-intentioned but unin-formed middle-class readers who primarily learned about current events through mass magazines and newspapers, suffragists used the new arts of publicity and propaganda to create a press sensation that brought the movement into these readers' parlors and living rooms. To influence the seemingly irrational and heterogeneous masses who crowded into city spaces and longed for emotional release through spectacle and illusion, suffragists staged public displays that used beauty and sentimentality to overwhelm onlookers' negative impressions of women voters.

But as the capitalist origins of suffrage window displays suggest, spec-tacle was a means not only of emotional control but also of commercial appeal. This appeal resonated powerfully with how suffragists—and other Americans—looked at and understood the physical landscape. As William Taylor argues, late nineteenth-century urbanization and the growth of commercial capitalism reordered the visual culture of cities. Places like New York became "showcases" for both stimulating and grat-ifying "the mass of consumers" enveloped in urban life. Within this environment, businesses used architecture, exhibits, and public drama to celebrate commodities and consumption. In turn, public space became a zone of commercial spectacle and commercial spectatorship. For pedestrians and urban bystanders (especially middle-class women shoppers), scrutinizing commercial notices and displays became a primary way of participating in street life.[5] Suffrage windows and other commercially emulative suffrage displays tapped into these new modes of attraction through color, commodities, and artful design.

Suffragists' embrace of a theatrical side of consumerism was at odds with suffrage arguments focused on consumer rights and commodity-centered domestic privileges. We have already examined how the latter stressed the rationality and virtue of women shoppers. The theatrical side stressed the emotionality of onlookers and the visual appeal of fantasy and abundance. It stressed drama, excitement, "color and dash." In the end, however, it too emphasized a liberal conception of citizenship in which private individuals demanded government accountability for means of self-actualization and social services.

Public space has long served as an arena of theatricality and display. The carnivalesque juxtapositions of medieval markets and religious celebrations, the public and spectatorial nature of corporeal punishment before the nineteenth century, and the pomp of royal court ceremonies all demonstrate the extensive history of such drama in the Western world. The history of the early United States is replete with similar examples: workers, elite leaders, fraternal organizations, religious groups, and political partisans appropriated city streets and public buildings through parades and mass meetings; fiery preachers and politicians delivered hours-long sermons and speeches to huge outdoor crowds; marginalized groups, including poor whites, immigrants, and free African Americans in the North, organized public events that gave them temporary reign over public spaces. In each of these cases, street theater became what scholar Susan Davis calls a "tool for building, maintaining, and confronting power relations."[6] Events like partisan parades played out public dramas of class relations that pitted working-class voters against elite political leaders in delicate games of reciprocity and one-upmanship. Similarly, parades by Irish Catholics and free blacks revealed ethnic and racial divisions that white, nonimmigrant Americans fought ferociously to maintain and contain.[7]

Although street theater may have highlighted conflicts over class and race, it universally confirmed the social hierarchy of gender relations. Partisan processions in particular served as rituals of manhood. They helped demonstrate men's authority over the public sphere, that arena of discourse and debate focused on commerce, politics, and the state. Women rarely joined parades; they remained on the sidelines and cheered marchers from windows and balconies. Nineteenth-century domestic ideology substantiated women's limited participation in such events by assigning them to society's private sphere, which by the 1830s meant the spatial confines of the home.[8] There, women's "natural" talents and virtues—such as domesticity, gentility, morality, and spirituality—were expected to blossom. Women who rejected—by choice or circumstance—that family-centered, economically dependent life became known as "public" women. As Davis and other scholars attest, few terms carried such opprobrium. "Public" women were synonymous with prostitutes—the one group of women who flaunted their bodies in their own form of commercial street theater.[9]

Nevertheless, the confined nature of the private sphere did not mean women barricaded themselves in parlors. Domestic ideology seldom matched the complex reality of nineteenth-century life, particularly for poor and laboring women. Historian Christine Stansell calls antebellum New York a "city of women" because of the many poor women whose "domestic lives spread out to the hallways of their tenements, to adjoining apartments and the streets below," and for whom urban neighborhoods rather than private homes became key markers of identity.[10] Even "respectable" middle-class women traversed the centers of cities and towns. Errands, shopping trips, religious services, and neighborly visits meant daily incursions into public space. Moreover, what scholar Lori Ginzberg calls "benevolent femininity" led to an explosion of publicly oriented female moral and social reform organizations. Benevolent femininity grew out of the idealized notions of women's natural virtue and moral superiority that undergirded domestic ideology, and out of the activist, evangelical zeal of the Second Great Awakening. Taking its cue from religious calls for personal salvation and conversion, this ideology exhorted women to "heal or transform the world."[11] To that end, "respectable" middle-class white women distributed religious tracts to the unconverted, acted as "friendly visitors" in some of the most disreputable quarters of town, served on mixed-sex charitable committees, lobbied politicians in the corridors of state legislatures, and delivered public lectures.[12] Only when radical women reformers adopted similar tactics did social critics question the propriety of such methods.[13] Thus, rather than fully describing reality or even the preferred way of living, domestic ideology bolstered specific ideas about social organization. It provided the ideological means for socially conservative middle-class whites to police the behavior of other groups and to assign legitimacy— or illegitimacy—to competing beliefs.

Women in the early suffrage movement clearly *did* challenge the political and social hierarchy of the sexes. They sought to make democracy inclusive of women and, as a result, to permanently incorporate women into one of the most male-centered and sanctified activities: voting. Moreover, suffragists pursued their objectives in very public ways. They gave lectures and attended conventions; met in public halls, churches, and other well-trafficked sites; went door-to-door passing suffrage petitions and querying men and women's opinions about female enfranchisement; visited state legislators; and encouraged influential people to support the movement.

Few suffragists more boldly appropriated public space than Susan B. Anthony. In 1872, she and sixteen female colleagues created an uproar by attempting to vote for president at a Rochester, New York polling station.[14] Four years later, during the American Centennial, she and four compatriots disrupted a huge fourth of July ceremony by suddenly ascending the speaker's platform and handing a "Declaration of Rights for Women" to the event's chair.[15] As these examples suggest, suffragists did not simply behave like radicalized benevolent workers. They took actions other women deemed outrageous. Perceiving public space as the site of active citizenship, they took their demands to the most symbolic of political spaces and events: the polling place and the civic celebration. By breaking men's monopoly on political ritual, Anthony and her associates declared women equal citizens and equal claimants of public space.[16]

Such actions did not go answered. Antisuffragists routinely accused suffragists of breaching the boundaries of the private, domestic sphere. They ridiculed their femininity and stereotyped movement followers as manly, strident, abrasive shrews. Facing such invective was the least of suffragists' problems, however. Individuals of both sexes often presumed that women in public relinquished the right to "genteel" treatment. Rochester officials indicted Anthony for trying to vote and forced her to sit through a shockingly improper trial.[17] Less well-known women sometimes faced physical threats. During the 1870s, suffrage speaker

Margaret Campbell and her husband (who arranged and advertised many of his wife's talks) confronted a maze of pranks and scares as they traveled across the country on behalf of woman suffrage. In one Colorado village, someone even sabotaged their horse-buggy so that a potentially dangerous "accident" would occur on the road.[18]

Suffragists fought harassment with logic and argument. They lambasted the notion of a unique center of women's work. Early on, they identified their right to *fight* for suffrage, like suffrage itself, as a natural right of all citizens—male or female. Physician Ann Preston took liberal individualism as her cue when she protested "against the tyranny of that public sentiment which assigns any arbitrary sphere to Woman." Rather, she insisted, "we believe that the woman who is obeying the convictions of her own soul, and whose ability is commensurate with her employment, is ever in her own true sphere."[19] Lydia Maria Child, another pioneering crusader for women's rights, challenged the basis of domestic ideology—and benevolent femininity—by downplaying ideas about woman's unique nature. "It is urged that if women participated in public affairs, puddings would be spoiled, and stockings neglected. Doubtless some such cases might occur; for we have the same human nature as men, [and] as men are sometimes so taken up with elections as to neglect their business for a while," so might women.[20]

As the movement became more conservative in the years after the Civil War, some suffragists countered criticism by emphasizing socially acceptable standards of femininity. Suffrage lecturer Cora Scott Pond of Massachusetts balanced politicking with proselytizing. At each stop on an 1884 speaking tour of Cape Cod towns, she and minister Anna Shaw introduced themselves to the clergy, engaged a hall for speaking, and asked the local newspaper editor to promote Pond's talk. They posted notices of the upcoming event in post offices and store windows, and on trees, fences, bridges, sign boards, and telegraph poles. Yet if these preparations revealed a pragmatic and savvy salesmanship, the event itself emulated a friendly and unintimidating center for women: the Protestant church—one of the ideological wellsprings of organized female benevolency and one of the few institutions that warmly welcomed and encouraged women's attendance. Just like a prayer meeting, Pond's presentation included a suffrage sermon, religious hymns, and requests for "offerings."[21] Other suffrage events radiated a sense of gentility, refinement, and domesticity. The organizers of the 1878 New England Woman Suffrage Association Festival promised to fill their gathering with beautiful flowers, vines, "and other green and growing things," thus tapping into associations between women and nature, beauty, and regeneration.[22] Likewise, when Iowa suffragists constructed a woman suffrage pavilion at their state's 1889 fair, they named it a "Woman Suffrage Home" and proudly touted it as "the neatest, the cosiest [sic], the most homelike place upon the grounds."[23]

Efforts such as these often raised the ire of remaining radicals. Anthony expressed disdain for a colleague who wanted to make " 'the suffrage conventions a little more aesthetic.' " "Well now, perhaps if we could paint injustice in delicate tints set in a framework of political argument, we might more easily entrap the Senator Edmunds and Oscar Wilde types of Adam's sons," she sarcastically wrote her good friend Elizabeth Cady Stanton. "Suppose at our next convention all of us dress in pale greens, have a faint and subdued gaslight with pink shades, write our speeches in verse and chant them to guitar accompaniment. Ah me! Alas! How can we reform the world aesthetically?"[24]

Disagreement over the best ways to promote the cause also strained the twentieth-century suffrage movement. As in the past, radicals worked to incorporate themselves into male-defined discourses, sites, and rituals. However, mainstream suffragists had become even more determined to highlight their commitment to traditional standards of femininity. Couching demands for enfranchisement in conservative calls to motherhood and domestic duty, these suffragists represented themselves as paragons of womanly virtue who selflessly put family and community needs above personal interests.

Despite continuing tensions, however, the dynamics of the movement had changed in important ways. In the early years of the new century, dramatic and bold English suffragists gained international attention by actively appropriating urban spaces and adopting traditionally male-defined methods of political protest. Such actions helped embolden and revitalize the U.S. movement. Although American suffragists of all ideological stripes began to reconsider their strategies for winning the vote, none did so with more alacrity than radicals.[25] After working firsthand with English suffragists, both Harriot Stanton Blatch and Alice Paul urged Americans to follow English women into the world of political spectacle. Blatch's cross-class, New York City-based Equality League of Self-Supporting Women (founded in 1907 and renamed the Women's Political Union in 1910) pioneered what historian Ellen DuBois calls a "proud and aggressive" style of agitation. With elite members drawing inspiration from the English suffrage movement and working-class members from "the militant tradition of the labor movement," the League regularly laid claim to public space through male-defined political rituals. The League held mass meetings, crowded New York state legislature suffrage hearings, and arranged the first large-scale U.S. woman suffrage parade.[26]

Mainstream suffragists responded more ambivalently to the English example. They recognized that English radicals' emphasis on spectacle brought tremendous and well-needed publicity to the cause, but they feared that the wrong kind of spectacle would reaffirm popular stereotypes about strident, shrewish suffragists. Mainstream suffragists thus rejected radicals as wholly other than themselves. Radical Lydia Kingmill Commander prided herself on being one of the first American militants to speak "night after night on the streets, and in the dancehalls" on behalf of suffrage. Yet nonradicals in the movement rebuffed and insulted Commander by characterizing "suffragettes" like her as "almost a disgrace to womanhood."[27] However, mainstream activists responded less confidently to the actual tactics of radicals. When Blatch invited the anti-radically inclined NAWSA to join her first parade, its leaders warned that such an event "would set suffrage back fifty years." Ultimately, NAWSA principals cooperated with Blatch—but only after she agreed to have participants ride ladylike in cars rather than march brazenly on foot. Furthermore, at the last minute several leaders (including soon-to-be NAWSA president Carrie Chapman Catt) excused themselves from the parade with dubious claims of poor health.[28]

Twentieth-century suffragists who took up traditionally male means of political protest also found critics outside the fold. In 1908, suffragists addressing an outdoor crowd on Wall Street found themselves pelted with "apple-cores, wet sponges, coils of ticker tape, and bags of water dropped from upper windows."[29] In 1912, women in a New York parade were "jostled," "crowded out of line," subjected to "ribald jests and insults," and "robbed by pickpockets, some of whom grabbed handbags right under the noses of" on-duty police officers.[30] The worst instance of violence directed at suffragists occurred at the mammoth 1913 Washington, D.C. suffrage procession, at which approximately 300,000 onlookers watched more than 5,000 suffragists march down Pennsylvania Avenue the day before Woodrow Wilson's presidential inauguration. More than three hundred people—mostly woman suffragists—were injured when thousands of spectators rioted.[31] Male—and even some female—bystanders verbally abused, physically assaulted, and fondled parade marchers. Several men jumped on parade floats and tried to accost terrified women riders (fig. 2.1).[32] When suffragists forced Congress to investigate the incident, antisuffragists blamed parade participants for the situation. After calling the entire idea of a suffrage parade an "aggressive vulgarity," one antisuffrage editorialist concluded that

> Womanhood can not have its cake and eat it. If women want the kind of consideration to which they have been accustomed they must live by the conventional standards. When women cease to conduct themselves as "ladies"—when they adopt the motives and antics and methods of the circus—they must not expect delicate consideration.[33]

In other words, women in public could still be deemed unworthy of respect and courtesy.

FIGURE 2.1 *1913 Washington, D.C. parade.*
Suffragists found themselves surrounded by unfriendly and aggressive onlookers during this NAWSA-sponsored event.
"Exhibit 1," Suffrage Parade Hearings 1.

By the time the Washington, D.C. procession occurred, however, mainstream suffragists had abandoned their ambivalence toward many forms of public protest. Indeed, the NAWSA—the group that blanched at Blatch's first suffrage parade—sponsored the spectacular, violence-marred, capital event. Historians have attributed mainstream suffragists' acceptance of political street theater to renewed interest in the cause. Certainly, the excitement of the times inspired some women to try almost anything that would bring attention to the movement. Even conservative suffragists quickly came to realize that parades and other colorful stunts offered effective means of publicity.

Nothing demonstrated this point more convincingly than the successful California woman suffrage campaign of 1911. Fearing that votes for women would lead to prohibition, California's powerful liquor industry had long stonewalled the state's active suffrage movement. In 1911, California women worked to outwit and out-organize their opponents by running the boldest, most dramatic campaign yet held in the United States. Impeccable timing gave the cause momentum. In 1910, Washington State women raised the first successful suffrage campaign in sixteen years. When California women followed suit, fellow American suffragists—still buoyed with excitement—eagerly offered assistance. For the first time, organizations across the nation enthusiastically sent money and paid speakers to another campaign state. With aid coming from all quarters and with English precedent setting the tone, suffragists in California made the appropriation of public space an important component of their work. Using traditional forms of political ritual, they took to the streets in voter canvasses, parades, pageants, rallies, mass meetings, and street speeches. They experimented with automobile caravans; they put up billboards, electric signs, and broadsides; and they made full use of suffrage buttons and badges. When the dust from the campaign had settled, a breathtakingly small electoral margin gave California women the vote.[34]

The closeness of the race did not dampen the enthusiasm of out-of-state women, however. Suffragists across the nation sought copies of Golden State literature, buttons, pennants, and paraphernalia. NAWSA officer Mary Ware Dennett asked the California Campaign Committee to send her "one sample . . . of everything issued by every suffrage association which is represented on your campaign committee. Anything in fact, that will show the character and variety of methods used in California." She expressed particular interest in the "propaganda" that publicly heralded the cause, like the "small 'snipe' posters," the "street-car mottoes," and the "big street posters 10 feet by 8." Convinced that many suffragists could learn from California's strategy, Dennett organized a display of its promotional material at the upcoming NAWSA annual convention in Louisville, Kentucky. "You have no idea," wrote Dennett, "how the delegates to the Convention . . . will be thrilled and interested by these things."[35] The newly enfranchised women responded eagerly to such requests. Palo Alto suffragist Alice Park constantly advised her disfranchised friends to embrace spectacle. She told Iowa women how to prepare advance publicity for visiting suffrage speakers, and she encouraged New York women to embolden their approach to street meetings. In 1912, she set up shop in Arizona and helped women in that state run their successful suffrage campaign. Wherever she went, she praised all the inventive and dramatic political tactics she encountered.[36]

Suffragists did not adopt such methods merely because they seemed effective. People seldom abandon long-held concerns about propriety just because new ideas seem advantageous. Indeed, nonradicals could have emulated Washington women, who won the vote through a quiet and thoroughly respectable campaign. Something else made the California campaign compelling. Several variables had conjoined to make the appropriation of public space and the embrace of political ritual seem valuable and possible. To begin with, new definitions of the "public" encouraged suffragists to reevaluate how they spread the suffrage message. At the same time, an emerging equation between the urban landscape and the commercial landscape led to new ideas about spectacle and spectatorship that suffragists eagerly tapped and exploited.

Michael Schudson argues that the United States never possessed a Habermasian public sphere in which a large cross-section of the population actively engaged in critical-rational debate.[37] But at one time, white Americans generally did define the "public" as a collection of white, male, republican citizens who approached civic duties independently, assertively, and wisely.[38] Although nineteenth-century partisanship had long demonstrated the fantasy of this ideal, it was not until the 1870s that many thinkers began to reevaluate this optimistic faith in public citizens. Numerous forces contributed to the intellectual shift. To some extent, the growing commercialization of public space had already begun to usurp civic rituals and memorials as the dominant ideological markers of the physical landscape. In addition, many

Americans viewed urbanization, immigration, class and ethnic differences, and political corruption and machine politics as profound threats to the idea of an independent citizenry devoted first and foremost to the republic's well-being. These forces, along with a powerful domestic ideology that had long identified the home as the center of meaningful life, made many white, middle-class Americans feel estranged from urban life. As crowded city streets became the sparring grounds of intercultural conflict over language, religion, dress, and custom, the white middle class sought to isolate itself in homogeneous suburban enclaves.[39] Refuge, however, was hampered by muckraking journalists like Jacob Riis, who brought cultural comparisons into private middle-class homes through increasingly prosperous and sensationalist newspapers and magazines.

Stuart Ewen argues that reform-minded writers in the 1870s began to identify homebound readers as a powerful and unique type of public. Drawing from early notions about civic-minded republican citizens, these writers defined the new public as educated and well-intentioned victims of an increasingly complex world that occluded the truth about social conditions. Ultimately hopeful, however, these reformers believed that if magazines, books, and newspapers could uncover the truth about poverty, political intrigue, or any assortment of social ills, the reading public would fight for change. The late nineteenth-century explosion in the publishing industry (a phenomenon discussed more fully in chapter 5) contributed to the idea that readers comprised an earnest but uninformed and isolated public. Eager to exploit the sensationalistic possibilities of muckraking journalism, newspapers and national magazines eagerly printed exposés on corruption, graft, and social hardship. By the twentieth century, using the press to create interest in—and reveal the "truth" about—specific topics had become a standard tactic of progressive reformers. A new name for attracting—and managing—the reading public's attention had even evolved: publicity.[40]

The English suffrage movement and the successful California campaign convinced a growing number of suffragists to court publicity. Like earlier reform-minded journalists and other contemporary reformers, women in the twentieth-century movement began to argue that "publicity and propaganda" would not only make the reading public aware of their struggle, but also prove the movement's virtue. "As I get it," explained Rose Young, director of New York's 1915 Empire State Campaign Committee's Press department, the concern of suffragists with organization, with publicity, and with propaganda is one and the same—to insure the education of the voter on the question of suffrage, make him see what it means in principle, how it works in practice, correlate the impending political enfranchisement of woman with her other already achieved enfranchisements, make him see that suffrage is not a sidestep that stands out with a sinister detachment from the world's progress, but is part of that progress.[41]

Lacking the insider status of reform-minded writers who could easily use the press to promote change, however, suffragists like Young had to think creatively about how they could get the press to spread the suffrage message. As Young noted, "If you concede that you want to keep suffrage before the public as a live issue, as the livest issue of the times, you must concede that you've got to keep it in the newspapers. To keep it in the newspapers you must relate it acceptably to the news of the day."[42] That took planning. By the 1910s, the NAWSA in particular had become much more astute about organizational structure and campaign strategizing. According to historian Sara Hunter Graham, this turnaround in operations made the NAWSA an effective player at pressure politics, and part of that politics included carefully managed, press-oriented publicity. In 1912, the Association launched a publicity bureau with a budget of $3,000.[43] Like the publicity committees and departments of other suffrage groups, the bureau focused on turning public space into a setting for "spectacular affairs" and stunts that caught the press's imagination through "beauty, picturesqueness or oddity." The Empire State Campaign committee's press department proved especially adept at this tactic. Under Young's direction, it staged a Carnegie Hall Mass Meeting, a parade, a pageant, a suffrage baseball game, a "made-in-the USA Exposition" of goods, a May Day celebration, and a "One-Day" women's "strike" in which women refused to perform the paid and unpaid labor they contributed to families and society. Gearing each event more toward readers at home than eyewitness bystanders, the publicity workers in the department struggled to see that "each and every" stunt received "adequate press reaction."[44]

Not all stunts received the type of media coverage suffragists desired. In the end, the editors and publishers who controlled newspapers and magazines retained tremendous influence over how the reading public perceived suffragists. As women in the mainstream movement came to realize, even carefully contrived scenarios could backfire. Iowa suffragists, for example, firmly rebuffed NAWSA offers of assistance after reading about the dramatic activities it sponsored in cities like New York. According to NAWSA president Carrie Chapman Catt, negative news reports convinced Iowans that the Association "would queer the whole situation" if it sent people into their state. "My belief," she argued, "is substantiated by the timidity of the women concerning open-air meetings. Many local leaders would not allow them at all."[45] This incident underscores the substantial differences that often existed between urban and rural suffrage movements, but it also demonstrates the press's ability to control what readers learned about events. Without a positive response from the press, even the most eye-catching publicity stunts could achieve limited—even contrary—results.

The reading public represented only one of the audiences that suffragists sought to influence. They also had to contend with what they and many other reformers defined as the irrational, undifferentiated, heterogeneous, urbanized mass public who crowded suffrage spectacles and displays in search of amusement, enlightenment, or perhaps simply a shorter trek to work, home, or the market.[46] The reduction of public citizens to a senseless crowd signified a major intellectual departure from the past, one that reflected not only white, middle-class anxieties about urbanization and immigration, but also new social scientific theories about group dynamics. French social psychologist Gustave Le Bon explained that crowds possessed a collective mentality that made them resistant to logic and reason. Instead, he argued, crowds acted out of instinct and longed for spectacle and emotional release. Le Bon was not entirely cynical about the rise of this debased public, however. He suggested that a managerial elite could control the urban masses' opinions by tapping into their love of amusement and illusion.[47] Stuart Ewen concludes that Le Bon's work became highly influential among American progressives in part because it rationalized popular fears about immigrants and city life.[48]

Harriot Stanton Blatch's initial justification for organizing suffrage parades reflected the popularity of these ideas. Convinced "that mankind is moved to action by emotion, not by argument and reason," Blatch concluded that the color and dash of parades offered unbeatable tools of persuasion. "What could be more stirring," she asked, "than hundreds of women, carrying banners, marching—marching—marching?"[49] Other suffragists agreed. Glenna Tinnin, chair of the 1913 Washington, D.C. pageant committee, stressed that suffragists needed to court voters with dramatic, visual appeals to emotion. Caught up in the nationwide pageantry craze of the early 1900s, Tinnin argued that "a pageant can be immeasurably more convincing than the best of lectures, for it can say the same thing to the public the lecturer says, and in that 'that same thing' is presented pictorially, it goes forth with power." She concluded that "an idea that is driven home to the mind through the eye produces a more striking and lasting impression than any that goest [sic] through the ear."[50]

Le Bon's theories found resonance with suffragists and other American progressives not only because definitions of the public had changed, but also because similar ideas about the allure of spectacle and illusion had already found support in nearby quarters. Le Bon simply gave these beliefs the imprimatur of social science. Since at least the 1880s, a new breed of consumer capitalist (including department store owners and mass producers of cheap consumer goods) and a growing cadre of consumer industry support staff (including department store managers, advertisers, trade journalists, and merchandise display experts) had concluded that visual appeals to fantasy and emotion could convince middle-class women shoppers to buy almost anything. Le Bon's theories thus extended already popular ideas about the gullibility and irrationality of women to other socially suspect groups, such as immigrants and members of the working class, and confirmed retailers' previous assumption that the thoughts and actions of such individuals could be managed by trained professionals.

As large-scale consumer capitalism exploded in the late nineteenth century and the commercial emphasis on spectacle ballooned, the visual context of the urban landscape changed—and so did perceptions of public space. According to historian Michael Booth, the growth of a consumer economy, new urban forms, and large-scale urban institu-tions helped acclimate mid-nineteenth century English citizens to a commercialized public sphere. These forces "conditioned" city dwellers into accepting "mass grandeur and elaborate ornamentation" as parts of daily life.[51] Similar forces were at work in the urbanizing United States. Mammoth department stores with fanciful plate-glass window displays, elaborate commercial theaters, gigantic painted and electric signs, sen-sationalist newspapers, and other commercial markers of public space insinuated consumer-oriented spectacle into the quotidian routines of many Americans. Not only did these marvels imply that virtually all populated settings could be transformed into commercial venues, but they also suggested that the spectacular was simultaneously fantastic and commonplace, extraordinary yet mundane.

The naturalization of commercial spectacle provided a new lens through which to view the world. Film theorist Anne Friedberg calls this mode of perception a "mobilized virtual gaze," which she defines as a "received perception mediated through representation" that "travels in an imaginary *flânerie* through an imaginary elsewhere and an imaginary elsewhen."[52] Newspaper photography, early forms of cinema, and elaborate department store re-creations of Parisian streets, Egyptian temples, and Arabian nights all created fantastic visions that transported onlookers to imaginary times and places.[53] Men and women observers related to this mode of perception in different ways. Tradition gave the male spectator, or *flâneur*, the ability to wander in and out of public spaces with ease and without question. Moreover, the flâneur's possession of an objectifying "male gaze" allowed him to master the visual register and all that it contained. Some scholars conclude that women, as subjects of male objectification, were unable to assume this dominating form of spectatorship.[54] But Friedberg disagrees, arguing that the identification of shopping as a socially acceptable form of leisure in the late nineteenth century gave urban women a new sense of public freedom that, in turn, translated into a new kind of spectator: the *flâneuse*, the female observer. Like the flâneur, the flâneuse possessed a mobilized gaze that stemmed from her pedestrian orientation. However, she only assumed a controlling gaze in the new public spaces that treasured women's consumption—places like department stores and amusement parks.[55] Perhaps it is more accurate, therefore, to see the flâneuse as someone who indeed possessed greater public freedom, but remained oddly positioned between public spectator and public spectacle. The shopper's recognized right to observe and participate in the consumer marketplace gave the flâneuse public respectability, but because she had limited access to a controlling form of spectatorship, she remained subject to the dominating, objectifying gaze of the flâneur.

The California campaign's willingness to go beyond traditional forms of political ritual by embracing commercially derivative uses of public space—such as electric signs—suggests that women in the revitalized suffrage movement had keyed into both the naturalization of commercial spectacle and the emphasis on commercial spectatorship. Moreover, like the businesses that sought to capture the observing gaze of the flâneur and flâneuse via vibrant and dramatic architecture, windows, and billboards, suffragists recognized urban geography and topography as advertising space. Other activists had followed commercial institutions down this path. In 1888, the Democratic party of New York leased advertising space on Manhattan streetcars.[56] In 1913, supporters of the radical International Workers of the World labor union rented Madison Square Garden for a pageant reenacting the famous Paterson, New Jersey silk strike. Publicity for the event included red electric lights spelling out i.w.w. on the Garden tower.[57] But no political party, union, or social cause during the progressive period utilized the advertising potential of public space as fully as did suffragists, especially urban suffragists.

The most dramatic indication of suffragists' new understanding of public space followed the relocation of the NAWSA headquarters from Warren, Ohio to New York City in late 1909 (the new headquarters became functional in 1910). Wealthy suffrage supporter Alva Belmont underwrote the move's cost and paid a year's rent for NAWSA office space in a Broadway skyscraper. But the ambitious Belmont wanted to do more than establish the NAWSA in a prominent location. She wanted to make its presence visible and dramatic, wanted to capture the gaze of the workers, shoppers, and passersby who hurried along Broadway each day. Belmont proposed placing an eye-catching NAWSA electric sign on top the office building housing the Association, but the property's owners refused her request. Undaunted, she bought a nearby building and hung her sign proudly from its pinnacle.[58]

By the mid-1910s, suffragists had become experts at advertising suffrage events, campaigns, and groups by incorporating movement messages into well-trafficked sites. In 1915, the NAWSA and local Chicago suffragists used "practically every advertising medium available" to publicize that city's upcoming suffrage parade. They painted billboards, showed promotional slides in movie theaters, and even installed a large electric sign on Michigan Avenue—one of the busiest and most renowned shopping streets in the country. For the entire week preceding the parade the sign encouraged women to HELP NAIL THE SUFFRAGE PLANK. ATTEND NATIONAL SUFFRAGE CONFERENCE, PRINCESS THEATRE, JUNE 6. MARCH IN THE SUFFRAGE PARADE, JUNE 7. (fig. 2.2).[59]

Nothing, however, compared to the "Empire State Campaign." In response to the New York State woman suffrage referendum of 1915, the Empire State Campaign Committee formed a press and publicity council dedicated to making the movement visible. One hundred

FIGURE 2.2 *1916 suffrage billboard.*
Constructed across from the Chicago Coliseum, where the Republican Party
held its presidential nominating convention.
Reproduced by permission of the Susan B. Anthony Ephemera Collection,
Huntington Library, San Marino, California.

volunteers made it virtually impossible for pedestrians, motorists, and onlookers to ignore the suffrage message. Suffragists covered the visual landscape with advertisements. They distributed 149,533 posters— "thousands" hung from trees, on fences, and in the windows of houses, apartments, and storefronts. Other posters decorated the interiors of banks, moving picture and vaudeville theaters, and other businesses (fig. 2.3). New York women gave away a million suffrage buttons. They convinced "hundreds" of movie house operators to show suffrage slides between entertainments. In the last weeks of the campaign they placed 400 small electric signs in shop windows, and they hung "large net campaign banners" at Fifth Avenue and Thirty-first Street and at Columbus Circle. The Street Railways Advertising Company gave suffragists $8,000 worth of free advertising space on city streetcars. When antisuffragist "discrimination" frustrated attempts to rent similar spaces on the subway, hundreds of suffragists rode the lines wearing cardboard "lapboards" that spelled out suffrage slogans. In happy contrast to the harassment they often faced when performing such acts, these women were treated with "great courtesy and respect" by the "public."[60]

The embrace of commercially inspired spectacles did more than add new life to suffragists' political methods, however. It also influenced how suffragists represented themselves within a world of commercialized public drama. Like the flâneuse, the suffragist who participated in stunts and political rituals occupied that oddly dual position between spectacle and spectator. When women wore lapboards, sandwich boards, suffrage buttons, and even suffrage fashions the female body in public was a unique form of spectacle; it attracted notice and remained constantly susceptible to the controlling gaze of the flâneur/male voter (fig. 2.4). As a male parade watcher disappointed at the appearance of a group of marchers disparagingly put it, "These are nothing but hens. We came out to see chickens."[61]

While an earlier generation of women might have feared the rebukes and opprobrium that accompanied such conspicuousness, twentieth-century suffragists redefined notoriety as free advertising and embraced their status as spectacle. Transplanted English suffragist Elisabeth Freeman explained this ideological shift while justifying her work as a New York "newsy" (an outdoor newspaper vendor) for the *Woman's Journal.* When a Wall Street businessman scolded Freeman and asked why she did " 'not stay home . . . and try nice quiet means to get your

FIGURE 2.3 *"Vote" poster.*
Posters like this advertised the 1915 New York suffrage campaign.
Courtesy United States History, Local History & Genealogy Division, The New York Public Library, Astor, Lenox and Tilden Foundations.

vote?' " she replied that " 'women have tried that way for over 60 years and it did not work.' " But just " 'look at this fine method of advertising,'"she continued. " 'It would be worth several thousand dollars to any

FIGURE 2.4 *Suffrage sandwich board.*
Sandwich boards and other devices transformed women's bodies into explicit advertisements for the cause.
Courtesy NAWSA Papers, Library of Congress.

business.' " Indeed, it would. Newsies not only provoked immediate attention, but also proved a favorite subject of newspaper photographers (fig. 2.5).[62]

Suffragists who took to the streets also identified themselves as observers of spectacle. They watched parades and pageants, attended mass meetings and rallies, walked by suffrage windows, broadsides, and billboards, and looked for friendly pedestrians wearing suffrage buttons and pins. Yet, like the gaze of the flâneuse, the gaze of the suffragist often seemed to uphold commercial standards of looking. The same emphasis on fantasy, color, and abundance in descriptions of department store displays and windows found its way into accounts and reminiscences of suffrage events, especially parades. In recalling her arrival at the site of the 1913 Washington, D.C. procession, Rhode Island suffrage leader Sara Algeo described the parade route as "transformed" into "a creation mostly of Alladin's [sic] lamp."[63] Clearly familiar with the commercial resonance of her metaphor, she added that "the power of the magicians [sic] touch began boldly to show itself on Saturday, March 3d. Mingled with the Inaugural decorations of gay bunting and stars and stripes, the suffrage colors appeared on the shop fronts. Great bunches of Votes for Women pennants were for sale in the hands of every street-vendor."[64] People outside the movement made similar allusions. A San Francisco newspaper tapped into the imagery of popular and exotic new department store displays when it noted that a 1912 torchlight suffrage parade on New York's Fifth Avenue resembled "the lawn of a Chinese Mandarin on fete night."[65] One cartoonist made the association even more explicit. In a drawing entitled "On to Albany," vendors line a suffrage parade route. Political and consumer desire literally merge as women shop and peruse merchandise while marching for their rights (fig. 2.6).

Businesses compounded the associations between political and commercial spectacle. During the 1910s, a number of retailers exploited the growing popularity of the suffrage movement by incorporating suffrage symbols, colors, and commodities into their store decorations. Algeo noted that merchants in Washington, D.C. prepared for the 1913 suffrage parade by bedecking their shop fronts in suffrage hues. Likewise, the elite Fifth Avenue stores lining New York suffrage parade routes "bloomed in suffrage colors" on the days before processions.[66] In 1912, Macy's department store created an elaborate window display to herald

FIGURE 2.5

Woman suffrage newsies.

Courtesy NAWSA Papers, Library of Congress.

an upcoming parade. "But here was a window," wrote F. F. Purdy in the trade journal *Merchants Record and Show Window*:

a fine scheme in orange with a large portrait of Julia Ward Howe high in center, draped with an American flag and ornamented by a big orange bow with flowing ends. The official white hats with

FIGURE 2.6 *"On to Albany."*
As in this cartoon, suffragists and nonsuffragists often associated the spectacle of suffrage parades with the spectacle of consumerism.
Reproduced by permission of the Susan B. Anthony Ephemera Collection,
Huntington Library, San Marino, California.

yellow [the traditional suffrage color] trimming were numerous. There were many pennants, of various colleges and universities, as well as the familiar "Votes for women" pennant. It was a golden window, down to the gilt buttons, and even the fixtures, and a saddle in center, of russet leather, harmonizing, many women riding horseback in the parade, especially the officers and organizers of the parade.[67]

Paying tribute to the suffrage movement through such displays did more than confuse the boundaries between political and commercial spectacle; it incorporated the movement into a lifestyle fantasy centered around commodity consumption. Macy's collapsed the differences between commercial and political longings by creating a vision of proud, educated, and stylishly outfitted women citizens. To give further credence to that fantasy, almost everything in the window was for sale. Indeed, the discriminating Macy's shopper could even buy a complete parade marching outfit including "war bonnet, hat pins, lanterns, wide sash, chrysanthemum, stole, two buttons, [and a] pennant" for only $1.68.[68]

Suffragists celebrated and encouraged the spatial mingling of commercial and political fantasy. In 1912, they named Macy's "headquarters for suffrage supplies" and encouraged supporters to stock up on proper regalia. Numerous suffrage groups, including the NAWSA, opened suffrage stores in bustling shopping districts. In 1915, New York women sponsored a summer carnival sport at the popular amusement zone Luna Park.[69] Some suffragists even revealed their own commodity-centered lifestyle fantasies. Hoping to dramatically convince onlookers of suffragists' unity, dignity, and respectability, a number of suffrage parade organizers imposed dress requirements on marchers. Organizers of a 1916 New Haven, Connecticut parade insisted that marchers wear white and buy twenty-cent parade hats and ten-cent parade lanterns, both of which were conveniently sold at suffrage headquarters. They also urged college students to rent caps, gowns, and hoods for $1.50.[70] Even in less rigidly planned processions, smaller groups of suffragists managed to tie their public identities to commodities. Although the organizers of the Boston Woman Suffrage Victory Parade of 1915 explicitly rejected obligatory marching costumes, participating suffragists from the Middlesex County Conference required members to don a twenty-five-cent "Middlesex sash" worn "from right shoulder to left hip."[71] Similarly, one young woman prepared for an upcoming New York parade by indulging in campaign paraphernalia. At the city's suffrage headquarters, she "laid in a stock of flags, buttons, buttercups and a parade hat" just in time for the event.[72] In each case, activists implied that the absence of certain goods hampered the ability to demand public attention—to become the spectacle. Without the right hat or sash, a woman had no place in the New Haven parade or in the Middlesex County Conference—her presence in the public sphere simply did not count.

If suffragists had come to define the commercially outfitted body as an important component of respectable public life, however, much of its potency stemmed from its underlying message about class. No factor influenced the use of commodities more than money. Historian Nan Enstad describes how progressive-era working-class women attempted to erase their class status by indulging in "elaborate fashion, conspicuous consumption, and a pleasure seeking style." Middle-class women often resented what they saw as working girls' inappropriate and wasteful attempts to "play the lady."[73] Suffrage parade dress requirements gave material weight to such concerns by immediately categorizing women according to financial means. A 1912 *New York Tribune* article perceptively captured this subtext. A "little shop girl" watching one parade could not even afford a small, fifteen-cent "Votes for Women" flag, let alone a thirty-seven-cent hat designed for marchers. Conversely, Miss Cora Martin, a worker at the NAWSA Madison Avenue headquarters, could easily buy such an accessory—but she opposed it strongly. "This association," she noted, "believes in a woman wearing the hat that she looks best in, whether it costs 37 cents or $37."[74]

While some suffragists used commodities to publicly acknowledge the social and spatial privileges of middle-class and elite women, others disavowed the economic inequities of consumer culture. They implied that the public display of goods made the drama and excitement of commercial culture accessible to all through spectatorship. Automobiles made this suggestion explicit. Cars were uncommon in many parts of the United States during the 1910s; thus, suffragists created quite a stir when they delivered speeches from motor vehicles. Yet automobiles remained the expensive toys of the elite, and their use called to mind stereotypes of the moneyed class. Some suffragists welcomed such evocations. The same women who insisted on uniform dress in the 1916 New Haven procession invited wealthy supporters to enter cars in the event and to lease available seats for the steep fee of one dollar. For other suffragists, however, such stereotypes interfered with efforts to reach a diverse audience of potential voters. Consequently, some women represented cars not as symbols of class status but as providers of mass public entertainment. One group of suffragists driving through Ohio, for example, temporarily joined a visiting circus. When a circus manager invited the women to speak at his show they pulled their car "behind the elephants" and drove to the big top.[75] Suffragists passing through Clinton, Massachusetts turned their caravan into a miniparade. They strung their Buick "stem to stern" with "yard-wide strips of yellow cloth" advertising suffrage speaker HELEN TODD OF CALIFORNIA. Inside the car, recalled a former suffragist, sat "two of the best looking women in the district—and a trumpeter." As they traveled through the community, "only the blind and deaf . . . were unaware that the suffragists had hit the town," (figs. 2.7 and 2.8).[76]

As these examples suggest, suffragists had given life to a new kind of street theater that simultaneously highlighted and erased class conflict, conflated political protest and commercial spectacle, and merged public debate with commodity-centered fantasy. By tapping into new ideas about spectacle, spectatorship, and the urban landscape and relating their struggle to new definitions of the "public," mainstream suffragists came to see the appropriation of public space and traditional forms of public political protest as socially acceptable, even ladylike. Balancing educational with emotional messages, twentieth-century mainstream suffragists used public space to tell stories about why all Americans needed women to vote. They constructed parade floats bemoaning industrialization's effect on public/private spheres. They held banners emphasizing maternal duty, municipal housekeeping, and consumer rights (fig. 2.9). They stood on street corners and talked about the self-sacrifice of mothers and the difficult lives of poor laboring women. Evoking the spirits of their more propriety-minded nineteenth-century predecessors, they constructed carefully controlled representations of womanhood. Paraders countered mannish stereotypes of suffragists by marching hand-in-hand with children and grandchildren. Young suffragists in particular used fashion and appearance to declare themselves arbiters of beauty, style, and modern femininity. Melodramatic pageants compared miserable, shackled, disfranchised women with beautiful, strong, and starry-eyed women voters. Suffrage movies shown in commercial theaters concocted elaborate narratives about the pluck and sex appeal of suffragists.

FIGURE 2.7

Suffragist Margaret Foley campaigning in Cleveland, 1912. Automobiles made
suffrage speeches a form of education and entertainment.
Courtesy NAWSA Papers, Library of Congress.

FIGURE 2.8 *"Getting Ready for the Washington Hike."*
American Press Association.

*Courtesy United States History, Local History & Genealogy Division, The New
York Public Library, Astor, Lenox and Tilden Foundations.*

FIGURE 2.9 *Typical banners.*

Parade banners for this New York procession distilled suffrage arguments into easy-to-read slogans. Note the banner addressing consumer needs. American Press Association.

Courtesy United States History, Local History & Genealogy Division, The New York Public Library, Astor, Lenox and Tilden Foundations.

The new ways in which mainstream suffragists entered political rituals and public space demonstrate how much ideas about citizenship and public life had changed since the beginning of the movement. As in the past—and as radical suffragists had always understood—public space was still a site for acting out the public requirements of citizenship. But citizenship was no longer defined in the narrow masculinist terms of nineteenth-century individualism and partisanship. The death of old-style party activism confirmed this transition. By 1908, once widely popular partisan-sponsored parades had become rare events, and by 1912, partisan marching companies had become virtually extinct.[77] Groups that continued to take to the streets on behalf of political and social struggles, like suffragists and striking workers, used their identities as women, workers, consumers, and patriots to demand accountability from industry, government, and the consumer marketplace.

But these new-style activists did more than take *to* the streets. Suffragists in particular took over the streets. Emulating the commercial marketplace that had attempted to visually stimulate women since at least the 1880s, suffragists covered the urban landscape with billboards, placards, electric signs, window displays, banners, buttons, and badges. They tapped into a commercial aesthetic that offered new ways of seeing and of being seen. They participated in blurring the boundaries between the commercial and the civic environments and in the merging of commercial and civic discourse, adding a new dimension to the politicization of public space, the meanings of political ritual, and the culture of women's politics.

Chapter 3

*On Stage: Personality, the Performing Self, and the
Representation of Woman Suffragists*

As a drama instructor, interpreter of dramatic and lyric poetry, playwright, and pageant producer, Glenna Smith Tinnin believed that public performances—particularly pageants—were the best way to promote
woman suffrage. With their visual, emotional nature, pageants' capacity
for "stirring sentiments" and "making appeals" was limitless. Plus, she
added, pageants allowed participants to subsume their identities (and
thus their inhibitions) "in an idea, a message or a story."[1] As chair of the
pageant committee for the 1913 Washington, D.C. Woman Suffrage
Procession, Tinnin set out to prove her theory. Assembling a talented
crew of professional theatrical artists who supported woman suffrage,
Tinnin attempted to transform the ideals of the movement into a visual
feast. The result was *The Allegory*, an extravagant series of pantomimes
set to music and performed on the steps of the federal treasury building.
With classically costumed women representing mythological and symbolic figures, the pageant tied concepts of peace, justice, charity, liberty,
and hope to women's enfranchisement (fig. 3.1).[2]

Sympathetic observers called the performance breathtaking. The
renowned playwright and pageant master Percy MacKaye, who enthusiastically supported the movement and whose sister Hazel had designed
and directed the event, remarked that its "majestic and sensuous beauty"
kept thousands of spectators enthralled. Even the apparently lowbrow
"frequenters of nondescript vaudeville and 'movies' " watched the story
"like the audience of a cathedral ritual." MacKaye himself contended
that *The Allegory* exuded a sense of magic and spontaneity that made
it almost hypnotizing. However, that too was part of the show, for as

FIGURE 3.1

Liberty and Her Attendants: Suffrage tableau, 1913 Washington, D.C.
Suffrage Pageant.
Courtesy NAWSA Papers, Library of Congress.

MacKaye readily acknowledged, the pageant's allure was both predictable and carefully orchestrated by skilled professionals "applying expert imagination to a definite end."[3]

The public presentation of *The Allegory* demonstrates clearly that as public space increasingly served as a stage for woman suffrage spectacles during the 1910s, suffragists increasingly saw themselves as public performers capable of both appropriating that space and manipulating impressions and representations of themselves and the cause. Pageantry was but one forum for expression. Plays, motion pictures, parades, public speaking events, and even fashion allowed suffragists to act out public, political identities and aspirations.

Recently, scholars have documented several types of suffrage performances. Kay Sloan has analyzed woman suffrage films, some of which suffrage groups produced in order to counteract negative stereotypes associated with supporters of votes for women.[4] Works by Karen Blair and Martin Tackel describe the colorful and theatrical woman suffrage pageants and tie them to the popular pageantry movement of the early twentieth century. Moreover, by closely documenting the democratic, anticommercial, and civic-minded philosophy behind pageants, their research reveals the continuing influence of republicanism on concepts of citizenship. As Blair writes, the individuals behind these inspirational dramas believed that "communal endeavors [such as pageants] nurtured a democratic society, and that the nation and its citizens would be stronger for the people's willingness to act together, toward common goals." Woman-suffrage pageants demonstrated that women could carve out meaningful public roles by contributing to these goals.[5]

Without exception, however, this scholarship overlooks two essential features of suffrage performances. One, these performances were not new in the 1910s. They had a long and impressive history within the movement and within the larger context of American reform tactics. Two, despite what Tackel in particular calls the anticommercial ideology of the pageantry movement, all types of twentieth-century suffrage performances reflected the evolving consumer culture's influence on constructions of modern identity. In conjunction with developments in advertising, public relations, psychology, and political thought, consumer culture extolled—and suffrage performances brought to life—new ideas about personality and the performing self.

As scholars note, the emotional culture of the early twentieth-century United States became increasingly obsessed with individual personality.

Writers, physicians, and advertisers encouraged men and women to develop winsome, charismatic personas that would supposedly foster intimate relationships, emotional vitality, and personal and business success. This "culture of personality" contrasted greatly with earlier generations' regard for character, defined by integrity, honor, reputation, and self-restraint. But the difference between character and personality went beyond these traits. The terms implied entirely different temperaments: while strength of character promised emotional and psychological stability, a vibrant personality assured a rich and varied emotional and social life. Just as significantly, while cultural critics in the nineteenth century emphasized the inherent nature of character, those in the twentieth stressed the ability to improve and hone personality through the right dress, manners, and behavior.[6]

The culture of personality had special implications for women. As Lary May has demonstrated, the vivacious, energetic traits of the modern personality fused with a Victorian ideal of female virtue to produce a powerful reconceptualization of womanhood. The much-discussed "new woman" combined the age-old virgin and whore archetypes into a model of fun-loving, modern, youthful, yet morally pure femininity. Movies, magazines, stores, and other vehicles of mass culture associated this new gender construct with consumerism by equating modernity with commodities such as makeup and fashionable attire. They likewise advised the "new woman" to follow the advice of advertisers and so-called celebrity experts such as Mary Pickford, whose regular newspaper column told women how to stay young, beautiful, and sexually desirable by purchasing the right merchandise.[7]

The belief that a more attractive personality could be assumed or projected through careful attention to looks and behavior formed the foundation of the modern concept of the performing self.[8] This idea was by no means new. As Richard Sennett argues, the tradition of *theatrum mundi*—wherein the world represents a stage upon which people act out various social roles—is almost as old as Western civilization itself. Philosophers as diverse as Plato, Petronius, Rousseau, and Diderot all expounded upon this thesis.[9] When the idea of the performing self became intertwined with the culture of personality in the late nineteenth and early twentieth centuries, however, it became inextricably associated with commodities, resulting in a new definition of the performing self. This definition accepted the nineteenth-century belief that appearance represented a social map of the body revealing one's nature and moral worth, but rejected the concomitant belief that these attributes were unalterable and inherent. Instead, new ideas about the performing self included popular social scientific and psychological theories about the malleability of personal identity and increasingly common commercial claims about the reified emotional qualities imparted by mass-produced goods. Together, these concepts implied that individuals could use commodities to highlight and improve different aspects of personality. Indeed, when combined with carefully practiced mannerisms and character traits, commodities could effectively control what the social map of the body said and how it was read.[10] Indeed, as Karen Halttunen's work on interior decorating suggests, commodities could extend that social map beyond the body and into physical spaces like the home.[11]

Vehicles of suffrage performance during the 1910s—including parades, plays, pageants, movies, public speaking events, and fashion—reveal how deeply the culture of personality and the idea of the performing self had influenced ideas about personal identity, political life, and women's political activism. Intent on overcoming disparaging preconceptions of suffrage campaigners, performance participants assumed an idealized public identity in much the same way consumers assumed a performing self. As this chapter will demonstrate, suffragists used physical appearance, dress, and personality to suggest that woman suffragists (and thus potential woman voters) were attractive, stylish, charming, dignified, and virtuous. They used such representations symbolically, implying that women's enfranchisement was a positive goal because woman suffragists were personable, likable, and modern individuals. In selling this image to the public, suffragists mimicked contemporary leaders of consumer industries. Like these business mavericks, they contended that identity could be a matter of fashion—that with the right commodities and advice, one's sense of self could be molded, retooled, compartmentalized, and reified. And like business leaders, suffragists suggested that projecting the right personality and the right performing self were not mere matters of luck or whim. The idealized representations suffragists created through performance required a careful attention to image, a skillful management of impressions, and a savvy willingness to both manipulate emotion and exploit the growing consumer culture's narcissistic preoccupation with looks, self-presentation, and outside approval.

Drawing upon the culture of personality and the performing self allowed suffragists to create a positive public image, reach a mass and diverse audience on its own turf, and associate their cause with highly admired contemporary values. Woman suffrage performances helped make the modern movement seem dynamic and exciting. That suffrage performance could stress democracy (as Tackel and Blair argue) while simultaneously contriving stage-managed constructions of the self suggests the emergence of a complex new vision of female citizenship. Women's political participation reflected a growing cultural preoccupation with the authority of scientific, expert, and celebrity advice and opinion—necessary components in the search for the best self-presentation. In addition to its other uses, therefore, suffrage performance became another component wedding the language and worldview of twentieth-century consumerism to that of American politics. This unlikely marriage was inscribed and played out upon the body. The performer—the suffragist—became the star.

Although Percy MacKaye characterized pageantry as a new and novel tool for civic reform, suffragists—as well as other reformers—had included dramatic performance in their repertoire of political tactics for some time.[12] As early as the 1880s, Massachusetts suffragists searched for plays with a "strong woman's rights moral." When they found only a few, leaders of the movement encouraged supporters to take up the pen and become playwrights themselves. Soon, short skits and plays became common features at suffrage sociables and meetings.[13] But suffrage drama extended beyond these modest efforts. The Massachusetts Woman Suffrage Association's 1889 *Historical Pageant* offered a spectacle of enormous scale and scope. Consisting of twenty tableaux enacting the history of Massachusetts, the pageant featured 500 male and female participants and lasted over five hours. After depicting the legendary meeting between Queen Isabella and Christopher Columbus and a series of other nationally significant events, the pageant ended with three pantomimes tracing the social progress of nineteenth-century American women.[14] Viewed by a sold-out audience at Boston's Hollis Street Theatre, the pageant received positive reviews from the Boston press and netted a profit of $1,115.95. Inspired by this success, pageant director Cora Scott Pond resigned her position as the Association's state organizer and took the play on the road, producing the *Historical Pageant* in Newport, Providence, and Hartford. Members of the Massachusetts Woman Suffrage Association organized another elaborate pageant the following year (this time celebrating the history of marriage).[15]

Ironically, the concept of woman suffrage often proved incidental to early suffrage performances. Although three of the twenty scenes in the *Historical Pageant* centered on women's progress, none dealt specifically with the movement, and a fourth was cut from the play at the last minute.[16] Instead, these dramas focused on the steadfast progress of the United States and its mainstream white civilization. Promoting woman suffrage in this fashion entailed plotting it obliquely along the trajectory of national advancement.

The nature of woman suffrage performance began to change in the early 1900s. Pageantry had suddenly become popular with a variety of townships, artists, and social reformers. According to David Glassberg, civic boosters and recreational workers saw pageants as a way of bringing communities together and fostering a greater sense of patriotism and local pride.[17] Other groups also recognized pageants as a means of social enlightenment. The radical I.W.W. staged one of the most renowned spectacles of the time: the Paterson Silk Strike Pageant of 1913. Held at New York's Madison Square Garden and featuring actual participants in the infamous New Jersey strike, the event provided tremendous publicity for the strikers and helped strengthen ties among workers.[18] African Americans joined the pageantry craze with W.E.B. DuBois's *The Star of Ethiopia*, which included a cast of more than a thousand people and used positive depictions of historically significant Africans and African Americans to instill racial pride and counter prejudice.[19]

Sparked by the new interest in pageantry, prosuffrage pageants and plays became widely performed and easily accessible. *The Woman's Journal* and several other women's rights periodicals began printing new plays for readers to perform. During the 1910s, the NAWSA made it even easier to find scripts for such shows by selling them through a series of catalogs. In some cases, the catalog's synopsis is all that remains of these dramas. But even these brief records reveal that the theme of woman suffrage was no longer a minor component of plots.[20] Woman-suffrage performances now dealt directly with this subject. Often, the new plays and pageants reflected the movement's growing emphasis on expediency. Charlotte Perkins Gilman's *Something to Vote For*, for example, exposed the dangers of impure milk and suggested that voting women could enforce dairy industry regulations. Likewise, *Put to the Test*, by Mrs. Oreola Williams Haskell, used expediency defenses to comically demonstrate the hollowness of antisuffragists' "indirect influence" argument, which contended that women influenced public policy through private entreaty and prayer and therefore did not need the ballot.[21]

The new dramas also included more fully developed characters. As the nineteenth-century Massachusetts Woman Suffrage Association's pageants suggest, early suffrage performances privileged themes, such as marriage or national progress, over characterization. The tableaux and imagery, not the actors, stole the show. Later works, however, centered on the personal effects of disfranchisement. In Gilman's play, one character's son dies from contaminated milk. A young man in English suffragist Cicily Hamilton's *How the Vote Was Won* realizes that helping woman suffrage means helping himself, since living by the maxim "a woman's place is in the home" would make him fiscally responsible for his unmarried female relatives.[22]

Even pageants—by nature thematically oriented—highlighted the individual impact of disfranchisement. One NAWSA-sponsored St. Louis pageant contrasted nonvoting women dressed in shackles and long, black mourning clothes with "tall, splendid blondes and brunettes, gold-crowned and brightly-garbed" female voters. The disfranchised women stood physically below their more fortunate sisters, despairing about their inability to ascend to the higher plane of civilization (fig. 3.2). Other pageants used similar imagery to stress the personal humiliation of being denied a further role in the nation's aggrandizement.[23] Shackles served as a common prop. Symbols of bondage and servitude, they brought the meaning of disfranchisement to a personal, material level that associated women with the lowest members of a society: slaves, criminals, traitors.

Suffrage pageants' emphasis on shackled women also perpetuated a visual narrative that had long highlighted concerns about female vulnerability. As work by art historian Joy Kasson demonstrates, representations of women in captivity were often evasive, obscuring actual threats to womanhood but implying savage transitions from "virginity to sexual experience, from the known to the unknown, from domesticity to wildness, [and] from control to loss of control."[24] These connotations—like those suggesting the debasement of women as citizens—also called to mind the personal implications of disfranchisement. Like the chained women in figure 3.2, women without votes could neither protect themselves from danger nor expect to be protected. Only women with votes—like those "golden-crowned" exemplars of liberty—could literally shield themselves from the problems facing modern America.

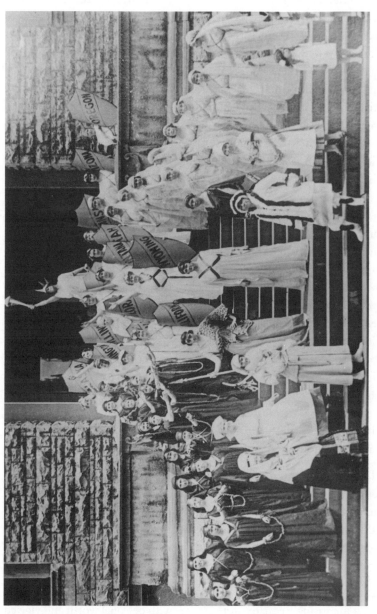

FIGURE 3.2

St. Louis Suffrage Pageant tableau, 1916. Note shackled women on left.
American Press Association.

Courtesy United States History, Local History & Genealogy Division, The New York Public Library, Astor, Lenox and Tilden Foundations.

This new emphasis on the individual consequences of disfranchise-ment reflected a growing concern with issues of representation. Particularly in the last decade of the movement, suffrage performances revealed a commitment to controlling how, why, and when woman suffragists were shown in public. This concern stemmed from a number of factors. The virulence of organized antisuffragists forced advocates of female enfranchisement to take issues of representation seriously. Antisuffragism and negative stereotypes of suffragists were as old as women's fight for the ballot, but with the revitalization of the woman suffrage movement in the 1910s, opponents had become increasingly vitriolic. In what Alice Stone Blackwell called "A Campaign of Slander," antisuffragists portrayed leaders of the movement as disparagingly as possible.[25] Depicted as unsexed, unattractive, and selfish dangers to family, home, and nation, rank-and-file suffrage supporters were equally denigrated. Magazines and newspapers matched these stereotypes by regularly lampooning and caricaturing prosuffrage forces. Even early filmmakers got into the act. Kay Sloan describes one Charlie Chaplin movie in which the famed comedian dresses in women's clothing and plays a shrewish suffragist who accosts anyone who gets in his/her way.[26] Twentieth-century suffragists, therefore, faced a multimedia barrage of criticism unknown to their predecessors.

But modern suffragists also found unprecedented ways of fighting their opponents. Earlier suffragists had countered foes by recalling the promises of the Declaration of Independence and the revolutionary cry for "no taxation without representation." They had also emphasized their supporters' high moral character. As Elizabeth Cady Stanton, Susan B. Anthony, and Matilda Joslyn Gage wrote in 1881,

> The leaders in this movement have been women of superior mental and physical organization, of good social standing and education, remarkably alike for their domestic virtues, knowledge of public affairs, and rare executive ability; good speakers and writers, inspir-ing and conducting the genuine reforms of the day; everywhere exerting themselves to promote the best interests of society. . . .[27]

Latter-day suffragists never abandoned these arguments, but in a soci-ety that increasingly equated appearances with personal worth and viewed personality as a brand of social credit, they responded to antisuffragists in much more vibrant and visible—and even superficial—ways.[28] Many suf-fragists would have agreed with the film critic who identified the appearance and personality of the movement's supporters as critical to its success. "If all suffragettes were as fair to look upon" as the woman who portrayed Equal Suffrage in the NAWSA film *Your Girl and Mine*, he noted, female enfranchisement "would be a reality in every state in the Union today."[29]

Suffrage performances, therefore, not only challenged negative preconceptions of movement activists but also tapped into a larger context of ideas about personality and the performing self. Suffrage plays, pageants, films, speeches, and fashions all relayed an image that fit into and bolstered the cultural preoccupation with personality. This image could take a variety of forms: the heroic mother, the working girl, the college student, the militant, or the patriot, for example.[30] Although these archetypes might differ on the surface, they all shared a common spirit; each embodied an irrepressible charisma, beauty, energy, commitment, and dignity that attempted to alleviate doubts about the movement's worth.

The protagonist in Selina Solomon's play, *The Girl from Colorado or The Conversion of Aunty Suffridge*, for instance, is young, attractive and level-headed—the perfect example (as her relatives learn) of a "womanly" voter. Yet her natural beauty and allure also demonstrate her ability to win a man's heart.[31] Similarly, the vibrant Aunt Jane in the suffrage movie *Your Girl and Mine* manifests a love for family and children that extends beyond the bonds of kinship to a passion for improving society and women's livelihood. And Mabel, the spunky young heroine in the WPU's film *What Eighty Million Women Want—?*, proves that political commitment is compatible with not only romantic love, but also quick thinking and daring feats of courage.[32] As these examples suggest, suffragists from a variety of perspectives could represent the standards of womanly personality most valued by early twentieth-century Americans: moral purity and heterosexual (or at the very least motherly) love combined with passion, charisma, and a zeal for life.

Perhaps no suffragists gave more life to this representation than professional actresses. After all, these women were experts at fashioning public identities and personalizing large-scale spectacles. With their glamour, youth, and beauty they personified the "new woman." By the 1910s, they captured the hearts of young men and women and assumed a widely influential presence in working- and middle-class urban communities. During this decade, numerous actresses—including Mary Pickford and Ethel Barrymore—publicly supported suffrage. Barrymore even acted in a woman suffrage play and donated the proceeds to the movement.[33]

One actress, Fola La Follette, made an entire career out of performing suffrage plays. The daughter of maverick Wisconsin governor Robert La Follette, she moved to New York in 1904 hoping to find fame and fortune. Although her father's political reputation helped her land a few small parts, La Follette experienced little success until she began giving private readings of Cicily Hamilton's one-act woman suffrage play *How the Vote Was Won* in 1910. Assuming a different persona for each character, La Follette turned the popular English program into an energetic one-woman show. She was soon in constant demand, performing the play before suffragists, college students, churchgoers, and even vaudeville audiences. For suffragists, the best thing about the show was the actress herself. Described by Maud Wood Park as having a behavior, appearance, and style that ran "counter to all the conventional traditional 'suffragists' who are the butt of the comic-joke maker," La Follette made personality a defining aspect of public identity.[34] As a professional actress, she regarded this as her role. But for audiences, the distinction between the actress and her stage presence became somewhat obscure. To them, as Park's remark indicates, she *was* the wry, gracious persona she assumed on stage. Her peers saw her as the living embodiment of the public image they sought to convey.

Actresses who advocated woman suffrage infused the movement with their unique cultural cachet. They helped an old cause seem modern and exciting by suggesting that suffragists were modern and exciting. While not all women could achieve the success of Ethel Barrymore or even Fola La Follette, they could emulate their idols' spirit and strength of personality by supporting the woman suffrage movement. By association, these fans could gain the glamour and appeal of famous actresses. This is best demonstrated by the enormous flurry of attention that accompanied suffrage events hosted by professional performers. Whenever the musicians and actresses in Gertrude Foster Brown's New York Woman Suffrage Study Club sponsored teas and parties, for example, the public response proved overwhelming. According to Brown, "the public loved the opportunity to talk to their favorite actresses" and attended in droves. Such events offered unparalleled opportunities to mix with celebrities, talk with them, and perhaps take some of their sparkle home. For their part, wrote Brown, the "leading theatrical stars loved the publicity these occasions gave them" and gladly devoted time and energy to the club (fig. 3.3).[35]

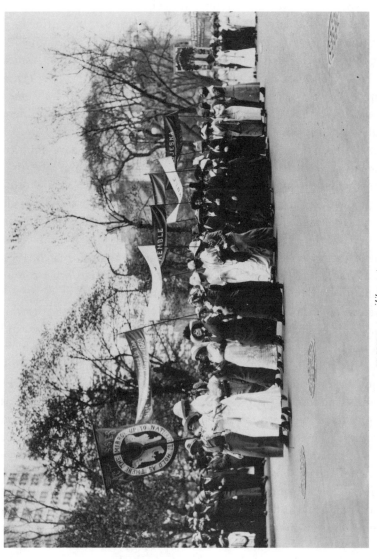

FIGURE 3.3 *The actresses.*

Actresses marching in a New York parade. They brought a sense of style and modernity to the movement. American Press Association. *Courtesy United States History, Local History & Genealogy Division, The New York Public Library, Astor, Lenox and Tilden Foundations.*

The concept of the performing self, however, implied that anyone could act like the ideal suffragist—actresses simply magnified this concept through their professional status. Almost every nationally prominent woman suffrage leader attempted to tap into the pre-existing association between charismatic personality and performers by starring in at least one prosuffrage movie.[36] Harriot Stanton Blatch and Emmeline Pankhurst saved the day in the WPU's *What Eighty Million Women Want—?*; the Woman Suffrage Party of New York's *The Ruling Power* featured Carrie Chapman Catt; and the NAWSA's *Votes for Women* showcased Jane Addams, Anna Howard Shaw, and other prominent leaders.[37] Shaw also appeared in the NAWSA's 1914 film *Your Girl and Mine*. Although suffrage supporters themselves might have doubted some of their leaders' allure and personal magnetism, film advertisements noted the presence and hawked the names of well-known suffragists with dramatic flourish. One full-page ad in the popular trade journal *Moving Picture World* boldly declared that *What Eighty Million Women Want—?* "FEATURES MRS. EMMELINE PANKHURST, the Great English Militant Suffragette, and Mrs. Harriot Stanton Blatch, Pres. Women's Political Union. . . . No more advertised personages can be found to-day than those *featured* here" (italics orig.).[38]

However, the notion of the performing self also presupposed that this ideal could be showcased in any context, not just in dramatic shows, and not just by leaders of the movement. Indeed, with the right dress, look, style, and personality, the suffragist's female body became the only prerequisite for assuming this identity. "Remember," noted Harriet B. Laidlaw, "no time or place can detract from the dignity of the cause as long as the suffragist who represents it is dignified, gracious, tactful, and earnest."[39] Thus parades, public speaking events, and more personal affairs permitted women of all backgrounds to assume public suffrage identities and personalities.

Parade participants represented this ideal en masse. They did not march randomly. Instead, organizers carefully separated and classified suffragists into like groups in order to demonstrate the movement's diverse appeal. Women of similar backgrounds or occupations marched together and highlighted different arguments for suffrage: housewives and mothers emphasized the struggle to protect families from harmful outside influences; college students stressed women's advanced intellect; separate units of teachers, nurses, factory workers, and a host of other working women called attention to the struggle for economic and professional equality; natives of different countries and states demonstrated the movement's global reach.[40] Along the parade route, these component parts of identity became totalizing. A marcher became a Wyoming voter or a college student, a factory worker or a mother, but seldom a hybrid of these choices. Perhaps this is why some suffragists felt completely subsumed by the parade. As one suffragist assured anxious participants, the parade would erase their individual involvement. "You'll pick friend after friend who is watching carefully for you. In nine cases out of ten, he will not see you; for his eyes have to speed across a line of women in an instant's time. . . . It is [as] though everybody else were there in the flesh, but you were disembodied."[41] Each woman became the generic suffragist image under which she marched: perhaps a working girl or college student, but not a complex, multifaceted person.

Marchers from other types of parades understood this process. Participants in nineteenth-century labor parades also marched as members of collective, usually artisanal, groups rather than as discrete individuals. And like suffragists, workers and voluntary association members who joined parades attempted to emphasize their public respectability and their commitment to the social good.[42] But suffragists, true to the priorities of personality and the performing self, were much more calculated about the construction of a public identity. Even walking came under the careful scrutiny and management of suffrage parade organizers. Harriot Stanton Blatch urged parade participants to take classes in the "art of walking" so that even their stride would meaningfully reflect upon their identities as suffragists and their potential roles as voters. Believing that marchers physically symbolized "courage and discipline," she attempted to ban automobiles from New York suffrage parades and make all participants parade on foot.[43] She likewise justified punctuality, not for the sake of the parade, but because of the visual message a flurry of late arrivals might signal. "REMEMBER," advised Blatch, "THE PUBLIC WILL JUDGE, QUITE ILLOGICALLY, OF COURSE, BUT NO LESS STRICTLY, YOUR QALIFICATION [sic] AS A VOTER BY YOUR PROMPTNESS."[44]

Parades, plays, movies, and pageants also inscribed the bodies of suffrage performers with clear racial messages. Reflecting the xenophobia and racism that had come to dominate much of the nonradical suffrage movement, whiteness stood as the unspoken standard of woman suffrage identity.[45] Vehicles of suffrage performance seldom included nonwhite, or even ethnically "undesirable," suffragists. Several dramas featured Irish immigrant women characters, but they were stereotyped as either domestic workers or poor, desperate individuals. Moreover, since most early twentieth-century immigrants came not from Ireland but from southern and eastern Europe, this characterization assumed its own racial cast by making whiteness synonymous with northern-European heritage. As Gwendolyn Mink suggests, a language of white republicanism privileged racial over gender identity by suggesting that white Americans and white supremacy would receive the real rewards of an extended franchise.[46] By constantly erasing people of color and ethnic identity, woman suffrage performances gave material weight to that idea.

Although parades sometimes included or mentioned nonwhite women, their involvement proved limited. Some parade organizers discouraged or complicated the marching efforts of African American women. In the famous 1913 Washington, D.C. parade and pageant, white NAWSA delegates from the South pressured organizers to racially segregate marchers. Black participants were excluded from the regular order of procession and relegated to the very back of the parade.[47] Several parades exploited racial ideology by comparing the status of white women with that of women from other ethnic nationalities. When Mrs. Loo Lin (identified as the " 'boss of Chinatown' ") carried a flag reading WOMEN VOTE IN CHINA, WHY NOT HERE? in one New York suffrage procession, she immediately drew attention to the racial hierarchy between northern-European-descended American and Chinese women.[48] A banner held by suffrage leader Anna Howard Shaw, reading N.A.W.S.A. CATCHING UP WITH CHINA, made a similar point.[49] For white women reared according to the ugly racial politics of the era, the humiliation of having fewer political privileges than women in this supposedly less civilized nation needed no further explanation. Pageants also stressed this theme. In the St. Louis pageant described earlier, "tall, splendid [white] blondes and [white] brunettes" embodied the best models of womanhood. They stood atop a clearly demarcated society in which white men and women led the nation's progress. The humiliation of their mournful, shackled sisters thus stemmed not only from disfranchisement, but also from a more degraded political status than men who were deemed racially and ethnically subordinate.

The most visible manipulation of body images, however, resulted from fashion. The previous chapter noted that parade organizers went to great lengths to control how participants looked. They established a variety of dress codes, ranging from mere color to specific apparel requirements. Organizers almost always encouraged marchers to wear white clothing.[50] Although the reasoning behind this choice of color went unexplained, white's historic associations with women's virtue and purity seem unavoidable. The belief among many Americans that personality was best expressed through color lends support to this supposition.[51] Dressed in this powerful signifier of femininity, woman suffragists could both contest stereotypes depicting them as unsexed and defuse lingering associations between women in public and immorality. White garb implied that woman suffragists embodied a standard of womanhood conjoining traditional ideals of virtue and morality with an inescapable public presence and identity. Moreover, by draping almost all marchers in this symbolically powerful color, suffragists effectively highlighted the bonds of gender uniting them despite their diverse backgrounds and beliefs (fig. 3.4).[52]

The figure of the parade marshal heightened mental associations provoked by the color white. Unlike fellow marchers, the marshal did not try to blend in with the passing masses. Dressed as Joan of Arc, the symbolic embodiment of Victory, or some other inspiring role model, the marshal set the tone of the parade by signifying the dignity, virtue, dedication, and inherent beauty of the marchers. Although these qualities privileged traditional standards of feminine character, they also bespoke the more modern embrace of personality. Reflecting the awe-inspiring spectacle of the parade itself, the parade marshal became one of the most memorable parts of the event. Fellow suffragists looked up to her and found her dramatic presence overwhelming. Usually recalling her as someone of tremendous glamour and charisma, suffragists touted the parade marshal's personal magnetism in their records and, years later, in their memoirs.[53]

Brightly colored sashes, ribbons, parasols, and other personal effects hinted at a more complex reality, however. As the suffrage movement became more ideologically divided, its material culture adopted a rainbow of hues. NAWSA members signaled their institutional loyalties by accessorizing their marching gowns with the traditional suffrage color, yellow. Radical women rejected the old standard. Following the lead of English militants, women in the CU highlighted their white apparel with splashes of purple, white, and gold, while those in the WPU draped themselves in green, purple, and white.

Appearances also became intertwined with how public speakers represented themselves. Cognizant that dress could be read as an insight

FIGURE 3.4 *Suffragettes' Peace Parade, Fifth Avenue, New York.*
Most suffrage parade organizers encouraged marchers to wear white, but not all
women did. American Press Association.

*Courtesy United States History, Local History & Genealogy Division, The New York
Public Library, Astor, Lenox and Tilden Foundations.*

into personality and personal worth, some speakers paid detailed attention to self-presentation. When Ohio suffragist Florence Allen was invited to participate in a Boston debate, her colleagues took her choice of clothing "under advisement." They rejected her original idea of wearing a suit to the event and collaborated on making a black, formal evening gown. Usually unconcerned with matters of fashion, Allen initially doubted the difference her attire would make. But when she attended the debate and heard two strangers privately speculate that she was an actress, she knew her compatriots had made the right decision. Years later, she remembered this as one of the highlights of her days in the movement.[54]

Like Allen, Gertrude Foster Brown understood fashion's importance to issues of representation. An accomplished outdoor suffrage speaker, Brown chose to wear street clothes to her first speech in front of a vaudeville audience. Afterward, Brown could not forget the lovely young women she encountered in the theater. Wearing makeup and dressed in "tights and wisps of velvet tunics," they must have embodied a public ideal of femininity that Brown found both appealing and effective, because she followed their lead completely during her next vaudeville appearance. "This time," remarked Brown, "I made up my face for the footlights, and I wore my handsomest trained evening gown, with a big picture hat, trimmed with plumes, on top of piled-up hair."[55] By matching the look of the actresses—who, after all, competed with her for applause and attention—Brown implied that she too was a performer. Her job was not only to deliver a convincing speech, but also to sell the movement—and thus woman's citizenship—by affiliating it with femininity, good looks, and style.

Shy and more self-restrained suffragists could represent the movement by wearing nationally marketed suffrage fashions. During World War I, suffrage apparel of various types appeared in department stores and suffrage press advertisements. Although there was one "ready-to-wear-to-anything-and-not-at-all-expensive suffrage blouse" offered, most such garb appealed to women who had become home farmers in order to help the war effort. Taking on this patriotic duty did not mean that a woman had "to look like a frump," promised an article in *The Woman Citizen*. With the right outfit—such as the NAWSA-endorsed "WOMANALLS"—the "woman with the hoe" would be "easily discernible just back of the man with the gun." Her "service uniform" would mark her immediately as a suffragist, and therefore a patriot. Moreover, with terms like "chic" and "natty" used to describe these items, suffrage apparel also implied that dressing the part of the suffragist/woman citizen/patriot made one fashionable and stylish no matter what one's endeavors.[56] A prosuffrage cartoon linked fashion and citizenship even more directly. Representing "equal franchise" as a stylish hat, it noted that "If only [President Wilson] knew how becoming [enfranchisement] would be!" women would doubtless receive the vote (figs. 3.5 and 3.6).[57]

As this attention to style and femininity suggests, suffragists attempted to carefully craft personality for public consumption. Suffrage leaders' efforts to find charismatic and winsome public speakers reflected this. Of course, there was nothing new about admiring or recruiting entertaining lecturers. Politicians and labor organizers had long recognized the importance of compelling oratory. And early suffrage leaders, including Susan B. Anthony, Elizabeth Cady Stanton, and Lucy Stone, certainly knew that their public influence sometimes stemmed from their flair for the dramatic. As the movement expanded and embraced publicity and male-oriented political tactics like mass meetings, however, the call for dynamic suffrage speakers assumed a new urgency.[58] Some suffrage groups set up training programs to help women cultivate their skills as interesting and exciting lecturers.[59] Historian Sara Hunter Graham describes one program that separated potential speakers into "agitators" who appealed to emotions and "educators" who emphasized logic and rational arguments for the vote. Another program used professional actresses and public speakers as teachers and even included a class on "The Psychology of an Audience."[60] But experience itself often provided the only preparation available. Many women found themselves clamoring for the vote on soapboxes and stages without ever having spoken in public.

Numerous suffragists argued that all a good speaker really needed was a strong personality. Suffrage organizations, advised Massachusetts activist Susan Fitzgerald in 1910, needed to find women whose "personality will [provoke] interest from the start"—individuals with good humor, spirit, and the ability to quickly gauge audience interest.[61] Women with these qualities gained fame on the suffrage lecture circuit and became known as "stars." Some stars turned their oratory into a profitable enterprise. When English suffragist Sylvia Pankhurst visited the United States in 1911, she had a professional theatrical agent book her engagements and charged $300 a lecture.[62] Most well-respected suffrage speakers merely asked host

FIGURE 3.5 "WOMANALLS."

Fashion became one way of representing the movement and its followers.
"WOMANALLS" were featured in a June 1917 edition of the *Woman Citizen.*
Reproduced by permission of Huntington Library, San Marino, California.

If He Only Knew How Becoming It Was

FIGURE 3.6 *"If he only knew."*
This cartoon compared woman suffrage to a stylish hat.
Reproduced by permission of the Susan B. Anthony Ephemera Collection,
Huntington Library, San Marino, California.

organizations to pick up their expenses and perhaps pay small stipends.[63] Lesser-known women secured only their colleagues' gratitude. When Rose Morgan French participated in the 1914 Ohio campaign, she resignedly noted that she "received no pay and little honor" for her suffrage speeches. She simply offered her "services to the Com[mittee]" to help " 'fill in the chinks,' " when it could get no one better or when someone" proved a disappointment.[64]

Leaders' interest in managing individual representations of the movement meant that—paid or unpaid—lecturers had to face the occasionally unwelcome authority of higher-ups. Women who organized sidewalk sermons and more formal public speaking events sometimes sought to control who spoke, what they said, how long they talked, and what subjects they discussed. In 1917, for example, Carrie Chapman Catt advised NAWSA affiliate-state presidents to choose their intended speakers for an upcoming series of meetings with state congressional delegations "with care," and she urged them to "coach" the women in what to say.[65] Such instructions undoubtedly proved useful. To the many suffragists inexperienced at organizing mass meetings and outdoor speaking events, clear directions probably provided a valuable organizational framework.

Yet even the best-laid plans faced challenges from unfriendly, aggressive crowds or hecklers. As former suffragist Miriam Allen DeFord remembered, speakers "expected" and "learned how to handle" jibes and interruptions.[66] Thus dependent upon public speakers' wits, these events often offered the most spontaneous forum for suffrage performance, where the speakers' individuality might regularly come to the fore. For the organizers of these events this could be a mixed blessing, however. In some cases, independence and quick thinking helped suffragists overcome the antipathy of entire crowds. One woman, for example, won over a street-corner audience after extemporaneously admonishing a system that gave the vote to a drunken heckler who had rudely accosted her colleagues but denied the vote to mothers.[67]

Occasionally, a speaker's independence presented its own problems. Suffragists in California's College League found themselves in a bind after hiring a lecturer who refused to follow direction. Upon growing "very fond of her own voice and of the pathos of her story," Margaret Haley repeatedly stole the "whole show" for herself by refusing to relinquish the stage. Despite frequent warnings and the knowledge that known "stars" waited in the wings, she spoke for up to an hour and a half at a time. The league passed her from manager to manager, but according to one source, "she would not be managed." Although the College League eventually dissolved its relationship with Haley, the group's experience highlights an important lesson: in order for the "show" to succeed, rules of organization, timing, and behavior had to be followed.[68] Sometimes, the performer's professionalism needed to keep the speaker's individuality in check.

As the College League learned, a speaker's ability to evoke sympathy was not an end in itself; its value was in breaking down resistance to the movement. Haley's pathos was not her problem. Ultimately, her inability to control emotion, rein it in, ration it, and use it as a tool for conversion proved her downfall. More experienced suffragists avoided this mistake, but they did not refrain from carefully manipulating emotions—both their own and those of their audiences. Suffrage leaders in the 1910s encouraged speakers and other suffrage performers to overcome opposition by stimulating their opponents' senses and feelings. Abolitionists and other radical reformers of the early nineteenth century would have called this strategy moral suasion. But twentieth-century suffragists, influenced by social scientific theories about crowd psychology and advertising and public relations experts' arguments about the importance of spectacle and visual display, articulated a much more cynical explanation for their methods.[69] Human beings, explained Blatch, are "moved to action, by emotion, not by argument and reason." "The enemy must be converted through his eyes." He must hear "music all the time."[70] New York NAWSA leader Maud Wood Park (herself an aspiring playwright) concurred, claiming that the "average opponent's objection to woman suffrage is not an objection of reason but an objection of sentiment." The key to winning suffrage, therefore, did not rest in fostering enlightenment rationality. "People can resist logic," she claimed, "but can they resist laughter, with youth and beauty to drive it home? Not often."[71]

Suffrage performances used drama and fantasy to make this emotional link with audiences. As Kaja Silverman's work on film suggests, the connection between spectator and actor occurs at the moment of "suture," the moment when the viewer not only identifies with the character being portrayed, but also unconsciously experiences that character's emotions and feelings. This happens regularly when we watch motion pictures: we feel the panic of the threatened protagonist, the melancholy of the star-crossed lover, and the exhilaration of the

triumphant hero (or, more rarely, heroine).[72] Woman suffrage performances aimed at politicizing suture. Ideally, once spectators confused
the suffragist character's feelings with their own, it would be harder for
them to accept negative stereotypes of woman suffragists or to remain
emotionally distant from the struggle for voting rights. The moment the
audience gave in to the heroine's grief, pain, melancholy, romance, or
triumph, it came closer to conversion. Although suffragists certainly did
not contemplate the nuances of modern film theory, they were savvy
enough to believe that dramatic narrative offered an effective way to
emotionally connect with people outside the movement.

Film, in particular, seemed a good way to touch people's hearts. For
one thing, it could deliver a diverse, mass audience. Although initially
popular with the working class, motion pictures had become a cross-
class and mixed-sex entertainment by the 1910s.[73] Moreover, because the
high demand for film led distributors to eagerly show whatever movie
reels they could find, woman suffragists knew their films would find a
way to these pleasure seekers.[74] Other reformers knew this as well.
Numerous progressive era associations and reformers—ranging from
the National Committee on Child Labor to birth control advocate
Margaret Sanger—collaborated with the open and free-wheeling early
film industry to produce one- and two-reel stories defending their
particular causes. But interest in this new medium stemmed from not
just its ability to deliver spectators. Reformers recognized film's potential for sympathetically connecting reformist ideas to dramatic narrative. For suffrage filmmakers, no genre served that purpose better than
melodrama. Already immensely popular with filmgoers, melodrama's
common glimpse into the lives of women and its overarching emotionalism meant that the connection of audiences with the pain and stigma
of disfranchisement could be fully exploited. Woman suffrage films
often associated that pain with the fear of loss, especially of life, love,
and offspring. In these dramas, the possibility of losing what one holds
most dear signifies the punishment for denying women the vote.
Enfranchisement offers the only path beyond personal devastation. It
alone guarantees a happy ending.

In the 1911 NAWSA film *Votes for Women*, for example, the near death
of a young suffragist rests upon the shoulders of her influential fiancé's
and her father's opposition to the movement. Not until the two men
face losing her to smallpox do they realize that woman suffrage might
have contributed to protective health and sanitation laws, and thus

spared them their grief. Their immediate conversion to the cause coincides with the young woman's recovery, which serves as their reward for supporting women's enfranchisement. The Association's 1914 film *Your Girl and Mine* upheld a similar threat. A horror story of one young bride's misfortune, the film focuses on Rosalie Fairlie, who loses her virtue, happiness, wealth, and ultimately her children to laws privileging the choices and rights of men over women. With the symbolic figure of Equal Justice superimposed on the action at crucial moments, *Your Girl and Mine* bluntly contended that Rosalie's fate could befall any woman, implying that until women voted, insecurity and uncertainty would cloud their futures (fig. 3.7).

Woman suffrage pageants sought to create a similar emotional connection between participants and audiences. Like commercial spectacles, pageants sought to induce feelings of sensory overload by emphasizing abundance, color, and the juxtaposition of images. Pageants could feature hundreds of individuals. They showed women in bright colors, or they grouped participants in bold patterns of white, black, or blue, which they interspersed with gold crowns and flowers, green wreaths of laurel, and balloons.[75] A mixture of fantasy, legend, and reality accompanied these decorations. Women adorned as mythological goddesses suddenly left their heavenly realm and joined a passing suffrage parade. Characters representing the American colonies stood side by side with those representing the modern United States. And performers draped in classical garb—representing the most ancient and prized of Western republics—stood complacently in recently constructed commercial theaters, or on the outdoor steps of art museums or government buildings, surrounded by onlookers dressed in the latest street fashions. In a New York event that mixed pageantry with speeches and skits, suffragists drove a car onto a vaudeville stage in order to reproduce the feel of a street meeting. Members of the Collegiate Equal Suffrage League followed this act by turning the proscenium into a "college campus on commencement day." College women dressed in caps and gowns sat and listened while gifted speakers gave suffrage/vaudeville/graduation addresses.[76]

This blend of fantasy, reality, color, and abundance allowed pageants to bypass rational discourse completely. Their emphasis on appearances gave them an unembarrassed emotional and sentimental quality. Glenna Smith Tinnin understood this completely. She insisted that "a pageant can be immeasurably more convincing than the best of lectures, for it can say

FIGURE 3.7

Promotional shot for the NAWSA film *Your Girl and Mine.*
Courtesy NAWSA Papers, Library of Congress.

the same thing to the public the lecturer says, and in that 'the same thing' is presented pictorially, it goes forth with power. An idea that is driven home to the mind through the eye produces a more striking and lasting impression than any that goest [sic] through the ear."[77] Although scant evidence of viewer responses to such spectacles exists, at least some bystanders seem to have been moved by the visual power of suffrage pageants. As a *Woman's Journal* review of the 1916 NAWSA St. Louis pageant noted: "It took an old, gray-haired man who stood for more than an hour watching the tableau to voice the sentiment of the crowd, and he did it in typical Missouri style. 'They're showing us . . . they're showing us right here in Missouri, and I'm for 'em.' "[78]

Creating an emotional audience response to any type of pageant required careful planning and orchestration.[79] The American Pageant Association, the primary professional organization for individuals involved in these performances, strongly suggested that trained and experienced "pageant masters" direct all such events. The townships, communities, and woman suffrage groups that organized pageants usually agreed. Moreover, they highly valued their associations with masters such as Percy MacKaye or, in the case of suffrage pageants, Hazel MacKaye and Virginia Tanner. Pageant hosts implied that the pageant masters' professionalism reflected positively upon their own cultural status.[80]

Suffrage films likewise emphasized their expert components. The NAWSA film *Your Girl and Mine* touted its professional credentials with pride. Gilson Willettes, the acclaimed writer of the popular silent film drama *The Adventures of Kathlyn*, wrote the scenario. Well-known and respected actors played the lead characters, and some of them received salaries running an astounding "four figures per week."[81] Finally, William N. Selig and the World Film company, two of the most important players in the early film industry, respectively co-produced and distributed the motion picture. Trade magazine writers concentrated on these facts and saw them as evidence of the film's potential for mass entertainment. This implies that the film's pedigree, not its story, secured its commercial viability and chance for market success.

Perhaps more important, however, critics and members of the NAWSA both interpreted the film's professional credentials as a sign of suffragists' professionalism—as proof that suffragists understood the value of training, expertise, and modern technology. The production of *Your Girl and Mine*, therefore, added further nuance to the idealization of suffragists: in addition to possessing charisma and virtue, the personality-enhanced suffragist knew the importance of professionalism and efficiency. Ironically, the organizing force behind the film, Ruth McCormick, belied the professionalism the film's marketing sought to convey. A leading figure in the NAWSA, McCormick initiated work on the film without the Association's knowledge. After learning about McCormick's project, NAWSA leaders begrudgingly scrapped plans for a previously approved motion picture.[82]

The expert management of woman suffrage performance vehicles such as films and pageants also manifested itself in propaganda. Like performance directors and managers, the writers promoting suffrage shows emphasized sentiment. Aware that commercial audiences sought amusement, the suffragists who sponsored various types of performance events promised entertainment and merriment, and suggested that politics was incidental to the show. Promotions for *Your Girl and Mine* implied that diversion reigned supreme. "First and foremost," McCormick told one reviewer, was the desire "to produce a photoplay that would appeal to every man and woman, regardless of whether they [sic] knew anything about the suffrage movement or cared anything about it."[83] And as a pamphlet advertising the motion picture asked, why worry about the moral "concealed in the very title of the play," when there was "an exciting hand-to-hand fight between a man and a woman in one of the earliest acts—when the quick march of events range from a wedding to a murder and an automobile abduction scene that breaks all former speed records"?[84]

Likewise, when New York's major suffrage associations combined forces to present a week-long program at Hammerstein's Victoria Theatre in 1912, they promised to mix suffrage entertainment with performances by vaudeville regulars such as Belle Baker and Mysterious Edna. Flyers for the celebration stressed spectacle and curiosity, including FIVE HUNDRED SUFFRAGISTS ON STAGE, INSTRUCTIVE AND ENTERTAINING, THE FIRST TIME IN VAUDEVILLE FOR THE SUFFRAGETTES, SOUVENIRS FOR EVERYBODY, A GREAT QUESTION PRESENTED IN THEATRICAL FORM, and PROGRESSIVE UP-TO-DATE METHODS EMBELLISHED WITH ATTRACTIVE SURROUNDINGS.[85] By implying that amusement had priority over polemic, these promotional strategies attempted to minimize the controversy surrounding suffrage performances. They also tried to lower the defenses of audience members who lacked any desire for political education but who might have been receptive to suffrage arguments wrapped in entertaining diversions.

The appeal to commercial amusement seekers highlights the democratic underpinnings of various types of suffrage performances. Blair and Tackel show how suffragists used pageants to reach a constituency far beyond the middle-class audience they had long courted. Films, parades, and sidewalk speeches sought a similar effect. The embrace and rise of suffrage shows thus served the larger strategy of creating a more heterogeneous movement. But woman suffrage performances also raise questions about how the culture of personality, the performing self, and commercialized performance may have influenced American politics.

Many kinds of suffrage presentations competed for attendants and revenues on the same basis as other commercial vehicles of entertainment: through publicity and advertising. The more money available, the more suffragists could market their spectacles—indeed, the more spectacles they could produce, the more they could control how suffragists were represented in front of mass audiences. This had positive benefits, but it also made money the key to winning political audiences, controlling political image, and disseminating information via the mass media. Suffrage pageants, parades, films, well-publicized speaking events, and fashions cost money. Parade organizers routinely complained about their tight financial straits.[86] In 1917, NAWSA President Carrie Chapman Catt bluntly admitted how central money had become to the movement. Blaming the situation on hostile and organized antisuffragists who had to be countered with increasingly inventive propaganda, Catt contended that state campaign expenses had grown out of control. She predicted that upcoming suffrage referenda in Oklahoma, Nebraska, Michigan, Massachusetts, and South Dakota would be impossible to win without a financial commitment of between at least $300,000 and $500,000. A hard-hitting federal campaign would require at least $2 million.[87]

Moreover, in marketing representations of suffrage identity, suffragists reified that identity. They implied that the ideal suffragist was one more product in the marketplace of mass consumer culture—one more commodity to be fashioned or refashioned for public consumption. Suffragists' representations of would-be women voters highlighted an ideal of citizenship that advocates of the movement promised to bring to the electorate. If they commercialized one, must not they have commercialized the other? Absolutely. By implying that suffrage identity could be packaged and sold, suffragists also implied that identity as a woman citizen could be packaged, sold, and redesigned as necessary. No woman citizen needed to be a "frump" as long as she had the right outfit to display her political status. Whether women were farming in WOMANALLS or voting, as the heroine in one play advised, "like a *truly womanly* girl" dressed in "a sensible skirt, and a real hat and shoes, with flat heels," citizenship became another part of their commodity-defined, other-directed sense of self.[88] Suffrage performances thus suggested that citizenship would continue as a gendered ideal: how women and men practiced their citizenship roles—even how they appeared in the voting booth—differed according to sex.

And what about suffragists' embrace of personality and the performing self? How, for example, did the personality-enhanced woman citizen depicted by suffragists compare with the civic-minded, self-actualizing citizen highlighted in chapter 1? As distinct as they might seem, these ideals shared at least one noteworthy similarity: both glorified self-realization. Writers contemplating liberalism in the early twentieth century were preoccupied with the self-realized citizen: the citizen with the desire and ability to reach his (and generally writers did mean *his*) full human potential, who understood civic duties as a widening expanse of social and community obligations. As the culture of personality's concomitant emphasis on self-realization suggests, this obsession with fulfilling selfhood was not just a political question but also part of a larger reorientation of personal identity. The writings of political theorists like John Dewey show the best that that reorientation had to offer. But the ideas behind the culture of personality show the slippery slope down which such high ideals could fall. Both concepts stressed the importance of social bonds to personal satisfaction, but they suggested different ways of maintaining those ties. For writers like Dewey, keeping in touch with and contributing to one's community was critical to self-actualization. For believers in the culture of personality, impressing others through looks and style—which increasingly meant through greater access to consumer goods—was the key to social acceptance. Suffrage performances that concentrated on the magnetic personalities of suffragists—plays and films, for example, that depicted the ideal new woman—provide further evidence of fragmented and contradictory ideas about women's citizenship coexisting within the nonradical movement. But when the personality-enhanced suffragist became identified as the conduit to individual and community-enhancing social reform, suffrage performances revealed how the lines between political and consumer-oriented means of self-realization could become confused.

In reality, however, the self-realized citizen and the self-realized, commodity-centered personality represent very different things. In a democratic society the citizens possess—at least in principle—a modicum of equality. But not all personalities are equally acceptable in modern consumer society. Industries and cultural leaders decide very undemocratically which public identities to herald. Herein rests the tyranny of the culture of personality. Those who do not, or cannot (for lack of resources), follow the advice of personality gurus or buy the "right" commodities struggle to find widespread social acceptance. Failure to live up to these standards is personalized. Social ostracism gets defined as the individual's fault; he or she must live with the shame and guilt of exclusion. The community-minded but ultimately free-thinking liberal citizen gives way to the stage-managed individual. While the first of these character types can work as his or her—or his or her community's—best advocate, the second depends upon and defers to expert opinion in order to make the best self-presentation in a status-conscious, image-saturated world. The citizen relinquishes free inquiry for a supervised image and social approval.

As suffrage performances demonstrate, however, this tells us more about how leaders and political activists came to represent themselves as citizens than it does about how everyday people defined their membership in the polity. In this respect, suffrage performances fit into a larger social and political context. Attempts to control representations of suffragists mirrored the careful handling of politicians by new partisan publicity experts, a phenomenon that continues—albeit in infinitely larger form—today.[89] Likewise, if woman suffragists commodified their representations of women citizens through such products as WOM-ANALLS, suffrage "stars," or commercial films, they proved no different than a political leadership that, during World War I, equated good citizenship with Liberty bond purchases and cited Hollywood celebrities Mary Pickford and Douglas Fairbanks as the embodiments of Americanism.[90]

As this growing concern with the stage management of personality, performance, and even citizenship suggests, suffragists took on pageants, films, plays, public speaking events, and suffrage fashions for a complex variety of reasons. Dramatic performance had a long and rich place in women's struggle for voting rights. Yet twentieth-century performances did vary considerably from earlier presentations. In addition to being more readily accessible and commercially oriented, they focused more specifically upon woman suffrage and its consequences in private life. They gave suffragists a way to control self-representation and to reach a diverse, mass audience. But they reflected more than a response to antisuffragism or a democratic effort to expand women's sphere. Suffrage performances registered women's adherence to the changing nature of personal and political identity. In new definitions of selfhood, personality and the performing self reigned supreme. Like advertisers, marketers, and consumer manufacturers, suffrage performances implied that identity could be a matter of style and fashion—easily changed, compartmentalized, classified, and reified.

And like admirers of the growing consumer culture, women who acted the part of the ideal suffragist identified personality and charisma as traits to be admired and cultivated. They believed such qualities revealed not only a person's internal worth, but also the value of his or her ideology and beliefs. In this scenario, woman suffrage was defined as right and good because suffragists (and therefore woman citizens) were seen as likable, charismatic, virtuous, and professional—thanks to a careful concern with managing impressions, appearances, and self-presentation. This concern highlighted the multiple and contradictory meanings of citizenship within the nonradical movement, but it also showed the troubling ways in which political and commercial constructions of identity could merge.

Chapter 4

From Sunflower Badges to Kewpie Dolls: Woman Suffrage Commodities and the Embrace of Consumer Capitalism

In 1894, longtime woman's rights activist Mary Livermore urged suffragists in her home state of Massachusetts to wear the suffrage color, yellow, to their annual festival. "Let every matron wear a knot of yellow ribbon on the left breast; every girl a bow of yellow ribbon, with long ends, on the left shoulder, and let every man who is of us, and with us, wear a yellow ribbon in the button hole, or on the lapel of his coat." As she explained to her friends and colleagues: "We have cultivated a 'severe plainness' long enough. It may be 'classic,' and it may be artistic, but it is desperately ugly. Let's have a change, and show our colors."[1]

By the time the Nineteenth Amendment finally passed in 1920, few suffragists needed such prodding. Showing the colors—proclaiming dedication to female enfranchisement through the use of woman suffrage merchandise—had become commonplace. Colored ribbons, however, had given way to largely inexpensive and mass-produced suffrage commodities, including hats, blouses, badges, pins, valentines, Kewpie dolls, playing cards, drinking cups, luggage tags, fans, hat pins, and much more.[2] Suffragists eagerly purchased these goods, and they used modern methods—including advertising, catalogs, and specialized suffrage shops—to market them.

Cultural historians and students of the woman suffrage movement have paid scant attention to these items. Although scholars point to a virtual explosion in woman suffrage commodities during the movement's revitalization in the 1910s, they have said little about these items' meaning or significance. Yet their historic presence and their sudden change in texture, tone, and scale in the 1910s are overwhelming evidence of their import and cultural context.

As theorists of popular culture would be quick to warn, the meanings of such items are not easily deciphered. Like popular movies and music, the allure of woman suffrage commodities is their open-ended connotations.[3] A suffrage badge or hat might have meant one thing to the woman wearing it and quite another to her family. It might have had further, different significance to a fellow suffragist marching in a parade, a businessman on the street, a conservative "anti" at home, or a commercial novelty manufacturer. The multiple meanings associated with these goods gave them their ultimate appeal and resonance within the increasingly heterogeneous movement and to the diverse audience it sought to attract. If this made the job of woman suffragists a little easier, it makes the work of the modern researcher that much harder, for the fluid character of woman suffrage commodities shrouds what they meant to the people who used and encountered them. Nevertheless, just as popular culture texts have *implied readings*—the dominant social messages encoded in works by their creators—so too do the items examined here. While we may never fully appreciate the diverse impact suffrage commodities had on early twentieth-century Americans, we can at least explore these readings.

The implied readings of suffrage goods changed with the movement and with the times. Especially before the 1910s, these items tended to express a rebelliousness that challenged traditional meanings of public and private life and that proclaimed a new political role for women. They sent a message of defiant unity and confidence to both suffragists and society at large. Nonetheless, suffrage commodities could just as easily undermine these ideals by reinforcing concepts of femininity and domesticity that had long been the basis of women's political dependence and social subordination. These two readings almost always existed in tension with each other. But as the movement blossomed in the 1910s, and suffragists reinterpreted goods as not just emblems of belief but also promotional lures and giveaways for uncommitted voters, woman suffrage commodities that legitimated the political and social status quo became increasingly common. By revealing and then neutralizing fears and anxieties about the effect votes for women would have on American society, these items made woman suffrage seem both less threatening and less significant.

Exploring only the implied readings of woman suffrage commodities, however, obscures one of their most important aspects: their money-making function. These goods allowed suffragists and businesses to earn money. Suffragists needed it to organize and run campaigns and businesses needed it to stay afloat. As consumer capitalism assumed economic and cultural dominance in the United States, and as the suffrage movement grew more popular, suffrage commodities acquired a unique cultural cast. They became signifiers of cultural legitimacy in a consumer-capitalist society. They suggested that nonradical suffragists were fully in tune with modern consumer values, including the celebration of material abundance and commodity-centered selfhood. There was nothing subtle about this act of legitimation. Suffragists applauded their ties to—and acknowledgments from—the market. Denied a political voice by government and political parties, suffragists sought validation in the commercial realm—one of the few highly public arenas that granted them widespread recognition and sometimes even respect.

The consequences of seeking authority within this economic and cultural context proved profound and lasting. By privileging the commercial realm as a site of political discourse, suffragists made consumerism a defining part of their movement. Indeed, by narrowing the possibilities for imagining American womanhood, consumerism helped shape a conservative vision of women's citizenship. By embracing a consumerist worldview, suffragists once again blurred the distinction between political and consumer identity and desires; by at least metaphorically equating participation in politics with participation in the marketplace, suffragists helped perpetuate a consumer-capitalist ideology that had already begun to privilege access to commodities over equal access to political power.

Suffragists were not the first activists to express their beliefs in material form. Mary Douglas and Baron Isherwood insist that commodities always serve as "visible parts of culture."[4] Since politics reflects the social tensions within a given society, its history is rich with physical artifacts. According to John Brewer, political memorabilia—including clothing, medals, and ceramics—had social and commercial implications in England as far back as the eighteenth century.[5] During the same time, American artisans attended public festivities dressed proudly in badges celebrating their trades, and by the early 1800s, American elections came replete with partisan pins, plates, and clothing. By the end of the nineteenth century, campaign souvenirs included such diverse objects as soap, jewelry, paperweights, and cigar holders.[6]

By the time Mary Livermore advised her colleagues to wear yellow ribbons, therefore, the concept of marking political identity through material objects had a long history. From the beginning, however, woman suffrage commodities expressed a different message from other types of political memorabilia. Objects distributed by political parties dwelled upon familiar motifs of American republicanism and manhood. Etchings and paintings of candidates emphasized their stern, forceful, and fully masculine qualities. Even a box holding a bar of soap shaped like a young child reminded citizens of the gendered nature of electoral politics by declaring "My Papa will Vote for McKinley" during the 1896 presidential election.[7]

The emphasis on manliness did not mean women were completely ignored by political parties. As work by historian Jean Baker explains, nineteenth-century partisanship was in many ways a family affair. Political parties appealed to their members' wives and daughters with ceramic dishes and glassware.[8] Some women worked tirelessly—although not always visibly—on political campaigns. Before she gained fame as a woman's rights and dress reform advocate, Amelia Bloomer actively aided the Whig party by making badges and writing mottos.[9] By the gilded age, women's groups had started fashioning their own emblems. Few symbols received more recognition than the WCTU's famous white ribbon, first adopted in 1877. More than a marker of WCTU membership, the ribbon carried powerful meaning for its wearers. As Frances Willard explained, "Our emblem holds within itself the colors of all nations and stands for universal purity and patriotism, universal prohibition and philanthropy, and universal peace."[10]

Suffragists drew from these diverse historical precedents when creating their own politically inspired goods. Like the white ribbons of the WCTU and the memorabilia routinely distributed by political parties, suffrage commodities allowed women in the movement to send a visible and explicit message to colleagues, opponents, and potential converts. According to one California woman, a badge designed by a Los Angeles suffrage club in 1892 served as an " 'object lesson.' It not only shows that the wearer is a woman suffragist, but is in itself an argument" for her enfranchisement. Featuring the NAWSA flag, a field of blue emblazoned with one gold star (representing the woman-enfranchised state of Wyoming), the badge served as a constant reminder that woman suffrage was not an abstract fantasy but a practical reality. Women in Wyoming had received the vote and aided their state. Why deny California women the same privilege? This argument, concluded the suffragist, was one "which thoughtful, consistent men cannot fail to understand and admit." Of course, not all viewers would recognize the symbolic quality of the badge, but that was part of its beauty, she argued. "By causing me to be questioned, my badge has many times led to conversation on the subject of woman's political position in the government, when otherwise there would have . . . been no opportunity or excuse for exchanging more than the few sentences necessary to the transaction of the business for which we met. In some cases, it has . . . made a convert to our cause."[11]

Like other types of political memorabilia, suffrage goods also celebrated the camaraderie and unity of the group for which they stood—equal suffrage supporters. But while men in the nineteenth century used political objects to tighten and highlight the bonds of partisanship—which in turn highlighted the bonds of manhood—woman suffragists used them to keep their largely homogeneous movement alive. Suffrage ribbons and badges appeared in the late 1880s, not in the intellectually heady years of the 1850s, when woman suffragists radically challenged the very nature of women's life and sphere. Often referred to as the "doldrums" of the woman suffrage movement, the period between roughly 1890 and 1910 was especially difficult due to campaign failures and the loss of aged and respected leaders. During these challenging years, woman suffrage commodities helped suffragists remain firm in their beliefs. Sociologist Michael Schudson notes that implicit beliefs and values need to be made explicit "because people need to see in pictures or hear in words even what they already know as deeply as they know anything, *especially* what they know as deeply as they know anything" (italics orig.).[12] Suffrage goods helped supporters express what they knew: that despite their losses the cause of woman suffrage was just and achievable. Commodities served as material emblems of the faith that remained the movement's greatest asset when success was uncertain.

When Kansas suffragists chose a yellow ribbon as their "distinctive sign" in 1887, they intended to express these exact ideals. They called the ribbon a "sunflower badge," for just as "the sunflower follows civilization, follows the wheel-tract and the plow, so woman suffrage inevitably follows civilized government." Their botanical analogy caught the attention of compatriots across the nation—including Mary Livermore. Massachusetts and Pennsylvania suffragists immediately adopted their own "sunflower badge."[13] Iowa women designed "pretty" sunflower-colored pincushions, and by 1896, the NAWSA was selling its own sunflower stationery and stickpins.[14] In one small act, the Kansas

women gave the movement a lasting symbol: without fanfare or organized discussion, yellow quickly became suffragists' "official color." It
served as a constant reminder of the link between progress and woman
suffrage, and of the inevitability of both.

Commodities likewise provided followers with an important sense
of community. An iconography united by color, for example, could
help suffragists identify—and identify with—one another. Similarly,
the lionization of suffrage pioneers through calendars, ink blotters,
photographs, postcards, and books helped create a collective past—a
shared history—for suffragists to cherish, placing the movement in a
linear framework from which followers could imagine a common
future. Indeed, like the symbolic sunflower, commemoratives of early
leaders such as Susan B. Anthony and Lucy Stone allowed colleagues to
envision that future and define suffrage and progress synonymously.
Few items exemplify this point better than the NAWSA's Woman's
Century Calendar of 1900, issued quarterly and sold for $1.45 per
annum. After acknowledging the movement's history with a nod to
Susan B. Anthony (in the form of a large photograph of the famed
leader), the calendar presents a year-by-year synopsis of the advances
made by women during the nineteenth century. An enumeration of the
key "Gains of the Century" and essays on women's "Progress in
Education," "Progress in Occupations and Professions," "Progress in
Social Liberty," and "Progress in Political Liberty" follow.[15] If, as the
front of the calendar promises and its contents imply, "The World Does
Move," then suffragists could rest assured that their patience and hard
work would be rewarded.

How individuals interpreted and responded to woman suffrage commodities depended upon where they encountered these objects. Bazaars,
for example, offered a plethora of suffrage goods. A longtime staple of
women's benevolent associations, and especially popular with abolitionists, bazaars signified women's traditional way to "raise money."[16] Usually
held in rented or donated halls, and often timed to coincide with the
Christmas shopping season, suffrage bazaars offered goods ranging from
woman suffrage books and photographs to food, linens, and other
household necessities—even farm animals. Planning for these events
began months in advance. Organizers appealed for donations through
the suffrage press, indicating just what items they preferred and how best
to deliver them. In the case of large bazaars, both individuals and suffrage
clubs often responded to such requests. Some groups staffed and stocked

their own booths, which they often named after their hometown or an admired suffrage leader.[17] Host organizations, usually umbrella groups such as the NAWSA or similar state associations, and participating local leagues generally split the proceeds.

Suffrage bazaars sent a message of defiant unity to individuals both inside and outside the movement. They boldly proclaimed women's willingness to mobilize on behalf of political equality and to question the social basis of electoral participation. This message was redoubled on the sales floor. Tables named after famous woman's rights leaders and goods proudly affixed with the word "suffrage" denoted an unmistakable sense of purpose and dedication. Bazaars likewise reconceptualized contemporary notions of politics and gender. At these events, homemade baked goods and hand-sewn linens acquired political connotations. Baking, sewing, and other tasks associated with private, domestic life became the tools for claiming and creating a greater public sphere for women. In this sense, suffrage commodities lived up to the radical potential outlined by anthropologist Grant McCracken. McCracken argues that individuals at odds with the dominant society can use commodities to "announce a new social identity." In doing so, "these groups are potentially the agents of a highly destabilizing social change. They defy the conventions according to which cultural categories are defined."[18]

However, McCracken also notes that while these agitators "give voice to their protest" through commodities, they usually leave the dominant social codes embedded in those goods unchallenged.[19] As a result, even the rebellious redefinition of objects can sometimes have conservative implications. Many goods sold at woman suffrage bazaars, for example, subtly reaffirmed antisuffrage arguments against votes for women. The sale of preserves, linens, and other household products reasserted that woman's sphere was indeed the home, not the public arena of politics and debate. The following verse, which welcomed visitors to an apron counter at an 1894 Massachusetts bazaar, exemplifies this point:

> Aprons here for young AND OLD;
> Who'll buy! Who'll buy!
> Cheap for cash they will be sold;
> Who'll buy! Who'll buy!
> Squire Currier bought one for his wife,
> For he can't make an apron to save his life.[20]

Although intended to help sell aprons, this piece of doggerel confirms a host of ideas about gender and domesticity that are concretized in the items themselves. Of course the aprons are for women (like the Squire's wife), and of course Squire Currier cannot make one "to save his life." Who would expect otherwise? This playful rhyme acknowledges what we already know: that commodities are themselves gendered. The apron epitomizes domestic ideology. It stands for nurturance, the sentimental home, domestic labor, and private life—the very concepts that antisuffragists believed made women uninterested in, and unfit for, public life. By promoting commodities such as this without first addressing the tensions between their gendered connotations and suffragists' political goals, nineteenth-century activists diluted the internal consistency of their ideology and objectives.

The paradoxical nature of woman suffrage bazaars also derived from their economic importance. Bazaars did indeed represent women's traditional way to "raise money," but there was nothing old-fashioned or staid about their administration.[21] They taught women at all levels of the movement important lessons about business management, organization, planning, publicity, and bookkeeping. Suffragists encouraged bazaar coordinators to conduct the events "in an entirely honorable and business-like manner." "All goods," noted one writer, "should be marked at the usual retail price, exactly corresponding with the price in stores where they can be ascertained." Nonetheless, prices could be expensive (five dollars was considered the upper limit) and profit margins counted (items needed to sell for "at least double the cost").[22] Successful bazaars definitely filled suffrage coffers. For example, an 1887 bazaar sponsored by the Massachusetts Woman Suffrage Association netted over $6,300, while a 1901 bazaar placed "upwards of $8,000 in the NAWSA treasury."[23]

Bazaars maximized sales by appealing to women's domestic identities. Often, entire sections specialized in items for "home economics" or "household science." They made it easier for mothers to shop by arranging displays and events for children, thus allowing women to browse unencumbered by rambunctious offspring. Cooking demonstrations accompanied the abundant supplies of food and kitchen wares for sale. Designed to make bazaars as profitable as possible, all these arrangements had the additional effect of cementing traditional ideas about the ties among domesticity, consumption, and gender.

Bazaars were not the only spots for finding suffrage commodities during the late nineteenth and early twentieth centuries. The NAWSA consistently offered a small variety of items. Likewise, individual women and smaller suffrage organizations sold homemade and made-to-order products at state fair suffrage pavilions, club and association headquarters, and through the mail. However, no standard method of promoting or producing such objects existed. Indeed, the publicizing of suffrage commodities in the text of woman suffrage newspapers, as opposed to in advertising space, suggests that they were viewed neither as part of an organized campaign for enfranchisement nor as a routine method of fundraising or propaganda. They were still unusual enough to warrant commentaries describing their appearance and cost, and from whom and where they could be purchased. Many newspaper writers felt it necessary to explain how potential buyers could use this merchandise. Suggestions ranged from distributing Lucy Stone ink blotters at birthday commemoratives for the famed leader to decorating state fair suffrage booths with postcards, pins, and statuettes.[24]

Like bazaar organizers, the women who sold these goods did not deny their financial objectives. As early as 1889, Iowa suffragists touted their success at creating "quite a source of income" by selling pincushions. In 1896, NAWSA leaders became convinced that they could turn a tidy profit through the continuous sale of suffrage paraphernalia. Optimists in the organization predicted such efforts would quickly bring in as much as $500. They justified their plan by noting that "other organizations have been able to make propaganda and at the same time help support their direct work, by the sale of articles relating to and advertising their principles, to be sold at a small profit to the Association itself." Unfortunately for the NAWSA, not all fundraising strategies worked as planned. Almost one year after offering its small array of merchandise to the suffrage community, the group's program had failed to break even.[25]

By adopting these methods, suffragists opened themselves up to a growing array of commercial ties.[26] Like women in other clubs and social movements, suffragists used their leverage as consumers to demand special treatment from businesses, requesting donations for upcoming bazaars. As one San Francisco woman noted, "merchants are in the habit of contributing to everything on every occasion, and would be willing to please a customer, even if they were not interested in the cause."[27] In some cases, however, businesses and city boosters courted suffragists. In 1879, the St. Louis Merchants' Exchange appealed to women with perhaps the very first badge commemorating the movement. Ever eager to promote the city's commercial fortunes, the Exchange invited members of the National Woman Suffrage Association—then in St. Louis for its annual convention—to tour its operation. Upon leaving, each delegate received a gold-lettered badge reading "N.W.S.A., May 10, 1879, Merchants' Exchange."[28] Similar incidents followed. In 1893, the Grand Rapids, Michigan Board of Trade bestowed programs upon woman suffragists holding a convention in their city. In addition, the Board "sent carriages to take the entire working convention for a drive through the city, a visit to one of the largest warehouses and to the carpet-sweeper factory," where each of the delegates received "specially made small carpet-sweepers, each marked 'National American Woman Suffrage Association' " in gilt.[29] As these examples suggest, woman suffrage gatherings promised a welcome source of revenue to cities and an opportunity to win over women consumers. These inducements probably convinced some business leaders to keep personal opposition to female enfranchisement in check. Chambers of commerce from across the country actively courted woman suffrage groups. In 1900 alone, civic leaders and business groups in Milwaukee, Detroit, San Antonio, Cleveland, and Cincinnati invited the NAWSA to hold its next annual meeting in their respective locales. The Association ultimately accepted a bid from Minneapolis. Not only did the Minnesota Woman Suffrage Association guarantee $600 or more toward the NAWSA's expenses, it also presented invitations from the mayor, the Board of Trade, and three of the city's papers—all of whom assured the state association "of financial backing."[30]

Accustomed to borrowing from political themes and mottos, businesses even appropriated the movement's rhetoric. In 1895, soap advertisements hung on Boston streetcars dramatically asked "Should Women Vote?"[31] A little over a decade latter, an article in the trade journal *The Western Electrician* advised readers to slightly alter militant English suffragists' "rallying cry": "Votes for Women." Why not raise another cheer calling attention "to the need of lifting the burden on the physical strength of women?" asked the author. "This cry may well be 'Motors for Women!'—motors to run the sewing machine, the carpet-sweepers, the laundry apparatus of the home; motors to operate the . . . machines of the brighter future, when household drudgery shall be a thing of the past, and motors to drive all the machinery in every factory where women are employed." This slogan, he declared, "has an inspiring sound. Let the electrical manufacturers, the new business champions, enlist the women of America under their new banner."[32]

With historical precedent to guide them, suffragists no doubt recognized the appropriation of their rhetoric for what it was: a way to attract the weary and visually overstimulated mass culture audience's attention. But rather than dismissing such commercial gimmicks, suffragists interpreted them as evidence of the movement's growing status. In equating acknowledgment from advertisers and businesses with public stature and respect, these women anticipated the attitude of later woman suffragists. However, during the last decade of the movement, the ties between commerce and suffragists grew into an intricate web. The significance of suffrage commodities changed. They still allowed suffragists to concretize their faith in the cause, and also, as one Massachusetts flyer suggested, to "show people HOW MUCH YOU WANT THE VOTE AND WHY."[33] Few twentieth-century suffragists expressed this point more eloquently than Alice Park. An active northern California suffragist, Park argued that

> the wearing of the badge is significant of progress. Few are worn where the suffrage movement is unpopular. Many are worn as it grows in favor. Every badge, pin or button is a help, arousing curiosity among strangers, stimulating conversation among acquaintances and discussion among friends and antis.
>
> Show your colors all day long—at home to the chance inquirer at the door, the caller and the tradesman; in the street and in the cars to the chance passer-by; and in all meetings to all who attend. Until women have the courage of their convictions, how can they expect to win recognition and approval?[34]

Park's confidence in the power of pins and badges stemmed from personal experience. In 1911, she started collecting and publicly displaying suffrage badges (fig. 4.1). As her collection grew, so did interest in her unique items. On a 1913 voyage to the International Woman Suffrage Conference in Budapest, Hungary, her "conspicuous badges"—and prominently placed VOTES FOR WOMEN luggage labels—brought her constant notice.[35]

By the 1910s, however, "showing your colors" signified more than an act of faith. The use of suffrage commodities had become intricately tied to the celebration of commercialism and material abundance. Familiar badges, postcards, and stationery supplies suddenly appeared alongside new woman suffrage pins, lockets, watch fobs, collar pins, veil pins, hat pins, cuff links, belt buckles, tea and coffee spoons, pennants, playing

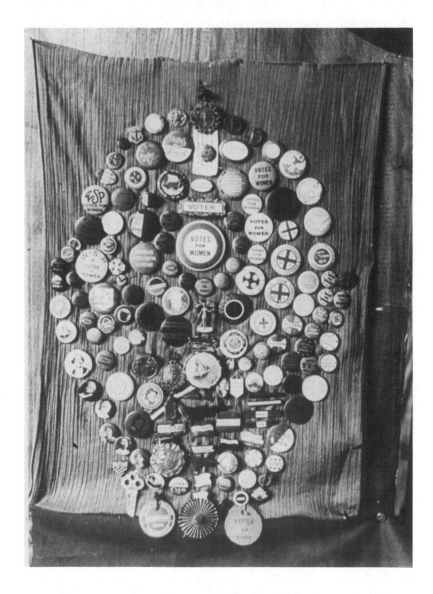

FIGURE 4.1
Alice Park collection of "votes for women" buttons and badges.
Courtesy Sophia Smith Collection, Smith College.

cards, balloons, fans, flyswatters, handkerchiefs, matchbooks, noise-makers, drinking cups, demitasse cups, hats, blouses, and more.[36] The scale on which suffrage commodities were produced and distributed also changed. Increasingly, highly organized, well-publicized systems for regularly marketing mass-produced goods replaced the ad hoc, sporadic sales methods of earlier activists. As late as 1909, buying suffrage merchandise could be complicated. In one case, *The Woman's Journal* encouraged a reader organizing a state fair suffrage booth to contact over a dozen sources in order to find a sufficient variety of postcards, cookbooks, badges, statuettes, matchboxes, and suffrage stamps.[37] No one group or individual sold all, or even many, of these goods. In the following decade, however, many suffrage associations offered a wide variety of objects.

The NAWSA, in particular, maintained a large and diverse supply of suffrage merchandise, which it promoted in the most modern ways. In addition to advertising in the suffrage press, the association established a national catalog service. Its regularly published "Catalog and Price List of Woman Suffrage Literature and Supplies" sold virtually anything an enterprising suffragist or suffrage league could desire.[38] The NAWSA even set up its own suffrage shops. Opened in New York City in 1913, the first store appealed to diverse interests by offering suffrage regalia, dry goods, and homemade comestibles. Described as a place WHERE BEAUTIFUL AND REAL BARGAINS ARE TO BE HAD, the store still existed as late as 1917.[39] A second store specializing in suffrage paraphernalia opened in Atlantic City in 1916—that year's location for the NAWSA's annual convention. Situated directly on the city's famed boardwalk—itself a commercial paradise of spectacle and consumer excess—the shop sold woman suffrage literature and novelties of all kinds, including "Votes for Women post-cards, pencils, stationery, drinking cups, yellow crepe paper caps, streamers and banners, favors, place cards, playing cards, horns, pins, paper napkins, doilies, Kewpies [sic] dolls, balloons, and fans."[40]

Unfortunately, the history of such stores remains obscure. We know little about their life spans, how they were founded, by whom, who shopped at them, and whether or not they profited. At least in the case of the Woman Suffrage Party Lunch Room—which sold home-cooked lunches, cosmetics, suffrage badges, and literature—research suggests that rich benefactors played an important role in supporting suffrage retailers. Housed in the Manhattan office building Alva Belmont bought for the NAWSA, the Lunch Room soon became a pet project of the wealthy suffragist. When Alice Park visited the establishment in 1915, she found Belmont standing at its door "like a head waiter."[41]

The growing diversity of suffrage goods and the expanding means of distributing them went hand-in-hand with suffragists' new commitment to public spectacle. Always a symbol of political identity, suffrage wares now represented a form of advertising. According to Park, each new suffrage group in the 1910s "wanted its own badge for local publicity."[42] Likewise, crepe paper caps, sandwich boards, lapboards and the like allowed women not only to commemorate their political identities, but also to transform their bodies into walking suffrage billboards.

But how did novelties like Kewpie dolls, fans, and objects unconnected to suffrage demonstrations promote woman suffrage? They certainly allowed women to express their beliefs and promote the movement under a variety of circumstances. But, perhaps most important, novelty goods brought the movement to a mass audience of nonsuffragists and allowed them to participate in suffragists' infectious spectacles. Often purchased in bulk and distributed either for free or at a minimum cost to passersby, street lecture attendants, parade watchers, theatergoers—whomever suffragists could attract to their forays in public space—these items became souvenirs, mementos of a day's adventure. During the Empire State campaign of 1915, for example, New York City suffragists distributed one million suffrage buttons, 200,000 cards of matches inscribed VOTE YES ON THE SUFFRAGE AMENDMENT, and 35,000 paper fans advising voters to KEEP COOL! THERE WILL BE NOTHING TO WORRY ABOUT AFTER WE GET VOTES FOR WOMEN.[43] Suffragists gave 500 such fans—and probably as many baby rattles and cool "peach sundaes"—to brokers and "animated capitalists" on one occasion at the "Votes for Women" restaurant on Wall Street.[44]

In some cases suffrage commodities might even be interpreted as "loss leaders" intended to maximize spectacle audiences. Such was the case at a series of events held at New York's Victoria theater that promised SOUVENIRS FOR EVERYBODY.[45] Undoubtedly, some recipients scoffed at these items and tossed them aside. But like the voters who eagerly collected partisan memorabilia, many men and women probably appreciated the novelties, or at least enjoyed the unusual context that made them available. Perhaps for some of these individuals suffrage commodities provided the first impulse toward a new, more positive opinion about the woman suffrage movement. Suffragists certainly hoped so. The "pleasing spectacle" of Wall Street workers snatching up fans and rattles and crowding "the tables and against the walls" of the "Votes for Women" restaurant must have convinced suffragists that the right bait could aid such transformations.[46]

In adopting these promotional methods, woman suffragists chose to emulate the commercial realm and privilege it as a locus for debate and appeal. Considering the degrading attention they often received from American politicians, suffragists wisely looked to other leaders and venues for validation. The organized and multifaceted sale of commodities was one more way to circumvent regular political processes and get their message across. Fans, badges, drinking cups, hats, and other types of memorabilia allowed suffragists to visually confront their opponents while attracting spectators to the drama and energy of their crusade. And mastering the organizational skills for running suffrage catalogs and stores and making financial decisions gave suffragists important tools for enhancing their movement and enriching their work as advocates for change.

If new modes of promotion and distribution altered the context for understanding and encountering suffrage commodities, however, so did the increasing number of businesses selling suffrage-oriented and -inspired merchandise. The emerging novelty industry latched on to the movement and capitalized upon its growth. Although little historical work has been done on this subject, the sudden appearance of novelty goods trade journals, catalogs, and retail stores during the early 1900s—especially the 1910s—indicates the tremendous expansion of this field.[47] Like other contemporary manufacturers, novelty goods makers took advantage of enormous economies of scale by pairing new tools of mass production with cheap labor. In searching for the right markets for their merchandise, many novelty makers targeted reform groups, including woman suffragists. The Holzapfel Publishing Company of Cleona, Pennsylvania, for example, rigorously promoted its pro-woman suffrage cartoon book to movement leaders in the northeast.[48] Likewise, The American Specialty Company marketed woman suffrage matchbooks to individuals active in the New York campaign of 1915, and insisted that few more persuasive forms of advertising existed. Boxes of matches labeled with a suffrage slogan and handed out to men, the company noted, would be "brought out by the smoker more than twenty times a day since he is obliged to strike the match on to the box in order to light. Your ad always strikes his attention when the box is brought and impresses his mind on the [upcoming New York woman suffrage] amendment."[49] Other businesses appealed directly to the average suffragist. In 1910, for instance, the Cargill Company and the Butler Brothers Jewelry Company urged women to consider their firms' respective supplies of suffrage postcards and jewelry.[50] Two years later, Macy's department store offered a suffrage marching outfit.[51] By 1917, other "leading Department Stores and Specialty Shops" sold official "suffragist blouses," stylishly designed in voile and crepe de chine by Max Kurzrok, Inc. (fig. 4.2).[52]

It is difficult to say whether these businesses and entrepreneurs felt motivated by potential profit or sincere interest in the cause. Rose O'Neill, the artist who created the popular "Kewpie" characters, was a devoted suffragist who donated her time and skills to drawing Kewpie postcards sold by the NAWSA's National Woman Suffrage Publishing Company.[53] In addition, several firms claimed admirable feminist credentials. The Cargill Company and the Butler Brothers Jewelry Company closed their advertisements with the inspiring motto: WE ARE OUT TO WIN THE VOTE—ARE YOU WITH US? Likewise, advertisers of the Beacon Manufacturing Company (makers of the "Beacon Marless" mop handle) proudly called themselves "Equal Suffragists" who "want to help you win, as well as to help our business grow."[54] But beyond these few examples, there is little evidence of the political ideology of suffrage commodity manufacturers. And even these cases are tainted by their clear commercial objectives.

What we do know is that suffragists blessed commercial forays into their world. New York women, for example, named Macy's their suffrage supply headquarters. Similarly, the NAWSA "recommended" Max Kurzrok's "suffragist blouse," and entered into a profit-sharing arrangement with the Butler Brothers Jewelry Company.[55] In many cases, suffragists went even further and urged followers to support retailers and manufacturers friendly to the cause. Like other publications dependent upon advertising revenue, *The Woman's Journal* continuously pressed readers to patronize its commercial sponsors. The paper even distorted the movement's own rhetoric by urging supporters to "vote and vote often" for the Johnson Educator Food Company's "Suffragette Cracker." "For upon the decision of the public," noted the paper, "depends the life of this Suffragette."[56] Special woman suffrage editions of commercial newspapers followed a similar strategy.[57] Generic "pattern advertisements," provided to local suffragists by the NAWSA,

THE SUFFRAGE BLOUSE

It was Miss Agnes Morgenthau, a leader among the "Y. S. S." (Younger Suffrage Set) who recommended that a "ready-to-wear - to - anything - and - not - at - all - expensive suffrage blouse" would meet a long-felt want among suffragists. A manufacturer has acted upon her suggestion and placed the above garment on the market.

FIGURE 4.2 *The suffrage blouse.*
Featured in the 2 June 1917 issue of the *Woman Citizen.*
Reproduced by permission of Huntington Library, San Marino, California.

allowed commercial sponsors of these papers to choose from a variety of slogans, including: "The Demand for SUFFRAGE and for (Blank's) Ice Cream may be resisted[.] It cannot be conquered"; and "WOMEN ATTENTION! Do your own voting[,] But Let me do your Building[.] John Blank." The most novel pattern advertisement turned English militants' famed motto DEEDS—NOT WORDS into a maxim for realtors.[58]

As we have seen, however, businesses needed few lessons on how to capitalize on woman suffrage rhetoric. With the expansion of the movement in the 1910s, this became far more common, and suffragists became far more cognizant of their struggle's growing commercial appeal. " 'All women vote for—' what? I'm sure I don't remember," wrote suffrage leader Mary Ware Dennett in 1911.

> It may have been a cereal, a tooth-paste, a carpet-sweeper, or anything else, but this I do remember, that it was an advertisement seen a few weeks ago in large letters, at the end of a car in the Hudson Tunnel, an advertisement which was bigger and more costly than any other in the car, and that it wouldn't have been there if it didn't pay to have it there, and it wouldn't have used those words if the suffrage movement had not become an asset to the commercial world.[59]

Five years later, another suffrage writer made a similar observation. "There have been plenty of signs of late that the advertising profession was awake to the publicity value of votes for women," noted Joe B. Hosmer in *The Woman's Journal.* "Suffrage parades have been typified in colors in the street car advertisements and the word 'Vote' has become almost a stock in trade."[60] One advertiser chose the image of the suffrage parade marcher to advertise a corn medication. If the product offered her relief from sore feet, suggested the ad, it might surely help the everyday consumer (fig. 4.3).

In retrospect, scholars might wonder whether the commercial appropriation of suffrage drama diluted the social and political content of the movement. Advertisers' skillful exploitation of feminism in the 1920s should make us suspicious of the consequences of similar actions a decade earlier.[61] But suffragists themselves did not recognize these concerns. For them, women's enfranchisement and consumerism went hand-in-hand. If anything, they applauded the piracy of suffrage slogans and spectacles, interpreting such acts as signs of their own success. Dennett, for example, believed that the commercial use of suffrage slogans created a mutually

Corns Quit, Pains Stop, With 'GETS-IT'

Quit Plasters, Salves and What-Nots.

After using "GETS-IT" once you will never again have occasion for asking, "What can I do to get rid of my corns?" "GETS-IT" is the first sure, certain corn-ender ever known. If you have

Why "Suffer-Yet" With Corns? Use "GETS-IT." They'll Vanish!

tried other things by the score and will now try "GETS-IT," you will realize this glorious fact.

You probably are tired sticking on tape that won't stay stuck, plasters that shift themselves right onto your corn, contraptions that make a bundle of your toe and press right down on the corn. Put two drops of "GETS-IT" on that corn in two seconds. The corn is then doomed as sure as night follows day. The corn shrivels. There's no pain, no fuss. If you think this sounds too good to be true try it tonight on any corn, callus, wart or bunion.

"GETS-IT" is sold by druggists everywhere, 25c a bottle, or sent direct by E. Lawrence & Co., Chicago.

"GETS-IT" is sold in San Francisco by the Owl Drug Co.—Advt.

FIGURE 4.3 *"Corns Quit."*
According to this advertisement, suffrage parade marchers could find relief
for sore feet with this corn medication.
Reproduced by permission of the Susan B. Anthony Ephemera Collection,
Huntington Library, San Marino, California.

satisfying relationship between advertisers and movement activists: "The suffragists are grateful because of just so much work done for them with no extra effort on their part, and the advertisers are grateful because it gives their poor, overworked, novelty-seeking brains one more chance to claim the attention of the public."[62] Agnes Ryan, managing editor of *The Woman's Journal*, seconded this opinion in an essay entitled "Valentines and Votes." "The latest evidence of the growing popularity of Votes for Women comes in the valentine," noted Ryan. "The fact that the commercial world begins to realize the value of Cupid, St. Valentine and the Suffragist in combination points to popular acceptance of the inevitableness [sic] of equal suffrage."[63]

In celebrating these trends, suffragists called attention to the intricate ties between the movement and consumer culture. Judging their struggle's impact on expressions of modern mass consumerism became one way for suffragists to measure their own success. That success proved greatest when suffragists noted that savvy business leaders, not politicians, gave the public what it really wanted. As Ryan concluded, the manufacturer has "his finger on the pulse of the nation," when he "makes his latest Valentine girl a Suffragist."[64] In this context, the boundaries between how people conceptualized their relationships to politics and to consumerism became somewhat blurred. Commerce seemed to sell not just merchandise, but equality and even democracy. Likewise, political rhetoric touted empowerment as well as access to abundant commodities.

By declaring the merger of politics and consumerism unproblematic, suffragists allowed businesses to freely undermine the integrity of suffrage campaign promises. As in the past, advertisers' appropriation of suffragists' notions of citizenship, political equality, and justice compromised the meanings of these ideas. Yet suffragists were uninterested in even questioning advertisements that started with slogans like "Women Want their *rights*," and concluded with backward-looking phrases like "Of course *votes* count—every four years or so, but *money* counts every day." Their acceptance of such slogans suggests that suffragists remained insensitive to the ways in which political and consumer choices had been redefined as indistinguishable. What were "Women's Rights?" asked the above-noted advertisement. "Broadly speaking," it continued, women wanted "the right to *enjoy life* in their way without infringing on the rights of others." They could practice that right only occasionally with the vote, but daily with money and consumption.[65]

Advertisers' trivialization of women voters continued in the postsuffrage period. Immediately preceding the presidential election of 1920—when American women citizens exercised their right to vote for the first time—a number of suffrage-inspired advertisements appeared. In one, Campbell's tomato soup stood for "a league of good cheer," for which the company's famous female, cherub-faced icon promised to "vote every day in the year" (fig. 4.4).[66] As late as 1932, an advertisement headed "When Lovely Women Vote" revealed the lasting fascination with female enfranchisement. As the advertising copy discloses, however, Listerine toothpaste, not the upcoming presidential election, had captured women's ballots.[67]

Suffragists' easy acceptance of the commercialization of suffrage rhetoric paralleled their embrace of a commercial aesthetic of spectacle, excess, and reconfigured public and private spaces, described in earlier chapters.[68] Suffrage commodities, however, reveal an unmentioned aspect of that aesthetic: its kitsch expression. Art historian Matei Calenescu describes kitsch as a uniquely capitalist art form whose "aesthetic charm is transparently commercial." Kitsch objects readily sacrifice originality, historic context, and artistic integrity for predictability, romanticism, emotionalism, and the promise of financial reward.[69] Defined thus, kitsch becomes the poor, degraded stepchild of supposedly noncommercial high art. It even stands as the negative, feminized model against which modern art and literature tried to define themselves during the first half of the twentieth century.[70] As critics like Andreas Huyssen warn, we should be wary of dichotomizing art in ways that sanction highbrow views of cultural boundaries. When we collaborate in the perpetuation of these boundaries we further entrench a wide range of social hierarchies.[71] But sensitivity to this problem should not make us uncritical of the ways in which commercial demands for mass appeal gave kitsch a certain familiar, sentimental, and uncontroversial aspect.

For woman suffragists, demands for mass appeal translated into ever fewer material reminders of the historic leaders who made the movement possible. Once-popular postcards of women like Susan B. Anthony, and even the NAWSA's contemporary visionary Carrie Chapman Catt, were replaced with mawkish illustrations and riveting photographs of spectacular parades and pageants—pictures replete with sentimental, emotional impact. Sometimes this imparted a liberating, fresh quality to suffrage goods. Even now, postcards showing long brigades of women marching in unity for suffrage deliver an impressive

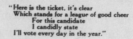

"Here is the ticket, it's clear
Which stands for a league of good cheer
For this candidate
I candidly state
I'll vote every day in the year."

EVERYBODY
FOR IT

The winning ticket

Campbell's Tomato Soup wins not only on its delicious flavor but on its wholesome quality and healthfulness.

It is one of the most valuable health-promoters you can have on your table.

The pure juice of vine-ripened tomatoes and the other choice ingredients with which we make it are nourishing in themselves and they also help to tone and regulate all the body processes which build up health and good condition.

Served as a Cream of Tomato, the usual way, its energy-yield is fifty per cent greater than that of milk.

Good soup once a day at least is a health rule which no one can afford to overlook.

Do not leave it to chance. Order a dozen of this appetizing soup at a time and have it handy.

21 kinds   15c a can

Campbell's SOUPS

LOOK FOR THE RED AND WHITE LABEL

FIGURE 4.4 *Campbell's soup advertisement.*
Advertisers sometimes appropriated the rhetoric and imagery
of the suffrage movement.
Good Housekeeping.

message of political commitment and courage. By bringing the movement and all of its dynamism into the purview of American society, suffrage commodities like these offered a clear challenge to individuals
resistant to political and social change. For some audiences, this challenge may have reaffirmed fears about how enfranchisement would
degrade and masculinize women. However, the kitsch nature of other
goods eased and deftly assuaged those anxieties by reaffirming older
ideas about women's emotional nature. If antisuffragists proposed that
enfranchisement would unsex women, suffrage clothing and gilded jewelry implied that the female sex's presupposed interest in fashion and
self-decoration would remain intact. If critics concluded that suffrage
would lead to race suicide, cloying postcards featuring happy, well-fed,
white children implied that the vote would not deter women from their
primary occupation: motherhood. And if skeptics suggested that suffragism was a synonym for lesbianism, candies called "Suffragette
Kisses" (advertised as "The Kiss That's Different") and woman suffrage
valentines proclaiming "Love Me, Love My Vote," and "Cupids [sic] put
his bow away, He has another task to-day. . . . Votes for Women" assured
Americans that romance and heterosexual norms faced little threat from
women voters (figs. 4.5–4.7).[72]

The ability of suffrage commodities to negotiate social tensions
through kitsch expression is perhaps best exemplified in a valentine
described by Agnes Ryan. The following verse accompanies a picture of
a female cupid dressed in a "yellow, orange and brown picture hat, yellow sash and long gloves [who] steps daintily along to the delight of two
boy Cupids":

> For my sweet Valentine.
> Cupid has no idea,
> How much I am oppressed,
> For, being a ward-leader,
> I'm compelled to be well-dressed.[73]

Embedded in this lighthearted, tongue-in-cheek rhyme is a host of
competing social constructs. The ambivalent image of the woman politico
surfaces immediately. For antisuffragists, few positions might seem more
contemptible than that of suffrage ward leader. Simultaneously canvasser,
cajoler, recruiter, administrator, and manager in the dirty world of local
city politics, she embodied all of the qualities that threatened to "unsex"
women and destabilize gender roles. While the valentine necessarily

FIGURE 4.5 *Suffrage valentine.*
Suffrage valentines like this helped neutralize fears of woman suffrage
by reasserting traditional gender ideals.
Reproduced by permission of the Susan B. Anthony Ephemera Collection,
Huntington Library, San Marino, California.

FIGURE 4.6 *Suffrage valentine.*
Reproduced by permission of the Susan B. Anthony Ephemera Collection,
Huntington Library, San Marino, California.

FIGURE 4.7 *Suffrage valentine.*
Reproduced by permission of the Susan B. Anthony Ephemera Collection,
Huntington Library, San Marino, California.

recognizes such concerns in its very mention of the ward leader, however, it quickly proceeds to neutralize them. Familiar concepts of oppression are turned playfully topsy-turvy. It is not political oppression—the lack of the vote—that causes the young cupid's lament, but the oppression of fashion. "Being a ward leader," she is "compelled" to be more fashionable, more feminine than other women. As the rapt attention of the two "boy Cupids" demonstrates, however, even this dilemma has its rewards: admiring male suitors.

By embodying a kitsch sentimentality, therefore, woman suffrage commodities maintained the paradoxical ability to advocate social change in a public forum unaccustomed to women's political presence, and simultaneously assure spectators that female enfranchisement would not be socially disruptive. Followers could turn their bodies into political billboards (via "yellow sashes" and the like), and yet imply that—as women—they differed little from their female detractors. For the mainstream suffragists examined in this study, these were important messages. In seeking to distance themselves from radicals, they presented eager homilies on the virtues of domesticity and motherhood, and enthusiastically represented suffragists as defenders of the home. If kitsch commodities aided that effort, so much the better.

In sanctioning the representation of women in predictable, sentimental, and romantic terms, nonradical suffragists ultimately settled for an uncontroversial and unremarkable standard of women's citizenship. Unlike the municipal housekeepers, socialists, and radical suffragists who saw votes for women as the first step in a larger transformation of self and society, this construction of political identity did not ask the newly enfranchised to redefine themselves, their capabilities, or their potential impact on American society. Instead it taught women to see the vote as one more way to center their lives around home, children, heterosexual romantic love, and consumerism.[74]

By tangibly representing the suffrage movement, woman suffrage commodities became the "visible part" of an American culture at odds over gender roles, politics, and the move toward a mass consumer society. In some ways, these artifacts represent the hope of a reimagined and regendered political sphere, reminding us that woman suffragists creatively used goods to foster a sense of community and faith, and to speak with unique resonance to American society. In the late nineteenth and early twentieth centuries, suffragists achieved these goals by using goods to represent natural, botanically inspired metaphors for civilization and progress. Commodities such as the sunflower badge embodied the high-minded ideals that helped followers endure difficult and uncertain times. Yet even in this period, acquiescence to the previously gendered nature of some commodities revealed a conservatism occasionally at odds with the political liberty women sought.

During the 1910s, suffrage goods expressed similar hopes and aspirations, but they had also become more in sync with the modern commercial era. Mass production and modern marketing techniques, including advertising and catalog sales, stamped their mark on suffrage items. Suffragists praised these changes and saw them as symbolic of the movement's progress. This shift in context had a profound influence on the significance of suffrage commodities. By associating progress with mass production and mass consumption, suffragists embraced a commercial ideology that glorified kitsch, sentimentality, and spectacle. In doing so, suffragists found yet another way of legitimizing their movement through consumer culture. They declared that their cause was modern, worthwhile, and wholly congruent with the celebration of consumer abundance and commodity-centered identity. Perhaps more important, suffrage merchandise allowed women in the movement to make these claims and simultaneously assuage the social anxieties of Americans. Many suffrage goods implied that while enfranchisement would extend women's political rights, women's involvement in consumer society would reaffirm traditional expectations of gender identity and social organization. Suffragists succeeded so well in sending a dramatic yet inviting message that businesses appropriated the rhetoric of the movement for commercial gain. The fact that woman suffragists not only permitted but embraced such exploitation indicates just how much nonradicals had accepted the evolving consumer-capitalist worldview. It also points to one more way the growth of consumer culture influenced nonradical suffragists' definitions of themselves, their cause, and the possible meanings of women's citizenship.

Chapter 5

Selling Suffrage News: Consumerism and
The Woman's Journal

In June 1931, eleven years after the Nineteenth Amendment guaranteed American women the right to vote, the final curtain fell on an old and influential player in the fight for women's political equality. After sixty-one and a half years, *The Woman's Journal,* the historic voice of the suffrage movement, issued its last number. Since its founding in 1870, the weekly newspaper-turned-monthly magazine had waged an unceasing battle on behalf of female enfranchisement and citizenship. It provided suffragists throughout the nation with campaign information, propaganda, camaraderie, and hope. And long before *Ms.* magazine offered modern feminists an alternative to the conservative gender ideology espoused in popular women's periodicals, *The Woman's Journal* gave their grandmothers a forum for serious political thought and discussion. As one *Journal* worker put it, the paper served as a "torchbearer." It offered a light of knowledge, unity, and—for a small cadre of working women—professional opportunity.[1] The fact that the *Journal* never missed an issue speaks to the commitment of its editors and writers and the faithful support of its readers.

But the *Journal* was more than a political polemic or inspirational organ. It was also a joint-stock corporation with economic imperatives, including raising revenues, paying bills, and avoiding debt. Unlike other corporate entities, however, the *Journal*'s business success or failure affected more than its own survival; it influenced women's struggle for voting rights. The founders of the paper believed its economic success would aid the woman suffrage movement and increase its financial resources. If lack of funding forced the *Journal* to stop printing, an important voice in the fight for woman suffrage would be lost. Thus, throughout its long history, a symbiotic relationship existed between the *Journal's* business and political objectives. Capitalist enterprise became not only a tool in the battle for enfranchisement, but also an intricate component of the movement itself. When the Woman's Journal Corporation used commercially inspired strategies to finance its product, it also meant to publicize and legitimize woman suffrage. And when it sold newspapers to raise interest in the cause, it likewise intended to raise money.

Yet if business and reform objectives were intricately connected, they were not equally successful. In over sixty years of operation, the publication never once broke even. Despite concerted efforts to make it profitable, the paper drained the resources of its owners and benefactors. At first this seemed an unfortunate, but acceptable and unavoidable, loss. During the nineteenth century, the *Journal's* proprietors excused its economic misfortunes and even valorized them as a sign of the paper's editorial integrity: its refusal to relinquish high-minded, if unpopular, ideals. Changes in the publishing world soon made it harder to ignore the paper's financial failings. By the end of the nineteenth century, advertising revenues and mass consumption were key to a publication's survival. Small newspapers were forced to keep pace with new, streamlined forms of labor, costly commercial standards of graphic design, and elaborate methods of promotion. With the *Journal's* controversial cause limiting both readers and sponsors, adapting to this environment proved a difficult—but not unwelcome—task. Numerous individuals dedicated themselves to updating the paper. Influenced by what cultural critic Sally Stein calls a new standard of visual orientation bent "on constructing an audience of spectators and by extension consumers," these women longed to make the *Journal* splashy and modern-looking.[2] They wanted it to emulate both the style of successful commercial periodicals and the tenor of the now more spectacular and popular suffrage movement. And they not only expected the *Journal* to make money, but also foresaw a time when it would stand as the premier political publication for American women. Much to the dismay of owner and editor Alice Stone Blackwell, ambitions such as these eventually began to overshadow the *Journal's* historic, if uneasy, balance between format and finance. Once Blackwell relinquished her hold on the paper and once women's enfranchisement became a reality, this balance seemed untenable and illogical. The paper was perceived increasingly as an economic albatross with no sustainable mass audience and few reasons for continuing publication. Its demise proved only a matter of time.

Despite its long history, the *Journal* was not the first periodical devoted to woman's rights and reform. Beginning in the 1850s, a consecutive series of newspapers including *The Lily, The Una, Saturday Visitor,* and *The Woman's Advocate* delivered regular doses of proto-feminism to politically minded women.[3] Nor is the *Journal* the most famous suffrage newspaper. That honor belongs to Susan B. Anthony and Elizabeth Cady Stanton's *The Revolution.* Although it lasted from only 1868 to 1870, *The Revolution's* unwavering support for a wide variety of woman's rights issues and financial backing by the eccentric segregationist George Train assured it instant, and ultimately historic, recognition.

The *Journal* began publication shortly before *The Revolution* folded. Like Stanton and Anthony, *Journal* founders Lucy Stone and her husband Henry B. Blackwell drew from the legacy of other women's newspapers. Nonetheless, abolitionist newspapers stood as their most important referent. Anthony, Stanton, Stone, and Blackwell had all witnessed the power of papers like *The Liberator* to spark discussion and advocate social change. Indeed, all four had been close friends before the Civil War and had worked with *Liberator* editor William Lloyd Garrison. Disagreement over the Fifteenth Amendment and Stanton and Anthony's increasing support for a wide platform of sometimes controversial woman's rights causes led Stone and Blackwell to break ranks with their former colleagues. The couple moved to Boston and helped found the moderate American Woman Suffrage Association (AWSA). Soon afterward, Stone and Blackwell started their own suffrage newspaper. With $1,000 of their own savings and $9,000 raised from two silent partners and a generous benefactor, they established the Woman's Journal Corporation, the joint-stock company responsible for publishing *The Woman's Journal.* They then rented a room in the Boston headquarters of the New England Woman Suffrage Association and went to work.[4]

Unlike *The Revolution,* the *Journal* avoided controversial aspects of the woman's movement. Instead, it concentrated on woman suffrage essays, campaign news, and fundraising and political proselytizing strategies. It also published book reviews, letters, proto-feminist short stories, editorials, accounts of expanding educational and professional opportunities for women, advice on dress reform and domestic science, and a variety of other topics appealing to reform-minded women.[5] By sticking to these more centrist aspects of the late nineteenth-century woman's movement, the *Journal* quickly became the AWSA's weekly organ and the mouthpiece for nonradical suffragists. Historian Eleanor Flexner contends that Stone and Blackwell proved so adept at reaching these women that the *Journal* drove the final nail in the failing *Revolution's* coffin.[6]

However, the founders were concerned with more than careful editorial planning as they immersed themselves in the unfamiliar waters of newspaper production. Blackwell, in particular, welcomed the economic success—even wealth—this undertaking might offer. Following the surprisingly strong demand for the paper's first few issues, Blackwell delightedly noted that

> for the first time in our lives we are beginning to experience what the French call "the embarrassment of riches." Indeed, we are told that some of our good friends, the working women, look a little suspiciously upon us as "bloated capitalists" and fear we are getting along too fast. They need not fear, for their cause is ours. Bread and the ballot go hand in hand.[7]

Blackwell had little reason to feel embarrassed. His optimistic financial projections soon floundered in a sea of low subscription rates and hard-to-meet debts. Stone, the guiding force behind the paper until her death in 1893, struggled to keep the enterprise afloat and to relieve her family and supporters from as many expenses as possible. Anthony could have warned her old colleagues of such difficulties. Similar problems had plagued *The Revolution*.[8]

Initially, Stone and Blackwell pinned the paper's financial success on subscription and advertising receipts. This was a relatively new idea, and it represents the *Journal's* first attempt to model itself after commercial, as opposed to reform, publications. During the first half of the nineteenth century, most papers met their expenses through the spoils of political partisanship, particularly through lucrative government printing contracts. As extensions of political parties, they aimed primarily at shaping politics, not making money. With urbanization, the rise of the penny press, and the decline of partisan financial support for newspapers, however, daily and weekly papers eschewed politics in favor of commerce. By the time the *Journal* entered the scene, circulation and advertising revenues had become the sole sources of support for most nonreform newspapers.[9]

Like commercial periodicals, the *Journal* used several strategies to maximize both types of income. It experimented with premium campaigns in which readers raised subscriptions in exchange for prizes. The more friends and neighbors persuaded to order the paper, the more—or better—items earned.[10] Attracting advertisers required a different tactic. Stone herself became the paper's first advertising agent. She dragged herself through the stores of Boston in search of local sponsors.[11] Although the *Journal's* refusal to accept notices for disreputable products, such as alcohol and tobacco, automatically limited its pool of potential advertisers, those businesses that supported the paper found an accommodating journalistic ally. The *Journal* regularly advanced clients' interests through "puffery." Although ethically suspect, this common practice "puffed up" advertisers by passing off product testimonials as news. In one case, the famous woman's rights pioneer Lydia Maria Child penned a seemingly innocuous advice article that promoted a local Boston merchant and *Journal* advertiser. Even fiction could assume a commercial slant. One anonymously penned short story advocated women's economic equality while simultaneously promoting two *Journal* sponsors: the makers of Doty's Washing Machine and the Universal Clothing Wringer.[12]

As this last example suggests, the newspaper also appealed to businesses by stressing the most gendered connotations of American consumerism. Explicitly recognizing its female readers as consumers, an 1899 *Journal* article promised "unrivaled facilities for reaching the women, who do nine tenths of the shopping in every community. . . . Every kind of manufacture, every article of commerce, every object of use or luxury,—dry goods, groceries, breadstuffs, millinery, clothing, furniture, carpets, house-furnishings—all these find buyers among the [paper's] wide-awake constituency."[13] Stone and Blackwell used such promotional strategies to keep hard-won advertisers satisfied with their investments. But these tactics also reaffirmed the paper's conservative leanings by limiting how readers might imagine consumerism's influence on women. A number of reformers—some of whom found a voice in the *Journal*—fantasized about consumer abundance liberating women from the constricting bonds of domestic drudgery, but the paper's gendered presentation of women buyers affirmed that consumption and domesticity went hand-in-hand.[14] Advertisers often compounded this message further by using *Journal* space to promote a paradigm of womanhood centered around shopping.

Despite the newspaper's adoption of commercial marketing strategies, interest in it remained low. Although no subscription figures for this period exist, evidence from the early twentieth century suggests that readership could not have exceeded 2,500, and was probably much lower.[15] In contrast, by 1890, the average daily newspaper sold approximately 5,200 copies.[16] Leading magazines that, like the *Journal*, had national circulations maintained readerships of over 100,000.[17] Advertisers also rejected the *Journal*. According to scholar Susan Schultz Huxman, local businesses saw little to gain by sponsoring a newspaper that catered to a national audience, maintained a small circulation, could not be found on newsstands, and used relatively poor-quality newsprint.[18] By 1909—the first year for which data is available—advertising equaled less than 8 percent of the *Journal's* annual revenues.[19]

Convinced, however, that the need for a suffrage organ outweighed its financial losses, the editors refused to stop publishing. Instead, the Stone/Blackwell family asked supporters to bridge the gap between income and expenses. Although they preferred direct donations or legacies, they also encouraged individuals and organizations of limited means to hold bazaars and other fundraising events on the paper's behalf. When outside resources proved insufficient, the family satisfied *Journal* creditors by dipping into its own pockets. Every year, through luck and perseverance, Blackwell and Stone managed to meet their fiscal obligations.[20] Although such trials proved difficult, the editors earnestly endeavored to put a bright face on a bad situation. Relinquishing Blackwell's premature dreams of wealth, they expressed pride in the *Journal's* financial losses. The priority they granted to the paper's reform mission became a badge of honor reflecting its dogged determination to enfranchise women. In celebration of the *Journal's* fifth anniversary in 1875, Blackwell touted the periodical's precarious fiscal health. While some might have viewed the "absence of pecuniary profit" as a sign of failure, he insisted that it proved the paper's editorial integrity and political success. These losses have "been the result of our fixed determination not to turn aside from the main purpose for which the paper was established," wrote Blackwell. "Without fear or favor we have expressed the honest convictions and deliberate judgment of a majority of the [*Journal's*] editors and proprietors."[21] An 1895 editorial commending the twenty-fifth anniversary of the paper rang a similar note: "We are proud of the fact that the paper has been published for a quarter of a century without profit—the correspondence and a large part of the editorial supervision having been a free-will offering to the best of all causes—equal rights for women."[22]

Within a few short years this perspective changed. The paper's annual deficit no longer elicited praise for the *Journal's* unbreakable will. Instead, it fostered accusations and finger-pointing. Writer Charlotte Perkins Gilman, who donated a year's service to the paper in 1904, blamed the paper's financial misfortunes on lackluster followers who neither subscribed to the *Journal* nor raised subscriptions for it.[23] Although this criticism seems unfair considering the organ's history, it points to a clear shift in the meaning and importance of the *Journal's* business operations. Once-justifiable economic losses now seemed unwarranted and inexcusable. The Stone/Blackwell family had begun to demand nothing less than the paper's self-sufficiency.

This demand reflected dramatic changes in the newspaper industry. The same business mentality that had begun privileging commercial over political influence spawned increasingly vigorous competition. By 1899, advertising (no longer in conjunction with subscriptions) had become the main source of income for newspapers. But that did not undermine the importance of circulation. Businesses—now largely working through advertising agencies—made ad placement decisions on the basis of readership figures. This, in turn, drove the search for consumers and helped inaugurate the sensationalism for which late nineteenth-century American journalism became renowned. Increased rivalry and commercialization also encouraged changes in the publishing process itself. Wealthy newspapers pushed for, and invested in, new technologies that made printing faster, more efficient, and more expensive. Forced to meet these improved standards, smaller newspapers faced dramatically increased start-up and operating costs, which further hampered their efforts to compete with larger, more successful publications. The drive for increased efficiency and profits also contributed to the subdivision of newspaper labor. Once-omnipotent editors found themselves challenged by new business and circulation managers who questioned commitment to strong editorial policies and worked with single-minded focus on commercial performance.[24]

As a small, weekly reform newspaper controlled largely by one family, the *Woman's Journal* suffered less from these developments than many low-circulation dailies. Nevertheless, the *Journal* could not ignore the new business standards; nor could its editors help but compare their product to the commercial publications that set those standards. In 1904, Gilman decried the increasingly high price of printing and typesetting. She likewise bemoaned the fact that, unlike commercial competitors, the paper could not pay writers. The combination of these problems caused Gilman to grimly contemplate the financially troubled periodical's condition. Noting that high-circulation newspapers and magazines succeeded by using subscription lists "as bait for advertisers," she complained that "the woman's movement is not yet sufficiently 'popular'—or those who consider it important are not yet sufficiently interested, or sufficiently beyond poverty—to have its organ attract advertisers." As a result, she noted, the *Journal* faltered while inferior publications "that find half-opened minds to nibble them" reaped profits.[25] To overcome this inequity, argued Gilman, the *Journal* needed to jump on the bandwagon and produce its own "bait." She insisted that higher circulation "would mean larger advertising, larger capital, power to engage the best writers and add many attractive features." It would mean, in effect, a more prosperous *Journal* and a more widely heralded suffrage movement.

The proprietors agreed. One week after running Gilman's critique, they announced a series of major changes. Emulating the mass magazines and metropolitan dailies that first realized that lower prices meant higher circulation, the family reduced the paper's annual subscription cost from $2.50 to $1.50 and waited for the now more affordable publication to attract an onslaught of new consumers and, in turn, coveted advertisers.[26] In addition, they counterbalanced the initial fall in revenue certain to accompany the lower price with lower operating costs. The eight-page weekly, which had changed little visually since 1870, was cut to four pages. By this time, the founders' only progeny, Alice Stone Blackwell, held sole authority over the paper's production.[27] As she informed readers, "for thirty-five years the editors of this paper have made it a rule not to go into debt, nor to contract any bill that they were not sure they [or their benefactors] could pay. They will not depart from that sound principle now."[28]

Although Alice Stone Blackwell regretted shortening the paper, no one could deny the new system's success. Within one year, an annual deficit averaging several thousand dollars fell to a few hundred. By 1906, the paper's economic prospects seemed so good that Blackwell exhibited some of her father's old optimism. "It is a common saying that no reform paper can ever be self supporting," she commented, "but things look as if the JOURNAL might become so within a few years."[29] Increased subscriptions (up to 2,400 in 1908) gave her further cause for satisfaction.[30] In early 1910, perhaps convinced that these improvements spelled a new day for the economically troubled venture, Blackwell answered the call of modern publishing practice and hired a full-time, paid business manager.[31]

Other suffragists also seemed impressed with the paper's apparent turnaround. The NAWSA watched the *Journal's* changing fortunes with growing interest. As early as 1893, Susan B. Anthony predicted that suffrage forces would not succeed until they sponsored "one great national daily newspaper, so we can sauce back our opponents every day in the year."[32] During the early twentieth century, the spectacular English woman suffrage movement seemed to prove her point. All three of the major British suffrage organizations maintained prosperous newspapers, which not only filled coffers but also provoked tremendous publicity. Moved by their success, numerous American suffrage groups began producing their own papers. The NAWSA initially considered turning its monthly newsletter into a weekly organ, but the prospect of high start-up costs forced it to consider other options. Acquiring a pre-existing periodical seemed cheaper; finding one verging on self-sufficiency, and that might eventually contribute to NAWSA finances, seemed perfect.[33]

In 1910, the NAWSA approached Blackwell and proposed adopting *The Woman's Journal* as its official publication. Close ties between the editor and the Association made prospects for affiliation bright. Blackwell served on the NAWSA board of directors, and she had almost single-handedly started the Association by negotiating the 1890 merger between the AWSA and the NWSA. Moreover, she had long demonstrated her support for the NAWSA by featuring it prominently in the *Journal's* columns. The two sides completed partnership discussions in July, and the final terms seemed equitable. For a relatively low cost, the NAWSA received a reputable, weekly suffrage paper equipped with a trained staff. Control over the paper's editorial policy went to the Association's board of directors. The *Journal* headquarters remained in Boston and Blackwell stayed on as editor (as in the past, she donated her services). The NAWSA agreed to pay the salaries of an assistant editor, the already contracted business manager, and a private secretary for Blackwell. It also agreed to cover future deficits.[34]

On the surface, Blackwell's belief that since "combination and consolidation give increased strength in every line of business . . . they are bound to give increased strength in reform," seemed to bode well for the new *Journal.* Circulation expanded rapidly. Before the partnership, readership still languished at 2,400, but by 1911, it had grown to 15,300 (see fig. 5.1).[35] Although inconsequential when compared to the over one million buyers of several leading national magazines, this increase signified a marked improvement, especially considering the paper's controversial objective.[36] A number of factors influenced this development. Since the greatest annual rate of increase directly followed affiliation, incorporating old NAWSA newsletter readers into the *Journal*'s subscription list—especially during a time of growing popularity for the movement—made a significant impact. Reducing the paper's yearly cost to $1.00 likewise bolstered circulation rates. By 1912, almost 20,000 people received the paper.

New business manager Agnes E. Ryan also had a tremendous impact on the *Journal*'s growth. Ryan gave the paper what it had never before had: publicity and an organized sales force. Through the use of "newsies" (female outdoor newspaper vendors), she gave the *Journal* and the movement a public and personal face. As early as 1909, several American suffragists emulated their English comrades by selling the *Journal* on the streets of Boston. Soon, most American suffrage papers employed roving peddlers of their own. But Ryan expanded and systematized newsy work. Articles and letters encouraged women throughout the nation to order the *Journal*'s trademark yellow and black canvas "newsy bags" and take to the streets. No training was necessary. Everything an enterprising suffragist needed to know could be found in Ryan's short pamphlet, "Selling the Woman's Journal."[37] It included basic suggestions (find out if sellers need permits; carry ample change; dress warmly in winter) as well as clever sales techniques (arrange for supporters to surround newsies and set an example of public consumption; work in cadres of up to twenty women to create a dramatic impression). Initially, some conservative suffragists questioned the propriety of such *Journal* promotions. But Ryan expressed little sympathy for their concerns:

> Now that we are used to street meetings, ope[n]-air campaigns, parades, and the hundreds of methods that resourceful suffragists have devised to bring equal suffrage to the attention of the public, it is difficult to consider the "dignity objection." Is it not well to ask in this connection, "What is dignity? Of what value is it in itself? And how does it compare in value with getting Votes for Women?" At best are we not in an undignified position before the world as long as we are disfranchised? Isn't the indignity of selling papers for the cause of passing moment as compared with the fundamental dignity of being free citizens?[38]

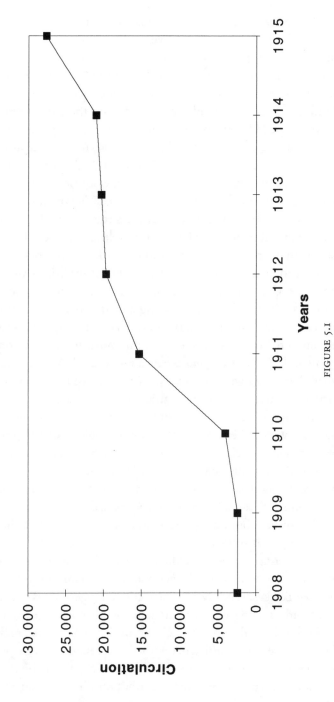

FIGURE 5.1
Woman's Journal circulation (1908–1915).
Agnes E. Ryan,
The Torchbearer.

Ryan attempted to further stimulate circulation by paying newsies on a commission basis. They received half the proceeds of each sale (two and a half cents per five-cent paper). An hour of work, which apparently averaged six sales, left vendors with about fifteen cents. Although these monetary rewards seem small, they often provided adequate incentive. Suffrage clubs in particular benefited from the commission arrangement. By peddling the paper in groups and devoting the profits to their organizations, clubs could build needed resources as well as visibly promote the movement. For individual women, the intersection between political commitment and economic necessity gave newsy work special allure. As an unpublished letter to *The Woman's Journal* from one prospective saleswoman indicates, the struggles for "bread and ballot" went hand-in-hand—as Henry Blackwell first proposed. "I am a self-supporting girl and am desirous to do work that is beneficial to society and yet to be able to earn my living," noted the young woman. "I am with the 'Cause' in heart and soul and if I can, by my efforts, help to propagate it, I shall feel I am doing a worthy deed."[39] By bringing the movement and its supporters to life for the mostly urban crowds that encountered newsies, women like this aided both the suffrage movement and *The Woman's Journal.* As a result, the NAWSA achieved more than Anthony's goal: it had a paper to "sauce back" opponents *and* heighten interest in both the cause and the Association.

Growing circulation and publicity, however, obscured mounting tensions within the partnership. Money problems once again provoked discord. Despite record sales figures, the *Journal's* annual deficit not only remained intact, but grew rapidly. Blackwell could have warned of as much. Unlike the fiscally conservative editor, the NAWSA accompanied its price reduction with a doubling of the paper's size. At least initially, expenses could not help but outpace revenues. As costs mounted, the dream of operating a self-sufficient suffrage paper dissipated. What had been an annual shortfall of several hundred dollars ballooned to $6,000 a mere two years into the affiliation.[40] Finger-pointing ran rampant. NAWSA leaders accused Blackwell and Ryan of ineffective management. Blackwell charged the board with unrealistic expectations and no long-range planning.

Both sides had reason to feel disgruntled. The *Journal* may not have been as close to self-sufficiency as the NAWSA believed. In 1909, despite five years of circulation increases, over 20 percent of the *Journal's* operating revenues came from contributions. In 1910, that figure rose to 28 percent—and the paper still ran a deficit (see figs. 5.2 and 5.3).[41]

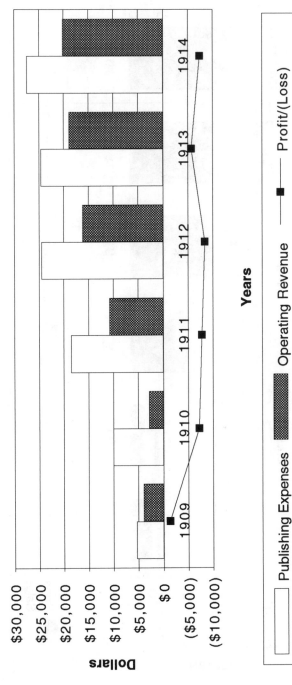

FIGURE 5.2

Woman's Journal revenue and expenses (1909–1914).

Agnes E. Ryan,

The Torchbearer and "A Woman's Journal Story."

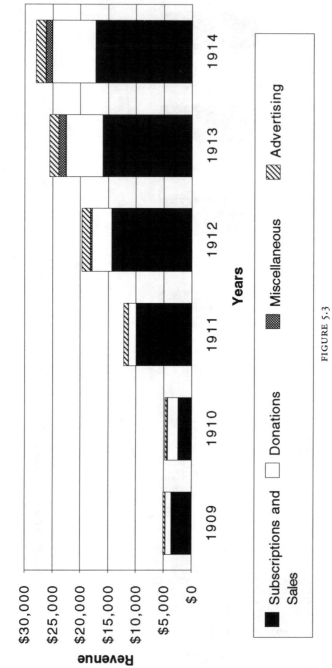

FIGURE 5.3
Woman's Journal revenue sources (1909–1914).
Ryan,
"A Woman's Journal Story."

Blackwell correctly argued that the NAWSA should have prepared for the paper's expenses in advance. Instead, it had no arrangements for handling immediate costs. Emboldened by several successful state campaigns and by growing interest in the suffrage question, the board had assumed that its guidance and national reputation, along with the increased circulation and advertising revenues supposedly fostered by the lower price, would eliminate the *Journal*'s liabilities.[42]

Other forces also exacerbated conflicts within the partnership. Indeed, tension may have been unavoidable. Since 1870, the Stone/Blackwell family had governed the newspaper with little interference. Despite protestations to the contrary, Blackwell proved unwilling to carry out one of the fundamental tenets of the partnership agreement. She simply would not relinquish editorial control to her fellow NAWSA board members. She firmly, albeit politely, voiced her objections to proposed changes in content and writing style, and resisted most of the board's advice on altering the paper's layout and graphic design. NAWSA leaders quickly began to resent their inability to dominate the *Journal*'s operation, and they used increasingly stringent measures to reduce Blackwell's influence. To begin with, they insisted upon moving the paper's production to New York's NAWSA headquarters. When Blackwell refused, the board tried isolating her from her staff so that she would either capitulate or collapse from exhaustion.[43]

Such hostility reflected both the power struggles within the partnership and the different visions of the *Journal*—as both a polemic and a business—each faction brought to the affiliation. Except for a greater willingness to address different aspects of the woman's movement, Blackwell's conceptualization of the paper mirrored that of her parents. Like them, she defined the *Journal*'s political mission as paramount. If sustaining the paper, and thus maintaining the heart of that mission, meant reducing its size and expense, that was an unfortunate necessity. The NAWSA board of directors never defined the paper so consistently or narrowly. They agreed the *Journal* should privilege the suffrage campaign, but they also longed to transform it into something more extravagant and impressive—something evocative of a big, commercial periodical. Board member Mary Ware Dennett foresaw it emerging as "the voice of the feminine movement."[44] Her colleague Mary Ritter Beard wanted to pattern the *Journal* after the *Saturday Evening Post* and staff it with the "best talent in the country."[45]

These ambitions reflected not only increased optimism about the movement's progress, but also a growing appreciation and acceptance of commercial packaging and style. Board members criticized the paper's writing. They said it lacked excitement; it gave little "live, fresh news," seldom included "any first class articles," and maintained a "timid" policy, even toward antisuffragists. "Most readers," remarked a board of directors clearly influenced by the lessons of sensationalist journalism, "would rather be shocked and displeased occasionally than bored all the time."[46] Most of all, however, the board attacked the paper's appearance. Large commercial publishers had begun altering the look of newspapers in the 1880s, when they started using banner headlines, different type sizes, and illustrations.[47] By the 1890s, magazines had adopted these and other new graphic design techniques.[48] In her study of early twentieth-century women's magazines, Sally Stein explains that such changes had a significant impact on the nature of periodical publishing and reading. Pictures and illustrations, revised typographical layouts, and reconceived approaches to story organization turned reading magazines into "a predominantly visual experience." The graphic reordering of periodicals transformed readers into "spectators, and by extension consumers" of images and a certain aesthetic style, and of mass-produced magazines and the goods advertised in their carefully arranged pages.[49] NAWSA board members sought to copy that graphic reordering, saying that the *Journal* " 'looks dull and unimportant,' that its 'news is not arranged with a sense of proportion—[that] one gets a muddled impression.' " They asked Blackwell to adopt a splashier, more modern-looking layout—with larger and clearer type, wider columns, better organization of stories, and cartoons on the front page of every issue.[50]

Significantly, the *Journal* was not the only reform-minded periodical affected by the alluring pull of commercial design standards. The left-wing paper *The Masses*—which grew out of the collaboration of a unique group of Greenwich Village intellectuals—displayed exactly the kind of dramatic visuality that NAWSA board members sought to incorporate into the *Journal.* As William Taylor notes, the proudly anti-capitalist and anticommercial *Masses* "drew heavily" on the design and layout principles of commercial magazines—including "colorful graphics, 'slick paper,' and handsome format."[51] NAWSA board members' emphasis on style thus reflected more than an astute appreciation of commodity packaging; it also represented a cultural shift in presumptions about what buyers desired and how they consumed information.

Of course, changes in the paper's design cost money. This too heightened tensions between Blackwell and the board. Blackwell could not understand why the board would lavish tight resources on matters of appearance. In 1911, for example, Blackwell tried to combat the *Journal's* mounting debt by switching to a less costly stock of paper, but one still used by what she called "dailies of a good class." The substitution promised to save the business $55 a week, or almost $3,000 a year. However, when NAWSA president Anna Howard Shaw objected to the appearance of the new paper, the whole plan had to be scrapped.[52] Yet while enthusiasm for commercial standards of design translated into generous spending, the board dragged its heels over other *Journal* expenses. Although the Association paid Ryan's salary, the board of directors never gave her money for publicity. It delayed disbursing newsy commissions, and—much to Blackwell's frustration—allowed unpaid bills to run for months on end.[53]

Ultimately, the differences between Blackwell and the board demonstrate distinct ideas about utilizing consumer culture on behalf of the suffrage movement. Far more familiar with the role of consumer than that of newspaper publisher, most board members associated commercial success with commercial style. From their perspective, graphically appealing publications attracted buyers. They believed that success meant following suit. But board members understood only part of commercial publishers' money-making strategy. Successful publications profited not only because they used layout and design to build up readership, but also because they used savvy business techniques centered around advertising, circulation, and promotion. While Blackwell may have lacked most board members' appreciation of how style motivated consumption, she did understand these important business realities. Blackwell knew that the production side of consumer culture mattered as much as the consumption side—that was why she hired Ryan. As Ryan recognized, the *Journal* needed money for promotion, advertising solicitations, and newsy commissions. Without these funds, the paper would languish due to lack of public exposure.

The small New York suffrage paper *The American Suffragette* had faced a similar problem. Worried that *The American Suffragette* simply "limped along" with subscription revenues barely covering publishing costs, editor Sofia Loebinger arranged for an advertising agency to take over the paper's publication. While she maintained editorial control, her "enterprising" new partners placed "the magazine on all newsstands in the city" and "past[ed] up large display cards everywhere."[54] Neither Blackwell nor Ryan proposed such a strategy for the *Journal*, but like the editor of *The American Suffragette* they sought business salvation through modern methods of publicity. Loebinger, Blackwell, and Ryan all concluded that cultivating consumption had as much to do with the final product as with the process of promotion and distribution.

Even had Blackwell and the board found a way to unite their different perspectives into a functional relationship, however, the *Journal* still would have lacked an important component aiding commercial success. Mass circulation magazines and newspapers succeeded, in part, because of extensive capitalization: secure financial backing, wealthy investors, and adequate resources for production, distribution, and promotion. The *Journal* had none of these things, and neither did the NAWSA. With inadequate funding limiting the *Journal*'s ability to compete with its perceived commercial rivals, the paper would never become the next *Saturday Evening Post* or "the voice of the feminine movement."

Convinced that NAWSA actions threatened the paper's fiscal and ideological reputation as well as her own authority, Blackwell dissolved the partnership in 1912. Sugarcoating tensions between the two sides, Ryan told buyers that the break-up "implies no lack of good will toward the NAWSA" and promised to "save the Association a substantial sum of money."[55] True feelings were hardly cordial, however. In a private letter to *Journal* benefactors, Blackwell denounced the board and accused certain members of plotting against her.[56] Relieved of responsibility for the *Journal*, the NAWSA returned to publishing a small, monthly newsletter. Nevertheless, the board did not relinquish hopes for a visually stimulating, grandiose organ. According to an aggrieved Blackwell, "the Headquarters officers still longed and planned for a big suffrage magazine in New York, and there was talk of securing this through an arrangement with the fashion magazine 'Dress.' "[57] As usual, however, the leadership's dreams proved bigger than the Association's pocketbook. Nothing came of the negotiations.

With Ryan retained as business manager, Blackwell resumed editorial authority over the *Journal*. But returning to the days of near self-sufficiency proved difficult. In part, the problem rested with the woman suffrage movement's growing popularity. With states across the nation embroiled in women's struggle for voting rights, suffragists depended on the newspaper for propaganda and advice. "When a call came for Journals or for information which the Journal workers could give . . . the call has been answered promptly," wrote Ryan. "We have not said . . . 'You must wait until we have raised the money to pay for what you ask.' . . . What else can we do when the need is so great?"[58]

As always, Blackwell and Ryan sought improved methods for meeting expenses. They once again pinned their hopes on increased advertising revenues. Ryan aggressively sought sponsors. She not only engaged commission-based, professional advertising agents, but also put subscribers to work. She penned articles urging readers to patronize *Journal* sponsors and acknowledge their support. She likewise encouraged suffragists to recommend *Journal* advertising space to local businesses. "Imagine what would happen if twenty suffragists in each city in the country were to call on the advertisers doing business there and urge them to advertise in the *Journal*," stressed Ryan. "They would simply put the *Journal* on the Advertiser's map."[59] Yet as a small operation, the newspaper faced the same difficulties that had always complicated the search for advertising revenue.

In some respects, matters had gotten worse. Ever-increasing competition made it more difficult for low-circulation, national publications to win over lucrative brand-name advertising accounts. Between 1900 and 1920, the number of monthly magazines in the United States increased by more than 1,000, and this did not even include weeklies and dailies. Periodicals with high sales figures set the standard. Time and again, publishing experts told Blackwell and Ryan that without a readership of 50,000 the *Journal* would have trouble attracting widely recognized, affluent advertisers.[60] In fact, in the two years after the dissolution of the NAWSA/Blackwell affiliation, advertising revenues remained a minuscule 6.4 percent of *Journal* receipts—a slightly lower percentage than in 1909 and during the ill-fated partnership of 1910–1912 (see fig. 5.3).[61]

Like Gilman, Ryan addressed this problem by trying to increase the number of weekly readers and subscribers. On "National Woman's Journal Day" in 1915, for example, she implemented "a plan to reach every suffragist in the country . . . and get her to subscribe." Drawing from promotional strategies used by colleagues to publicize upcoming suffrage events and garner newspaper attention, Ryan asked faithful readers to plan "a Round-up Meeting where everyone present is asked to subscribe; or a Tag Day, on which everyone who subscribes is tagged [probably with some sort of pin or ribbon]; or a Telephone Day, when every suffragist in town is called on the telephone to subscribe."[62] One year later, Ryan devised an even bolder policy. She proposed sending four carefully timed promotional letters to every known suffragist's residence. Recipients who failed to subscribe after this prodding would receive personal follow-up visits from local readers.[63] Tapping into the movement's growing emphasis on spectacle, Ryan also promoted the paper through elaborate publicity stunts. When a group of New York women began a "Suffrage Caravan" to Washington, D.C., she had one of her best newsies, Elisabeth Freeman, join the group and correspond with the paper via carrier pigeon. The pigeons, Ryan hoped, would "give the newspapers good copy and connect the *Journal* definitely with the expedition." Prewritten messages like the following placed the publication firmly at the center of attention: "We are off at 12 noon today. Huge crowd, delighted. Woman's Journal sold like hot cakes." And:

> We shall celebrate Lucy Stone's birth month in the most pic-
> turesque fashion this year. During the whole month of August we
> shall be celebrating in honor of the woman who brought the old-
> est suffrage paper in the world into existence. We are selling
> Journals at every stop and in between stops. What do you think
> Lucy Stone would say if she knew we are [sic] collecting our
> crowds by the music of a hurdy-gurdy, selling a Woman's Journal
> to every body and taking collections in a tambourine?[64]

Clarifying any doubts Freeman might have had about the gimmick's purpose, Ryan added one final piece of advice: "Manage the publicity end of it in your own way only do make a supreme effort to have the *Journal* get the publicity instead of having it simply go to suffrage. It will rather fall flat from our point of view if you don't."[65]

Although Stone's impression of this stunt must remain a mystery, she might easily have questioned Ryan's differentiation between publicizing the *Journal* and publicizing woman suffrage. To Stone, such distinctions would have seemed meaningless: the paper and enfranchisement went hand-in-hand. To privilege the *Journal* over the movement would have further confounded her, since the struggle for voting rights reigned supreme. Ryan's ease in abstracting the paper from the cause demonstrates how much conceptualizations of the publication had changed. By the 1910s, Ryan could view the *Journal* as a distinct entity: a commodity with its own function and commercial objectives.

This new conceptualization of the paper offered some rewards. By 1915, spectacular promotional strategies that capitalized on the movement's growing notoriety and popularity helped catapult circulation to over 27,000 (almost twice the readership as that achieved during the ill-fated partnership).[66] Moreover, if bolstering the cause had always stood as the paper's primary objective, co-opting commercial spectacle certainly did not hamper it. Through stunts and aggressive sales methods, Ryan and her workers mobilized support for enfranchisement, garnered publicity, and helped bring the suffrage message to a wider audience.

But the single-minded search for advertisers—via increased readers—occasionally undermined the paper's ideological grounding. In one case, the *Journal* printed an advertisement for *The Ladies Home Journal*—a die-hard opponent of woman suffrage.[67] When one reader asked why the paper accepted the notice of a known enemy, Ryan feebly contended that since the *Ladies Home Journal* was not "disreputable in the estimation of good people," the paper could not in good conscience reject its advertisement. Moreover, she continued,

> What we think of the "Ladies Home Journal" everyone who reads our paper knows and anyone who knows Miss Blackwell will understand that however much advertising the "Ladies Home Journal" gives us, we shall not change our tune in regard to the lies and misrepresentations it publishes.
>
> Now as for an advertisement in our column, it is so striking to have the chief anti-suffrage publication want to advertise in the chief suffrage publication in the country we knew it would amuse our readers and deceive no one.[68']

Although why the *Ladies Home Journal* would advertise in *The Woman's Journal* remains unclear, the negligible financial impact of such questionable endorsements is certain. The historic newspaper still met its deficits the old-fashioned way: by begging friends and benefactors. In 1915, the last year for which such data exists, almost one third of the paper's revenues came from contributions (see fig. 5.3).[69] One year later, in a 1916 book written for fundraising purposes, Ryan returned to the paper's money-making roots and urged "able women and friendly organizations in various towns and cities throughout the country to give a ball, banquet, bazaar, festival or other benefit or entertainment with the express purpose of sharing the proceeds" with the newspaper.[70] She likewise asked individuals to demonstrate support by purchasing stock in the Woman's Journal Corporation. Yet, since Ryan warned shareholders not to expect dividends, even this call for investment reads as a plea for donations.[71]

Plagued by a growing debt and obsessed with revenues, Blackwell made one last effort at improving the paper's circumstances. She finally modernized its layout and design. In December 1916, Ryan—by then managing editor—resigned from the *Journal.* An incomplete press release suggests that Ryan and her husband (an associate editor) left the paper under voluntary and amicable circumstances.[72] One month later, Blackwell hired a new business manager and publisher. George Brewster Gallup—"a thoroughly experienced newspaper man," an equal suffragist, and a devoted follower of civic affairs and city planning—quickly stamped his mark on the *Journal.*[73] Under his management, the paper's length expanded and its reading material almost doubled. It broadened its editorial focus by initiating a weekly column of NAWSA news and a department on city beautification and improvement.[74] The paper also sported a redesigned layout, widened columns, and more photographs and illustrations. Although still quite simple in design, the *Journal* had succumbed to the graphic standards of modern newspaper publishing. Like her old combatants on the NAWSA board of directors, Blackwell had accepted the fact that in the fight for consumers, looks mattered. Enticing buyers meant meeting their expectations of a newspaper's essence. And in the consumer society of the 1910s, that essence was largely defined by thickly paged, editorially diverse, easy to read, graphically stimulating commercial dailies. For reasons that remain unclear, however, Gallup's reign proved short-lived. Six months into his tenure, the *Journal*'s leadership changed permanently. Not only Gallup abdicated his position—so did Blackwell.

Ironically, after forty-seven years of family rule, Blackwell relinquished authority to an offshoot of her old detractors at NAWSA. Much to its own surprise, the Association had finally acquired what seemed like sufficient resources to launch the board of directors' long-desired "big suffrage magazine."[75] The money came from the wealthy and eccentric publishing magnate Mrs. Frank Leslie. Upon her death in 1914, she left the bulk of her almost $2 million estate to current NAWSA president Carrie Chapman Catt, requesting that Catt use the bequest on behalf of woman suffrage. Since Leslie had few ties to either the movement or Catt, her gift came as a shock to the suffrage community, as well as to the disgruntled associates and relatives of the deceased. After a long, bitter legal dispute over Leslie's will, Catt received a smaller settlement than originally anticipated, but one still totaling over $900,000. In honor of the donor, she immediately established the Leslie Woman Suffrage Commission, a bureau of "suffrage education"—or more accurately, publicity—inextricably tied to the NAWSA.[76]

Incorporated in March 1917, the Leslie Commission quickly set out to buy and consolidate the leading mainstream suffrage newspapers—including the *Journal.* Surprisingly, Blackwell quickly agreed to the commission's terms. Ryan's promotion to managing editor and Gallup's position as business manager and publisher indicate that Blackwell had loosened her grip on the paper's management and was ready to move on. In return for a $40,000 cash and stock buyout of Blackwell and one other investor and a guarantee allowing the long-reigning editor to write for the publication at an annual salary of $2,000, the daughter of Lucy Stone and Henry Blackwell relinquished all rights to the new venture.[77] On June 2, 1917, *The Woman's Journal* and two other suffrage publications (the New York Woman Suffrage Party's *The Woman Voter* and the NAWSA's newsletter *National Suffrage News*) combined to form the *Woman Citizen*, a weekly magazine of roughly twenty pages. Published in New York City, the new publication featured an illustrated front cover, an up-to-date appearance, and plenty of photographs and pictures. Like the commercial magazines it sought to copy, the *Citizen*'s visual orientation allowed consumers to concentrate on the act of looking, not just reading (figs. 5.4–5.6).

The new editor—novelist and magazine writer Rose Young—gloated over her predecessor's capitulation. "The Blackwells have gasped their last gasp and surrendered the Journal," noted one insider. "It is now the property of the Leslie Commission and Rose Young feels like a conqueror."[78] Young began her work by emphasizing the *Citizen*'s status as the NAWSA's new official organ. The magazine promised to print those "lively bits of information" that only the Association knew and that would allow readers to keep pace with the movement's acceleration. The *Citizen* also pledged to publicize local suffrage campaigns. Following the *Journal*'s long-running policy, one editorial asked NAWSA affiliates to send in press releases about their work. Those who refused, warned the article, would be "chagrined by an unfortunate comparison between the showing made by their own state and other states. And the fault will not be the *Woman Citizen*'s."[79]

But even as it began printing, the *Citizen*'s mission began to metamorphose. In 1917, Leslie Commission director Catt realized that the

Woman's Journal
And Suffrage News

VOL. 47. NO. 13   SATURDAY, MARCH 25, 1916   NEW ENGLAND EDITION

Chicago Women Insist That Spoils System Must Cease

Dramatic Meeting Packs Big Auditorium—3,000 New Voters Led by Noted Women, Draw Up Platform and Warn Mayor That City Hall Must Be Cleaned Up

In one of the most significant meetings ever held in the country, the women of Chicago on March 18 drew up a platform of municipal reform and threw down their gauge to the spoils system that has run rife at the City Hall. Three thousand women packed the huge Auditorium Theatre in what the Chicago Herald calls one of the "most dramatic political gatherings in the city's history."

"The women of Chicago yesterday sent their challenge to the City Hall," says the Herald. "It warned the mayor that spoils rule must cease. It gave him, in the form of a platform, a statement of the specific demands of the women of Chicago. It served notice that the 275,000 women voters of the city would call him to accounting for those demands. It was an impressive demonstration of the new force in Chicago politics."

The meeting was called after the split-salary exposures in the Welfare Bureau Department, but it did not by any means limit itself to them. The recognized leaders of the city in a series of telling five-minute speeches laid bare the administration's record and demanded that women's interests be considered.

The attempt to abolish the efficiency division of the Civil Service Commission, the condition revealed in the Department of Public Welfare, the introduction of politics into the Board of Education, the attempt to oust Major Funkhouser, the attack on the Municipal Voters' League—all were revealed in speeches by the heads of various civic organizations.

"We housekeepers want a machine that will collect our garbage in a clean, sanitary way, and we don't care at all about a machine to build up the mayor's political influence," was the final shot of Miss Mary McDowell, president of the Woman's City Club. "We don't want a machine that puts in as heads of departments men that know nothing about the work of the departments."

Miss Harriet Vittum charged that the removal of Mrs. Eva L. Slavetsky as head of the board of (Continued on page 98.)

NEW YORK BILL REPORTED 11 TO 1

Victory in Senate Committee Puts Amendment in Final Stage in Empire State

With only a single vote in the negative, the Whitney-Brereton suffrage amendment, providing for a referendum on woman suffrage in New York in 1917, was reported by the Senate Judiciary Committee on Tuesday evening. Eleven votes were cast in favor of reporting the measure, while Senator Brown cast the only vote in the negative. Senator Newton did not vote.

The amendment will now go on the general orders calendar, after which it will be made a special order for some day next week, when it will be debated and acted upon by the Senate.

"We are very well satisfied with the result," said Mrs. Norman de R. Whitehouse. "And we expect no further difficulty. The vote was the same as that by which the bill was reported from the Assembly committee, and we are confident that the measure will be passed with its relatively large majority that was accorded it in the Assembly. Our weeks of waiting outside the committee room at last have been rewarded."

There was no discussion of the amendment when it came before the committee. Senator Brown was not at the meeting, but he left word to be recorded in the negative.

Commenting editorially on the committee's action, the Tribune says:

"The vote they (the suffragists) failed last fall was large enough to deserve for the principle which called it forth liberal treatment at the hands of any body of lawmakers. It is certain that there has been no falling away from the suffrage standard. It is altogether likely that the votes-for-women forces are stronger numerically in ...

TAKES MEDICINE TO HELP CAUSE

All Attempts to Win Atlanta Girl Fail Until Experienced Woman Mentions Suffrage

Little Miss Gladys Corbitt, twelve years old, one of Atlanta's most enthusiastic suffragists, has proved her loyalty to the cause by taking some very bitter medicine. The little girl reads all the suffrage literature she can obtain, and is always on the watch for an opportunity to help.

She became ill recently and a physician prescribed a large dose of medicine, which she refused to take. An offer of $1 for taking the medicine was of no avail, until an older suffrage friend mentioned that the suffragists needed money with which to bring Senator Helen Ring Robinson to the city. Immediately the small suffragist changed her mind. She took the medicine, got the dollar and donated it to the fund which was used in bringing Senator Robinson to Atlanta for an address in behalf of municipal suf-

Tongues In Lamp Posts

SHAKESPEARE tells of "tongues in trees" and "sermons in stones," but it has remained for Mrs. R. B. Crowell, publicity chairman of the Alabama Equal Suffrage Association, to put a tongue in a lamp-post.

She writes: "I had this suffrage sign made and placed on one of the white way posts on one of the principal avenues in Tuscaloosa. It has suffrage sentiments on all four sides. The glass slides can be taken out and replaced by others at any time. The post carries its message day and night, and is ornamental."

MEXICAN PREDICTS VOTE IN YEAR

Carranza Officer, After Yucatan Congress of Women, Sees Great Awakening

In a report to President Carranza of the first congress of women in the Republic of Mexico, Sr. Alvarado, a representative of the de facto government in Yucatan, declares that within a year "the liberation of women will be seen." The congress, which was held in Merida, Yucatan, seems to have exceeded in size and importance the early newspaper accounts. The report, according to special correspondence in the Christian Science Monitor of March 15, indicates that 700 women delegates were present. The Monitor says:

WANT NO MORE WOMEN KILLED

Mass Meeting in Birmingham, First Ever Held by Women, Calls on Commission to Act

The death of a woman and her child after being struck by a jitney car has aroused the women of Birmingham, Ala., to the need of stricter traffic laws in that city. Mrs. W. C. Kilgore and her little daughter were run down by a car on Sunday evening two weeks ago after church.

A mass meeting, one of the first ever held by women in Birmingham to consider questions of moment, was called for the morning of March 14 at the City Hall. Resolutions were passed demanding that the City Commission take steps at once to put into strict regulation traffic laws on the ...

ALBERTA GRANTS EQUAL SUFFRAGE

Measure Passes Third Reading and Only Needs Lieutenant Governor's Assent to Be Law

Another victory has been won in Canada. The Alberta equal suffrage bill has passed its third reading and, according to the last news The Woman's Journal has, it now awaits only the assent of the Lieutenant-Governor. Since the suffrage bill was a government measure and the Lieutenant-Governor is a government man, there is practically no question but that the bill will get the necessary signature and become a statute.

Alberta will thus be the second province in Canada to give the women the vote since 1916 came in. Manitoba was the first. With the Lieutenant-Governor's signature for the second, both Alberta and Manitoba will have full provincial suffrage.

Alberta is bordered on the south by Montana, and is so near to the Dakotas that its influence will doubtless be felt there. According to the last census returns, the population of Alberta is 374,663. Its area is 255,285 square miles, which represents an area almost as large as Texas, and greater than California and Oregon combined. It is larger than the combined areas of Florida, Georgia, Alabama, Mississippi, South Carolina, Rhode Island and Connecticut.

CONVENTIONS TO SEE BIG PARADE

"Walkless Parade" Will Be Feature at St. Louis—40,000 Women In Chicago Line

More detailed plans for the demonstrations at the national Republican and Democratic conventions next June were announced last week by Mrs. Carrie Chapman Catt in New York.

A "walkless parade" will be the feature of the demonstration at the Democratic convention in St. Louis. Women from every State in the Union will stand on guard all day long on June 14, and, as the Democratic delegates come and go from the Jefferson Hotel to the Coliseum, they will find themselves at all times completely surrounded by women in white gowns, carrying picturesque yellow arm-bands, sashes, caps, and banners.

The National Association is calling for delegates not only from every State, but from every Congressional district in every State for the "walkless" parade.

In Chicago at the Republican convention the big parade, which (Continued on page 98.)

FIGURE 5.4

Front cover layout of *The Woman's Journal* soon before its 1916 redesign.
Reproduced by permission of Huntington Library, San Marino, California.

movement's impending success would eliminate the need for a suffrage newspaper. However, other commission members denied that female enfranchisement should mean the *Citizen*'s demise. From the start, Rose Young imagined the magazine extending beyond the struggle that gave

FIGURE 5.5

Front cover layout of *The Woman's Journal* during Gallup's tenure as editor and publisher.

Reproduced by permission of Huntington Library, San Marino, California.

it birth. As her ideas about its future became entangled with personal dreams for professional success, she saw herself transforming the *Citizen* into "a really great woman's newspaper." Remarked one colleague: "She is convinced that the world is ready for such an enterprise, and she is eager for the responsibility of putting this big new venture across."[80] After enfranchisement, Young continued championing the *Citizen*. She

FIGURE 5.6
Front cover layout of *The Woman Citizen.*
Reproduced by permission of Huntington Library, San Marino, California.

insisted that it could fulfill a vital purpose by providing the new woman voter with political information. Ready to exploit what many Americans assumed would be a period of political solidarity for women, Young argued that

> The demand for a magazine that can be a mouthpiece for modern women, a magazine that will attack controversial subjects, take sides for and against issues and people, unhampered by consideration for some particular propaganda, voice the woman view—the demand for that sort of magazine grows louder and louder. Whether the *WOMAN CITIZEN* is to be that magazine, or not, that magazine is to be.[81]

An unexpected illness forced Young to resign in 1920, but her argument proved persuasive. Convinced that the lack of magazines oriented to women as citizens—rather than as "wives, mothers, and housekeepers"[82]—threatened the very concept of "intelligent and informed" female voters, the Leslie Commission agreed to continue publishing the *Woman Citizen*: "the one magazine where women can express themselves politically, and in which they can discuss the questions of the day."[83]

Even with the Leslie Commission's substantial capital investment, however, the *Citizen* could not escape its financial dilemmas. Echoing the persistent confidence of past *Journal* enthusiasts, the commission initially predicted that it could make the magazine self-supporting. Yet as costs for the first three years of publication surpassed the entire expenditures of the suffrage campaign from 1848 to 1914, the Leslie Commission backed away from its optimistic projections.[84] Hoping to salvage the *Citizen*'s finances and preserve its postsuffrage mission, the group named member Gertrude Foster Brown general manager in 1920. A writer and musician whose marriage to a magazine art director gave her the closest thing to publishing experience of any of the commission's board members, Brown was asked to transform the *Citizen* into an economically viable periodical.[85] Despite having turned the paper's content over to a trained, commercial magazine editor, Brown quickly found herself in the same quagmire that plagued her predecessors. Brown's husband warned that the *Citizen* would never turn a profit until it received another large capital outlay. Unless it spent as much as well-financed women's magazines, it would not be able to compete with them. With the commission unwilling to make such an extensive monetary commitment, Brown could attempt only piecemeal efforts at improvement. To her credit, she decreased the deficit and increased circulation—but not nearly enough. During the 1920s, the magazine lost a minimum of $25,000 annually.[86] Per-issue circulation (the *Citizen* became a biweekly in 1923 and a monthly in 1925) still remained below 40,000—far less than the minimum 50,000 required to tap into key advertising accounts. In contrast, the average circulation of 365 magazines studied in one 1933 survey was over 86,000. And the monthly readership of leading periodicals had jumped to over two million.[87]

The persistent economic shortfall of the *Citizen* (renamed *The Woman's Journal* in 1928) made commission members ambivalent about continuing the magazine. In one four-year period alone, it voted five times on whether or not to suspend publication. Commitment to the periodical's new political mission kept the magazine afloat for a while. But as suffragists' long-fantasized women's voting bloc failed to materialize, and as tribalization and disagreement dispersed the always tenuous ranks of the suffrage movement, the idea of one "modern mouthpiece for women" creating a generation of "intelligent and informed" female voters seemed naive. Catt completely lost faith in the magazine: "We think there is a woman's point of view, but only a limited number of women think it necessary to get it in the Journal. . . . There appear to be hundreds of women's bulletins and magazines, each supplying a special or local constituency. Personally I am convinced that the aim of the paper has been attained."[88]

Considering the paper incapable of meeting the political needs of most women citizens, commission members could no longer excuse its financial drain on their organization. By 1929, the Leslie Commission's overriding commitment to educating women voters and offering them a forum for serious political discussion had collapsed. "The one and only aim in continuing the magazine," Catt concluded, "was to make it salable or disposable in some way that would return to the Leslie Commission some of the money it had expended."[89] A market-based definition of publishing success had once and for all triumphed over the *Journal's* historic reformist objectives. "The bare facts certainly are these," remarked a grim Catt. "If, for sixty years, a paper has been printed without sufficient receipts in any one year to pay its costs, it follows [that] that paper has never been wanted to the point of support."[90] The landmark publication could no longer forestall its demise. Out of respect to Brown, the commission (reorganized as the Leslie Continuing

Committee) agreed to let the general manager complete her last three-year plan.[91] Hard hit by the depression and still unable to surmount its financial problems, the *Journal* finally ceased printing in June 1931.

Years later, Brown reflected upon the magazine's suspension. "It was a keen disappointment to all of us," she wrote, "that we were not able to carry out our ideal of the successful publication of a serious woman's magazine, edited, published and controlled by women for women."[92] But although publishing success now meant commercial success, Brown kept the old regard for influencing public opinion. In the last weeks of publication hundreds of letters showing "the place which the magazine had filled, and the good it had done" poured into the *Journal*'s offices. "They came," noted Brown, "from libraries, teachers, women in responsible positions of all kinds, as well as from every part of private life, and they filled me with pride."[93] Lucy Stone and Henry Blackwell would have understood that pride. Like Brown, they realized that the *Journal*'s mission had always uneasily straddled economic imperatives and social good. Until the end, it offered an alternative voice for women readers to contemplate. Dispensing with the domestic homilies of commercial women's magazines, it offered political opinions and news and encouraged faith in the long fight for suffrage. As one suffragist wrote, "I would as soon think I could keep a house without a range as to be a suffrage worker without the *Woman's Journal*."[94]

Like other suffrage newspapers, the *Journal* also offered a small cadre of individuals an important opportunity for professional development and success. From Lucy Stone and Alice Stone Blackwell to Agnes Ryan and Rose Young, the *Journal* provided hard-to-find publishing experience for women, teaching them the essentials of newspaper writing, editing, sales, and business management. After the movement's end, experience working for the suffrage press still proved valuable. Recent work by Jennifer Scanlon documents the surprising number of suffrage newspaperwomen who went on to successful writing and advertising careers. One longtime copywriter for the J. Walter Thompson Advertising Company got her start as circulation manager for the NWP's newspaper, *The Suffragist*. Former *Citizen* editor Rose Young became a writer for the *Ladies Home Journal*.[95]

Even the humble task of selling papers on street corners could prove rewarding. Few newsies left detailed accounts of their work, but if Jessie Anthony's diary of her days peddling an English suffrage paper is representative of the experiences of newsies in general, and *Journal* newsies in particular, selling suffrage news could be an emboldening adventure. Anthony (the niece of Susan B. Anthony) begins her diary by describing her embarrassing—and thoroughly unsuccessful—first day hawking papers on the busy streets of London. Soon, however, she gained confidence in her work and delight in her new public visibility.[96] By the end of her tenure as a newsy, the young woman who had once stood "dumbly" on a street corner could talk freely with fellow vendors and potential converts, laugh gleefully at antisuffragists, and good-naturedly ignore impolite and pompous buffoons.

These successes, however, always existed in a complicated framework of financial loss and liability. The men and women who dedicated themselves to the *Journal's* operation found their work increasingly difficult in the rapidly changing publishing world of the late nineteenth and early twentieth centuries. During a time when most commercial publications survived by maintaining lucrative advertising accounts, the *Journal*—hampered by its small circulation and limited audience—barely scraped by. Nonetheless, the paper's proprietors and managers constantly sought to improve its performance and make it profitable, pinning their hopes on those things that seemed to make commercial periodicals popular. They struggled to raise circulation, and thus advertising revenues, and they adopted spectacular methods of promotion and publicity. Ultimately—after years of debate and a change in ownership—they copied the graphic design and layout strategies of mass magazines. Realizing that style attracted buyers, they made the act of looking an integral part of *Journal* consumption. Without adequate capital to compete with its commercial rivals, however, these changes never altered the paper's fortunes. Once the suffrage movement ended and the dream of a united bloc of women voters proved unattainable, the reformist zeal that kept the paper alive for sixty-one and a half years died. So too died the *Journal.*

Chapter 6

Ringing in a New Day

On August 26, 1920, the seventy-odd-year struggle to enfranchise American women came to a close when Secretary of State Bainbridge Colby signed a proclamation declaring federal adoption of the Nineteenth Amendment. Women citizens finally received the constitutional right to vote. To celebrate the end of their long fight, suffragists "from Cape Cod to Seattle" rang bells of triumph and blew horns of joy.[1] In one case, ratification leaders from East, West, North, and South gathered to peal "out the tiding of victory to the four winds of heaven." The sonorous chimes also paid tribute to consumer culture's intimate ties with the political movement that made votes for women possible. How did one bell deliver such dissonant messages? Easy. Suffragists borrowed it from Sears-Roebuck: the business that brought consumer fantasy and desire to every farm, village, township, and city, and that helped men, women, and children learn the gendered connotations of consumption. Suffragists had chosen a fitting symbol to ring in the new political era.[2]

The fight for suffrage had been difficult. By the time the amendment passed, a new generation of leaders had replaced pioneers like Susan B. Anthony and Lucy Stone. Ideology had expanded in a myriad of directions. While belief in women's natural right to vote still motivated suffragists, expedient arguments dealing with race, class, and reform had become powerful, and sometimes polarizing, weapons. Divisions between radicals and nonradicals, constitutionalists and states' rights advocates, and women of all classes and ethnicities threatened the movement's political cohesiveness and future attempts to mobilize the newly enfranchised. Nonetheless, suffragists convinced a nation of mostly male voters—Western states, in particular, had already enfranchised women by 1920—to share political power. Success stemmed from many sources, including cross-class political cooperation, persuasive expediency claims, sophisticated lobbying, expert political maneuvering, and effective fundraising and campaigning by both radicals and nonradicals.

Suffragists also appropriated and negotiated the boundaries of consumer culture. Whether this too contributed to their long-awaited victory is a difficult question. Women in the movement clearly used the methods and technologies of mass culture to promote their struggle, and they drew from various strands of consumer-capitalist ideology in order to represent themselves and justify votes for women. But the evidence gives fewer clues about how audiences responded to these strategies.

Moreover, few scholars have tried to account for the links between consumer culture and suffragists' political culture.[3] Those who have considered this issue have focused primarily on suffragists' uses of political spectacle—parades, pageants, and publicity stunts. And historians have disagreed about the effects of such tactics. In her study of women activists in Wisconsin, Genevieve McBride concludes that these methods proved "unsuited to the task of advancing public opinion."[4] Historian Michael McGerr, on the other hand, commends how suffragists embraced spectacle and views their bold and theatrical campaigns as a short-lived, alternative path for American women's political culture.[5]

Suffragists themselves were ambivalent. In 1910, Washington State women won the vote by cultivating a politics of respectability. In 1911, California women ignored this example and instigated the most sensational suffrage campaign to date. Not only did they win, but they urged colleagues to follow suit. New York women took their advice during the Empire State Campaign of 1915 and staged the most colorful suffrage effort ever seen. They failed. When the same women pushed a state suffrage referendum two years later they de-emphasized theatrics and stressed careful lobbying and grassroots political mobilization. They won. Finally, throughout their rancorous rivalry, radicals and nonradicals never agreed on the boundaries between acceptable and unacceptable public demonstrations and publicity stunts. Concern over image caused mainstream suffragists to reject campaign tactics that might not meet standards of femininity and patriotism.

Age, class, region, and competing reform cultures all contributed to suffragists' distinct outlooks. Timing also mattered. World War I, in particular, heightened conflicts over what schedule and type of stunts helped or hindered the movement. Eager to appear patriotic and afraid of seeming too radical, mainstream suffragists decreased their emphasis on spectacle and adopted a political style stressing insider and behind-the-scenes federal lobbying. The red scare that broke out after the war aggravated these tendencies and helped sound the death knell for the billboards, commodities, newsies, and other commercially inspired tactics that had advertised and promoted the progressive-era suffrage crusade.

Did the end of more artful campaigns mean the end of consumer culture's influence on nonradical suffragists and their movement? Not according to Harriet Taylor Upton. On the eve of federal enfranchisement, she declared that women voters wanted "lower prices," not fireworks and bands.[6] Upton understood what suffrage historians have not: Spectacle represented only one aspect of an American consumer culture that has always meant and offered different things to different people. Some nineteenth-century suffragists saw it as a path to liberation or refinement; others as a portal to degradation and enslavement. When envisioning a nation of enfranchised women, twentieth-century, nonradical suffragists predicted that consumerism would influence new voters in multiple ways. Suffragists claimed that consumer-oriented women voters would clean up government and industry, comparison shop between politicians and platforms, and exchange ballots for well-needed reforms. Like Upton, some suffragists believed enfranchised women would use their votes to protect the prerogatives of shoppers. But others subtly implied that women's consumerism confirmed the socially negligible effect of votes for women. Valentines and other examples of suffrage kitsch hinted at this by reaffirming gender hierarchies. Those suffragists most committed to political spectacle often defined voters as consumers who could be manipulated through color, theatricality, and careful stage management.

Despite these differences, supporters of the nonradical movement implicitly agreed that consumer culture—in all its guises—gave suffragists a vocabulary for explaining the world. It offered a widely accepted discourse for justifying goals and influencing opinion. Although other discursive traditions served the same function, consumer culture in particular allowed suffragists to creatively negotiate the cultural boundaries of politics, physical space, personal identity, and ideology. It gave them a new set of tools for identifying and representing themselves and their needs.

Recognizing consumer culture as a worldview embedded in mainstream suffragist political culture highlights the many ways ideologies become dominant. They insinuate themselves into all types of discourse, both verbal and material, seeming always and already existent. They become the very definition of common sense and everyday reality—just as consumerism became an implied and assumed component of twentieth-century suffragism. However, the real power of the culture and vocabulary of consumption ultimately stemmed from its ability to transcend the woman suffrage movement and become an accepted and unquestioned part of postsuffrage women's politics.

Citing women's low voter turnout and female activists' inability to politically mobilize women on a mass scale, most scholars stress the discontinuities between pre- and postsuffrage women's political culture.[7] Discontinuities certainly existed. The always tenuous unity of progressive-era suffragists dissolved after passage of the Nineteenth Amendment. The long-promised women's voting bloc never materialized. A voluntarist style of politics dominated by clubs that separated women by class, ethnicity, race, education, and religion became the most visible sign of mainstream women's continued political activism.[8] Former suffrage radicals—those most committed to advancing women's political rights—found their work hindered by growing social and political conservatism.[9]

But for many of the women who had once championed suffrage, the habits of consumption continued to provide an internal logic for the work of political activism and reform. Nowhere was this more apparent than in the League of Women Voters. The brainchild of Carrie Chapman Catt, the League grew directly out of the NAWSA. Like its predecessor, it unquestioningly utilized the tools of modern consumer society. Indeed, it used many of the same political tactics and strategies first perfected by commercially inspired suffragists. Like most suffrage groups, the League maintained a publicity department that promoted its functions and policies and that actively courted newspaper and magazine coverage.[10] And, like mainstream suffragists, the League joined forces with commercial businesses and leaders whenever possible. When attempting to raise $100,000 for its 1923 annual budget, the League called on retail leaders for support. Edward A. Filene, owner of Filene's department store in Boston, promised to provide the last $5,000 if League members could raise the rest.[11]

The League's commitment to consumer values proved most influential during the Get-Out-the-Vote canvasses of the 1920s. Concerned about the decade's low rate of voter turnout, the League and other civic and business groups encouraged voting through a series of publicity campaigns. According to historian Liette Gitlow, the League constructed voter education booths in department stores and small shops, and decorated store windows with festive designs centered around educational and promotional information. In addition, the League produced short films and slides that urged Americans of both sexes to vote.[12] None of these tactics was new, of course. Suffragists and other progressives had employed all of them more than a decade earlier.

The League also encouraged women voters to comparison shop before casting their votes for political candidates. In 1918, the New York League started sending office seekers questionnaires that addressed issues "especially important to women." Before primary elections, League members would post answers to the queries prominently in their office headquarters. After primaries, they would print and mail the final candidates' responses to registered women voters. By 1921, other local Leagues had also adopted this practice. With the mailing as a guide, women could weigh the pros and cons of political representation in systematic fashion. Indeed, women often "checked" the questionnaires and took them directly to the ballot box, just as they might take a shopping list to the market.[13]

Consumer culture more generally affected postsuffrage women's politics by providing an internal logic for political campaigns directed at all potential voters. As Michael McGerr argues, the commercialization of American elections began far before the 1920s, and indeed far before the revitalized suffrage movement took form.[14] But the 1920s saw a new maturation of this phenomenon. A growing body of literature confirms that the careful stage-management of political personality and the partisan use of increasingly sophisticated commercial marketing tools during this decade altered American political campaigns forever. Images, personas, sound bites, and money—always important variables—became more and more influential, especially as radio, film, and eventually television made politics an increasingly mass-marketed and technologically advanced process.[15] Lobbyists' and campaign managers' eager appropriations of these devices irrevocably integrated consumerism into the form and expression of partisan culture, just as suffragists' appropriations of contemporary technology and a consumer-capitalist ideology had integrated an earlier standard of consumerism into the struggle for voting rights.

Finally, for a number of suffragists, the incorporation of consumer values into politics provided a more personal connection between pre- and postsuffrage activity. For those most fully comfortable with the business of suffrage publicity, expertise in the arts of persuasion and salesmanship opened doors to professional careers otherwise closed to women. As noted earlier, work by Jennifer Scanlon confirms the startling number of suffragists who sought and found work in fields oriented toward women's consumption. Rose Young, chair of the Empire State Campaign Committee Publicity Department and one-time *Woman Citizen* editor, became a writer for that champion of consumerism *The Ladies Home Journal.* Numerous suffragists succeeded as copywriters for the famed J. Walter Thompson Advertising Company.[16]

In most cases, however, the personal connections between consumerism and the women who had worked for suffrage were more oblique. For those who had applauded commercial businesses' appropriations of suffrage slogans and representations of suffrage identity during the movement, the continuation of that practice after enfranchisement seemed unremarkable, even predictable. Consumer culture had already become a convenient tool for understanding women's identity. In a world shaped by buying and selling, voting simply extended women's consumerism into the realm of politics. Whether "voting" for Listerine, Campbell's Soup, or the Republican or Democratic parties, enfranchised women practiced their rights as consumers. And as consumers, they practiced their rights as women.

Notes

MANUSCRIPT COLLECTIONS

Anthony Family Papers. Huntington Library, San Marino, California.

Brown, Gertrude Foster. Papers. Women's Studies Manuscript Collection. Schlesinger Library, Radcliffe College. Series 1, Woman's Suffrage (microform, part B).

Laidlaw, Harriet Wright (Burton). Papers. Women's Studies Manuscript Collection. Schlesinger Library, Radcliffe College. Series 1, Woman's Suffrage (microform, part B).

McCulloch, Catherine Waugh. Papers. Women's Studies Manuscript Collection. Schlesinger Library, Radcliffe College. Series 1, Woman's Suffrage (microform, part B).

National American Woman Suffrage Association. Papers. Manuscript Division, Library of Congress, Washington, D.C. (microfilm edition).

National American Woman Suffrage Association. Papers. New York Public Library, New York.

Owens, Helen Brewster. Papers. Women's Studies Manuscript Collection. Schlesinger Library, Radcliffe College. Series 1, Woman's Suffrage (microform, part B).

Park, Alice. Papers. Huntington Library, San Marino, California.

Susan B. Anthony Ephemera Collection. Huntington Library, San Marino, California.

The Woman's Journal. Papers. Women's Studies Manuscript Collection. Schlesinger Library, Radcliffe College. Series 1, Woman's Suffrage (microform, part D).

INTRODUCTION

1. "Sufferin' Thru Suffrage," American Broadcasting Company, 1974.
2. I can think of no better discussion of the dialogical nature of history

than George Lipsitz's outstanding essays in *Time Passages: Collective Memory and American Popular Culture* (Minneapolis: University of Minnesota Press, 1990), especially the preface and chapters 1 and 2. Dominick LaCapra, however, is perhaps the most vocal advocate and theoretician of such a model. See, for example, *History and Criticism* (Ithaca: Cornell University Press, 1985), especially chapter 1. For a nice explication of LaCapra's work, see Lloyd S. Kramer, "Literature, Criticism, and Historical Imagination: The Literary Challenge of Hayden White and Dominick LaCapra" in Lynn Hunt, ed., *The New Cultural History* (Berkeley: University of California Press, 1989), 97–128.

3. Initially, the history of the movement was memorialized in a series of hagiographic works, including Harriot Stanton Blatch and Alma Lutz, *Challenging Years: The Memoirs of Harriot Stanton Blatch* (New York: G. Putnam's Sons, 1940), Carrie Chapman Catt and Nettie R. Shuler, *Woman Suffrage and Politics: The Inner Story of the Woman Suffrage Movement* (1929; reprint, Seattle: University of Washington Press, 1969), Ida Husted Harper, *Story of the National Amendment for Woman Suffrage* (New York: National Woman Suffrage Publishing Co., 1919), Ida Husted Harper, *The Life and Work of Susan B. Anthony* 1–3 (1898–1908; reprint eds., Indianapolis and Kansas City: Bowen-Merrill, 1983), Oreola Williams Haskell, *Banner Bearers: Tales of the Suffrage Campaigns* (Geneva, N.Y.: W. F. Humphrey, 1920), Inez Hanes Irwin, *Up Hill with Banners Flying* (Penobscot, Me.: Traversity, 1964), and Doris Stevens, *Jailed for Freedom* (New York: Boni and Liveright, 1920). During the 1950s, a more complex history of the movement emerged. Although works produced during this time recognized the intense schisms among suffragists, they saw woman suffrage as an inevitable part of human progress. The classic work in this tradition is Eleanor Flexner, *Century of Struggle: The Woman's Rights Movement in the United States*, rev. ed. (Cambridge, Mass.: Belknap Press, 1975), but Andrew Sinclair, *The Emancipation of the American Woman* (New York: Harper and Row, 1965) also follows this framework. During the 1960s, a less determinist and more critical historiographical trend arose. Aileen Kraditor's *Ideas of the Woman Suffrage Movement, 1890–1920* (New York: Columbia University Press, 1965) set the standard for questioning the different ideological, class, and racial motives of suffragists. Kraditor also affected the historiography by stressing the conservatism of the post-Civil War suffrage movement. Since the publication of her work, debate over the movement's conservatism and radicalism has become a major theme in the literature. Alan Grimes, *The Puritan Ethic and Woman Suffrage* (New York: Oxford University Press, 1967), Ellen Carol DuBois, *Feminism and Suffrage: The Emergence of an Independent Women's Movement in America, 1848–1869* (Ithaca: Cornell University Press, 1978), Steven M. Buechler, *The Transformation of the Woman*

Suffrage Movement: The Case of Illinois, 1850–1920 (New Brunswick, N.J.: Rutgers University Press, 1986), Nancy Cott, *The Grounding of Modern Feminism* (New Haven: Yale University Press, 1987); and Sara Hunter Graham, *Woman Suffrage and the New Democracy* (New Haven: Yale University Press, 1996) all deal with this subject.

4. The importance of the abolition movement to early suffragists is recalled in Flexner, *Century of Struggle*, chapter 4, and DuBois, *Feminism and Suffrage*, 31–52.

5. The Seneca Falls Declaration is reprinted in Elizabeth Cady Stanton, Susan B. Anthony, and Matilda Joslyn Gage, eds., *History of Woman Suffrage* I (1881; reprint, Salem, N.H.: Ayer Company, 1985), 70–71; the story of the Seneca Falls convention is detailed in Flexner, *Century of Struggle*, chapter 5.

6. The breakdown of the movement during Reconstruction is of primary importance to DuBois. Alice Stone Blackwell chronicles the growth of the American Woman Suffrage Association in *Lucy Stone: Pioneer Woman Suffragist* (Boston: Little, Brown, 1930).

7. For an excellent recent treatment of the NAWSA see Graham, *Woman Suffrage and the New Democracy*.

8. Anne F. Scott and Andrew M. Scott, eds., *One Half the People: The Fight for Woman Suffrage* (Philadelphia: J. B. Lippincott, 1975) and Mari Jo and Paul Buhle, eds., *The Concise History of Woman Suffrage* (Urbana: University of Illinois Press, 1978) both emphasize the reformist nature of the movement. See also Barbara Leslie Epstein, *The Politics of Domesticity: Women, Evangelism, and Temperance in Nineteenth-Century America* (Middletown, Conn.: Wesleyan University Press, 1981) and Ruth Bordin, *Woman and Temperance: The Quest for Power and Liberty, 1873–1900* (Philadelphia: Temple University Press, 1981).

9. Kraditor, *Ideas of the Woman Suffrage Movement* stresses the socially conservative overtones of the late-nineteenth and twentieth-century movement.

10. See, for example, Sandra Stanley Holton, " 'To Educate Women into Rebellion': Elizabeth Cady Stanton and the Creation of a Transatlantic Network of Radical Suffragists," *American Historical Review* 99 (October 1994): 1112–1136, and Ellen Carol DuBois, *Harriot Stanton Blatch and the Winning of Woman Suffrage* (New Haven: Yale University Press, 1997).

11. Ibid., 179.

12. Buechler, *Transformation of the Woman Suffrage Movement*, chapter five; Cott, *The Grounding of Modern Feminism*, chapter 3.

13. Graham calls the phrase "suffrage doldrums" a misnomer, and suggests the period from 1896 to 1910 might be better called a suffrage "renaissance"—characterized by active organizing and re-evaluation of suffrage tactics and political strategy. *Woman Suffrage and the New Democracy*, 33–52.

14. The rise of twentieth-century suffrage radicals is traced in: DuBois, *Harriot Stanton Blatch* and "Working Class Women, Class Relations, and Suffrage Militance: Harriot Stanton Blatch and the New York Woman Suffrage Movement, 1894–1909" in Ellen Carol DuBois and Vicki L. Ruiz, eds., *Unequal Sisters: A Multicultural Reader in U.S. Women's History* (New York: Routledge, 1990), 176–194; Christine A. Lunardini, *From Equal Suffrage to Equal Rights: Alice Paul and the National Woman's Party, 1910–1928* (New York: New York University Press, 1986); Linda G. Ford, *Iron-Jawed Angels: The Suffrage Militancy of the National Woman's Party, 1912–1920* (Lanham, N.Y.: University Press of America, 1991); and Holton, " 'To Educate Women into Rebellion.' " For Catt's impact on the NAWSA see Flexner, *Century of Struggle*, chapters 19 and 20, and Graham, *Woman Suffrage and the New Democracy*, chapters 5 and 6.

15. Ibid. represents an important recent exception. In addition, Cott and Buechler look at both nonradicals and radicals. Marjorie Spruill Wheeler, *New Women of the New South: The Leaders of the Woman Suffrage Movement in the Southern States* (New York: Oxford, 1993) looks at some of the most conservative members of the movement, especially in regard to race relations.

16. In her introduction, Graham calls this approach "insider" and "outsider" politics and calls the NAWSA's use of it a successful example of pressure politics.

17. Maud Park, "Report on Press Situation," 5 July 1917, NAWSA Papers, Library of Congress.

18. Buechler, *Transformation of the Woman Suffrage Movement*, 174.

19. William Leach, *Land of Desire: Merchants, Power, and the Rise of a New American Culture* (New York: Pantheon, 1993), 3.

20. Neil McKendrick, John Brewer, and J. H. Plumb, *The Birth of a Consumer Society: The Commercialization of Eighteenth-Century England* (London: Europa Publications Limited, 1982), chapters 1–4.

21. For the growth of modern consumer-capitalist culture see Leach, *Land of Desire*; Elaine Abelson, *When Ladies Go A-Thieving: Middle-Class Shoplifters in the Victorian Department Store* (New York: Oxford University Press, 1989); Lary May, *Screening Out the Past: The Birth of Mass Culture and the Motion Picture Industry* (Chicago: University of Chicago Press, 1980); Kathy Peiss, *Cheap Amusements: Working Women and Leisure in Turn-of-the-Century New York* (Philadelphia: Temple University Press, 1986); Roy Rosenzweig, *Eight Hours for What We Will: Workers and Leisure in an Industrial City, 1870–1920* (Cambridge: Cambridge University Press, 1983); Alan Trachtenberg, *The Incorporation of America: Culture and Society in the Gilded Age* (New York: Hill and Wang, 1982); Richard Wightman Fox and T. J. Jackson Lears, eds., *The Culture of Consumption: Critical Essays in American*

History, 1880–1980 (New York: Pantheon, 1983); T. J. Jackson Lears, *Fables of Abundance: A Cultural History of Advertising in America* (New York: Basic Books, 1994). For information on the managerial revolution critical to the growth of modern commercial institutions see Alfred D. Chandler, Jr., *The Visible Hand: The Managerial Revolution in American Business* (Cambridge, Mass.: Belknap Press, 1977).

22. T. J. Jackson Lears, "From Salvation to Self-Realization: Advertising and the Therapeutic Roots of the Consumer Culture, 1880–1930" in Fox and Lears, eds., *The Culture of Consumption*, 1–38; Warren Susman, *Culture as History: The Transformation of American Society in the Twentieth Century* (New York: Pantheon, 1984), especially chapter 14.

23. T. J. Jackson Lears, "The Concept of Cultural Hegemony: Problems and Possibilities," *American Historical Review* 90 (June 1985): 567–593. See also Stuart Hall, "Notes on Deconstructing 'The Popular'" in Raphael Samuel, ed., *People's History and Socialist Theory* (London: Routledge and Kegan Paul, 1981), 227–240, and George Lipsitz, "The Struggle for Hegemony," *Journal of American History* 75 (June 1988): 146–150.

24. Mary Ryan, *Cradle of the Middle Class: The Family in Oneida County, New York, 1790–1865* (Cambridge: Cambridge University Press, 1981), 200–201.

25. Works detailing the rise of the woman shopper include Leach, *Land of Desire*; Abelson, *When Ladies Go A-Thieving*; Rachel Bowlby, *Just Looking: Consumer Culture in Dreiser, Gissing and Zola* (New York: Methuen, 1985); William R. Leach, "Transformations in a Culture of Consumption: Women and Department Stores, 1890–1925," *Journal of American History* 71 (September 1984): 319–342; Susan Porter Benson, *Counter Cultures: Saleswomen, Managers and Customers in American Department Stores, 1890–1940* (Urbana: University of Illinois Press, 1986); and Victoria de Grazia and Ellen Furlough, eds., *The Sex of Things: Gender and Consumption in Historical Perspective* (Berkeley: University of California Press, 1996).

26. Abelson, *When Ladies Go A-Thieving*; Bowlby, *Just Looking*, especially chapter 2; Roland Marchand, *Advertising the American Dream: Making Way for Modernity, 1920–1940* (Berkeley: University of California Press, 1985).

27. Abelson, *When Ladies Go A-Thieving*, chapter 6.

1. Consumer Culture and Woman Suffrage Ideology

1. "Mrs. Harriet Upton Revered as Women's Rights Champion," unmarked newspaper clipping, Susan B. Anthony Ephemera Collection, Clippings 11, Huntington Library.

2. "Women Demand Lower Prices," *Woman Citizen*, 6 September 1919, 345.

3. Theda Skocpol, *Protecting Soldiers and Mothers: The Political Origins of Social Policy in the United States* (Cambridge, Mass.: Belknap Press, 1992), 521–522.

4. Jean Baker, *Affairs of Party: The Political Culture of Northern Democrats in the Mid-Nineteenth Century* (Ithaca: Cornell University Press, 1983).

5. For an excellent study of the early suffrage movement see DuBois, *Feminism and Suffrage.* Also see Eleanor Flexner's classic work, *Century of Struggle.*

6. Karen Halttunen, *Confidence Men and Painted Women: A Study of Middle-Class Culture in America, 1830–1870* (New Haven: Yale University Press, 1982); Richard L. Bushman, *The Refinement of America: Persons, Houses, Cities* (New York: Knopf, 1992).

7. Halttunen, *Confidence Men and Painted Women*; see chapter 5 in particular.

8. Thomas W. Higginson, "Featherses," [sic] *The Woman's Journal*, 12 February 1870, 44.

9. Stanton, Anthony, and Gage, eds., *History of Woman Suffrage* 3:99, and Susan B. Anthony and Ida Husted Harper, eds., *History of Woman Suffrage* 4 (1902; reprint, Salem, N.H.: Ayer, 1986), 56–57.

10. William Leach, *True Love and Perfect Union: The Feminist Reform of Sex and Society*, 2nd ed. (Middletown, Conn.: Wesleyan University Press, 1980), 255–256.

11. Ibid., 252.

12. Stanton, Anthony, and Gage, eds., *History of Woman Suffrage* 3:769.

13. "A Calico Dress Depot," *The Woman's Journal*, 15 January 1870, 10.

14. The literature on this subject is vast. For a beginning, see Ronald G. Walters, *American Reformers, 1815–1860* (New York: Hill and Wang, 1978).

15. For an interesting perspective on abolitionist and conservative charitable association fairs see Lori B. Ginzberg, *Women and the Work of Benevolence* (New Haven: Yale University Press, 1990), chapter 2.

16. Celia Burleigh, "Letter from New York," *The Woman's Journal*, 9 April 1870, 105.

17. Gerrit Smith, letter to the Dress Reform Association, 18 May 1857, NAWSA Papers, Library of Congress.

18. Olympia Brown, "Female Character" in Dana Greene, ed., *Suffrage and Religious Principles: Speeches and Writings of Olympia Brown* (1860; reprint, Metuchen, N.J.: Scarecrow Press, 1983), 43.

19. "A Working-Woman's Complaint," *The Woman's Journal*, 5 October 1871, 314.

20. Gerrit Smith, letter to the Dress Reform Association.

21. D. C. Bloomer, *Life and Writings of Amelia Bloomer* (Boston: Arena, 1895), 65–69.

22. "Dress Reform Convention Resolutions," *The Lilly*, 1 August 1858, 116.

23. Blackwell, *Lucy Stone*, 106–113.

24. Eleanor K. McDonnell, "Suffrage Then and Now, 1852–1917," *The Public Ledger*, 16 December 1917.

25. " 'Sojourner Truth' on the Fashions," *The Woman's Journal*, 12 November 1870, 356.

26. Bushman, *The Refinement of America*, 434–440.

27. See, for example, Paul E. Johnson, *A Shopkeeper's Millennium: Society and Revivals in Rochester, New York, 1815–1837* (New York: Hill and Wang, 1978); and Rosenzweig, *Eight Hours for What We Will.*

28. Bordin, *Woman and Temperance.*

29. Daniel Horowitz offers a detailed discussion of how some nineteenth-century reformers criticized drinking because it deprived families of money that could be spent on more uplifting pursuits. Daniel Horowitz, *The Morality of Spending: Attitudes Toward the Consumer Society in America, 1875–1940* (Baltimore: Johns Hopkins University Press, 1985; Chicago: Ivan R. Dee, Elephant Paperback, 1992).

30. Mrs. C.I.H. Nichols, quoted in *Proceedings of the Woman's Rights Convention Held at Worchester, Massachusetts* (New York: Fowler and Wells, 1852), 72.

31. Ryan, *Cradle of the Middle Class*, 200–201.

32. Leach, "Transformations in a Culture of Consumption," 319–342; Benson, *Counter Cultures.*

33. For more on Anthony and Stanton see DuBois, *Feminism and Suffrage*, chapter 3. For the conservatism and ethnocentrism of the later movement see Gwendolyn Mink, "The Lady and the Tramp: Gender, Race, and the Origins of the American Welfare State" in Linda Gordon, ed., *Women, the State, and Welfare* (Madison: University of Wisconsin Press, 1990), 92–122.

34. Dolores Hayden, *The Grand Domestic Revolution* (Cambridge: MIT Press, 1981), chapter 4.

35. "Farmer Brown's Wash-Day," *The Woman's Journal*, 2 July 1870, 202–203.

36. Leach, *True Love and Perfect Union*, 257.

37. Harper, *Life and Work of Susan B. Anthony* 2:844, 845.

38. Ibid., 932.

39. See, for example, Stanton, Anthony, and Gage, *History of Woman Suffrage* 1:109.

40. Carrie Chapman Catt, "Woman Suffrage and the Home," Leaflet (New York: Interurban Suffrage League, 1907), NAWSA Papers/LOC. For examples of how suffragists incorporated ideas about the rights of tax-

paying consumers into their movement, see "Political Equality [sic] Ass'n Makes Effective Reply to Opponents' Criticism," *Cambridge Times*, 24 May 1912, 1, 5; "Why Indiana Women Should Vote," Flyer (Indianapolis, Woman's Franchise League of Indiana, n.d.), NAWSA Papers/LOC.

41.   Frederick Jameson, "Reification and Utopia in Mass Culture," *Social Text* 1 (Winter 1979): 130–148.

42.   "Do You Use a Sewing Machine?" Leaflet (New York: New York Woman Suffrage Party, n.d.), NAWSA Papers/LOC.

43.   Mary Winsor, "A Suffrage Rummage Sale," (n.d.), 9.

44.   "A Fair Exchange," Flyer (The Suffrage Referendum League of Maine, n.d.), NAWSA Papers/LOC.

45.   Mary Garrett Hay, "Message to City Leaders," 15 October 1920, NAWSA Papers/LOC.

46.   Paula Baker describes this transition and its significance. See "The Domestication of Politics: Women and American Political Society, 1780–1920" in DuBois and Ruiz, eds., *Unequal Sisters*, 66–91.

47.   Miriam M. Cole, quoted in Stanton, Anthony, and Gage, eds., *History of Woman Suffrage* 3:501.

48.   Bordin, *Woman and Temperance*, 131. See also Epstein, *The Politics of Domesticity*, chapter 5. Not all suffragists approved of the close association between the movement and the WCTU. Some suffragists feared that by closing ranks with temperance reformers, the suffrage movement "rous[ed] the opposition of a very large and influential class" of brewers and distillers who not only sought to protect their economic interests, but also managed to control important state legislators. See Stanton, Anthony, and Gage, eds., *History of Woman Suffrage* 3:644.

49.   Frances E. Willard, pamphlet, "The Ballot for the Home: Reasons for Woman's Enfranchisement" (American Woman Suffrage Association: 1888), Susan B. Anthony Ephemera Collection, Clippings 8.

50.   Edward A. Stettner, *Shaping Modern Liberalism: Herbert Croly and Progressive Thought* (Lawrence: University of Kansas Press, 1993), 165; Robert B. Westbrook, *John Dewey and American Democracy* (Ithaca: Cornell University Press, 1991). See also James Kloppenberg, *Uncertain Victory: Social Democracy and Progressivism in European and American Thought, 1870–1920* (New York: Oxford University Press, 1986). For the tensions between women's politics and liberalism see Paula Baker, "The Domestication of Politics," and Joan Williams, "Domesticity as the Dangerous Supplement of Liberalism," *Journal of Women's History* 2 (Winter 1991): 69–88. Stettner and Westbrook are particularly good at discussing the significance of positive freedom to new liberal ideology.

51.   See, for example, "Plain Facts for the Working Man," flyer (New York: National Woman Suffrage Publishing Company, n.d.), NAWSA Papers/LOC; "What Illinois Women Have Accomplished with the

Vote," pamphlet, NAWSA Papers/LOC; Anthony and Harper, *History of Woman Suffrage* 4:536.

52. For other progressive-era articulations of this position see May, *Screening Out the Past*, especially chapters 2 and 3; Horowitz, *The Morality of Spending*, chapters 4 and 5.

53. For an excellent discussion of how these anxieties influenced middle-class families see Lisa Jacobson, "Raising Consumers: American Children and the Culture of Consumption, 1890–1940," Ph.D. dissertation, UCLA, 1997.

54. Elizabeth Ewen, *Immigrant Women in the Land of Dollars: Life and Culture on the Lower East Side, 1890–1925* (New York: Monthly Review Press, 1985); Peiss, *Cheap Amusements*; and Lewis Ehrenberg, *Steppin' Out: New York Nightlife and the Transformation of American Culture, 1890–1930* (Westport, Conn.: Greenwood, 1981).

55. Abelson, *When Ladies Go A-Thieving*, chapter 2.

56. "An Unexpected Effect," *Harper's Weekly*, 18 May 1920, 20.

57. "Campaign Literature," Susan B. Anthony Ephemera Collection, Clippings 18, 3.

58. Although not centered on women shoppers, Daniel Horowitz notes a similar, positive construction of progressive-era consumerism in *The Morality of Spending*, chapter 6.

59. Thomas W. Higginson, "Women as Economists," *The Woman's Journal*, 14 February 1880, 49.

60. Laura Shapiro, *Perfection Salad: Women and Cooking at the Turn of the Century* (New York: Farrar, Straus and Giroux, 1986), chapter 8.

61. Henry B. Blackwell, "Women Vs. Waste," *The Woman's Journal*, 26 September 1908, 154.

62. George Creel and Judge Ben B. Lindsey, "Measuring Up Equal Suffrage: An Authoritative Estimate of Results in Colorado," *The Delineator* (February 1911): 151.

63. Nathaniel C. Fowler, quoted in Alice Stone Blackwell, "Woman is Buyer," *The Woman's Journal*, 9 December 1916, 388.

64. Blackwell, "Women Vs. Waste."

65. In what must be one of the most oft-repeated quotes in U.S. women's history, suffragist Rheta Childe Dorr summed up the municipal housekeeping movement by agreeing that a "Woman's Place is Home. But Home is not contained within the four walls of an individual house. Home is the community. The city full of people is the family. . . . And badly do the Home and Family need their mother." Rheta Childe Dorr, *What Eight Million Women Want* (Boston: Small Maynard, 1910), 327.

66. Creel and Lindsey, "Measuring Up Equal Suffrage."

67. My summary of the founding of the NCL comes from Kathryn Kish Sklar, "Two Political Cultures in the Progressive Era: The National Consumers' League and the American Association for Labor Legis-

lation" in Linda K. Kerber, Alice Kessler-Harris, and Kathryn Kish Sklar, eds., *U.S. History as Women's History* (Chapel Hill: University of North Carolina Press, 1995), 43; and Joan Waugh, "Unsentimental Reformer: The Life of Josephine Shaw Lowell," Ph.D. dissertation, UCLA, 462–468.

68. John Graham Brooks, "The Morals of Shopping," *The Woman's Journal*, 22 December 1900, 401.

69. Kathryn Kish Sklar, *Florence Kelley and the Nation's Work: The Rise of Women's Political Culture* (New Haven: Yale University Press, 1994), 309.

70. Ibid., 50.

71. This event occurred in 1896. See Anthony and Harper, *History of Woman Suffrage* 4:753.

72. Mrs. Edward Costigan, "The Prices You Pay," *The Woman Citizen*, 5 June 1920, 10–11.

73. Charlotte Perkins Gilman, "Something to Vote For," *The Forerunner* 2 (June 1911): 151.

74. See, for example, Frederic C. Howe, "Why I Want Woman Suffrage," Leaflet (Warren: Ohio Woman Suffrage Association, n.d.), NAWSA Papers/LOC; "What Illinois Women Have Accomplished with the Vote," Leaflet, NAWSA Papers/LOC; "Political Equality [sic] Ass'n Makes Effective Reply to Opponents' Criticism," Caroline Bartlett Crane, "Business Versus the Home," Leaflet (New York: NAWSA, 1913), NAWSA Papers/LOC.

75. Susan W. Fitzgerald, "Statement of Mrs. Susan W. Fitzgerald, of Boston, Mass.," *Woman Suffrage: Hearing Before the Committee on the Judiciary (1910)*, NAWSA Papers/LOC.

76. Ibid.

77. Maud Nathan, "The Wage-Earner and the Ballot," *The Woman's Journal*, 5 March 1904, 78.

78. Laura A. Gregg, "Embalmed Milk for Babies," *Progress* 1 (October, 1900): 3, NAWSA Papers/LOC.

79. For more on early twentieth-century inflation see Horowitz, *The Morality of Spending*, 67, and Richard Hofstadter, *The Age of Reform* (New York: Vintage, 1955), 170–173.

80. Henry B. Blackwell, "Woman Suffrage an Economic Necessity," *The Woman's Journal*, 24 August 1907, 134.

81. Henry B. Blackwell, "The Conservatism of Women," *The Woman's Journal*, 17 August 1907, 130.

82. James Madison, *Federalist* number 10, Alexander Hamilton, James Madison, John Jay, *The Federalist Papers* (New York: New American Library, 1961), 77–84.

83. Alice Stone Blackwell, "Juggling with Our Food," *The Woman's Journal*, 9 December 1916, 396.

84. Blackwell, "The Conservatism of Women."

85. Mrs. Walter McNab Miller, quoted in Rose Young, " 'Conspicuous Thrift'—Slogan of Southern Suffragists," press release, 29 May 1917, NAWSA Papers, New York Public Library, Box 6, Folder: Leslie Woman Suffrage Committee Press Releases, 1917.

86. "Suffrage Aid in State Wide Food Saving," press release, n.d., NAWSA Papers/NYPL, Box 6, Press Releases Folder.

87. Partially complete, unnamed pamphlet, NAWSA Papers/NYPL, Box 6, Miscellaneous Papers Folder; "Suffragists Will Give Service for Nation's Welfare," *The Woman's Journal*, 24 March 1917, 67.

88. "Taking Your Town Off the Market," draft press release, n.d., NAWSA Papers/NYPL, Box 6, Press Releases Folder.

2. "So Much Color and Dash"

1. "Suffrage Window Draws Crowds," *The Woman's Journal*, 10 March 1917, 37.

2. Alice Park, *Autobiography of Alice Park I*, unpublished manuscript, 123. Park Collection, Box 8, Huntington Library.

3. *Annual Report: New York State Woman Suffrage Association*. 1915. 47th annual convention (New York: NYWSA, 1915), 25. NAWSA Papers, Library of Congress.

4. Craig Calhoun, "Introduction: Habermas and the Public Sphere" in Craig Calhoun, ed., *Habermas and the Public Sphere* (Cambridge: MIT Press, 1992), 7–9; Phillip J. Ethington, "Hypothesis from Habermas: Notes on Reconstructing American Political and Social History, 1890–1920," *Intellectual History Newsletter* 14 (1992), 21–40.

5. William Taylor, "The Evolution of Public Space in New York City: The Commercial Showcase of America" in Simon J. Bronner, ed., *Consuming Visions: Accumulation and Display of Goods in America, 1880–1920* (New York: Norton, 1989), 288.

6. Susan G. Davis, *Parades and Power: Street Theatre in Nineteenth-Century Philadelphia* (Berkeley: University of California Press, 1986), 6.

7. Ibid., 46–48.

8. Linda Kerber, "Separate Spheres, Female Worlds, Woman's Place: The Rhetoric of Women's History," *Journal of American History* 75 (June 1988): 9–39.

9. Davis, *Parades and Power*, 47.

10. Christine Stansell, *City of Women: Sex and Class in New York, 1789–1860* (New York: Knopf, 1986), 41.

11. Ginzberg, *Women and the Work of Benevolence*, 35.

12. Scholars have written extensively about how the religious fervor of the Second Great Awakening and the belief in women's moral superiority led to an explosion in moral reform efforts by women. See ibid.;

Stansell, *City of Women*; Ryan, *Cradle of the Middle Class*; and Epstein, *The Politics of Domesticity*.

13.   Ginzberg, *Women and the Work of Benevolence*, 40.

14.   Flexner, *Century of Struggle*, 168.

15.   Ibid., 174.

16.   Without doubt, incorporating women into men's political rituals was not Anthony's primary objective. Her attempt at voting, for example, was intended to test a theory about constitutional rights. But her actions also demonstrated an unwillingness to be denied the visible, public rewards of citizenship.

17.   The trial is described in Flexner, *Century of Struggle*, 168–171.

18.   Margaret W. Campbell, "Margaret M. Campbell," *The Woman's Journal*, 11 August 1894, 249–250. Suffragists were not the only women reformers to face such hardships. In the temperance "Crusades" of 1873–1875, in Dayton, Ohio male onlookers pelted women marchers with sausages and beer, while in Cleveland 500 women marchers were attacked by a mob that kicked and threw brickbats. Bordin, *Woman and Temperance*, 25.

19.   Ann Preston, quoted in Stanton, Anthony, and Gage, eds., *History of Woman Suffrage* 1:363.

20.   Lydia Maria Child, quoted in ibid., 3:519.

21.   Cora Scott Pond, "Cape Cod Work," *The Woman's Journal*, 20 September 1884, 301. Pond's companion, Anna Shaw, later became one of the foremost leaders of the American woman suffrage movement and president of the National American Woman Suffrage Association.

22.   Abby W. May, "For the Festival," *The Woman's Journal*, 25 May 1878, 164.

23.   Eliza H. Hunter, "American Annual Meeting: Twentieth Annual Meeting American Woman Suffrage Association," *The Woman's Journal*, 12 January 1889, 10.

24.   Quoted in Harper, *Life and Work of Susan B. Anthony* 2:605.

25.   Flexner, *Century of Struggle*, 259. The spectacular nature of the English movement is recounted in Lisa Tickner, *The Spectacle of Women: Imagery of the Suffrage Campaign, 1907–1914* (Chicago: University of Chicago Press, 1988).

26.   Blatch and Lutz, *Challenging Years*, 129. Blatch's parade took place in 1910. Suffrage processions actually occurred in the United States as early as 1908. The first parade was held in New York, but suffragists were forbidden from marching in formation because of an antiquated regulation against Sunday parades. On the whole, it was a rather hurried and disorganized affair; see Alice Stone Blackwell, "The Suffrage Parade," *The Woman's Journal*, 22 February 1908, 30. Later that year, "an army" of San Francisco suffragists marched from Golden Gate Park to The Chutes, a nearby amusement park; see "California," *The Woman's Journal*, 3

October 1908, 159. The first English woman suffrage parade occurred in 1907.

27. Lydia Kingmill Commander, letter to Alice Park, 13 February 1909, Park Collection, Box 1.

28. Blatch and Lutz, *Challenging Years*, 129–130. The NAWSA was not the only suffrage organization to criticize Blatch's plan. The "shocked" head of New York's Equal Franchise Society refused to participate in the parade.

29. "Editorial Notes," *The Woman's Journal*, 7 March 1908, 37.

30. "Police Routed By Suffragists Pledge Reform," 10 May 1912, newspaper clipping, Susan B. Anthony Ephemera Collection, Clippings 15, Huntington Library.

31. "Disorder Mars Suffrage Show," 4 March 1913, *Public Ledger*, 3; Percy MacKaye, "Art and the Woman's Movement: A Comment on the National Suffrage Pageant," *Forum* 49 (1913): 680–684.

32. "300 Injured in Wild Scenes at 'Votes' Parade," unnamed newspaper clipping, 5 March 1913, NAWSA Papers; "Probing Insults to Suffragists," 1913, newspaper clipping, Susan B. Anthony Ephemera Collection, Clippings 15, 54.

33. "The Suffragette Parade," *The Argonaut*, 29 March 1913, n.p., newspaper clipping, Susan B. Anthony Ephemera Collection, Clippings 15, 58. For more on the Washington, D.C. parade riot, see *Suffrage Parade Hearings: Hearings Before a Subcommittee of the Committee on the District of Columbia, United States Senate* I (Washington, D.C.: Government Printing Office, 1913).

34. This summary of the California campaign is derived from Sherry Jeanne Katz, "A Politics of Coalition: Socialist Women and the California Suffrage Movement, 1900–1911" in Marjorie Spruill Wheeler, ed., *One Woman One Vote* (Troutdale, Ore.: NewSage, 1995), 255; and Flexner, *Century of Struggle*, 263. For a more detailed look at the California movement see Sherry Jeanne Katz, "Dual Commitments: Feminism, Socialism, and Women's Political Activism in California, 1890–1920," Ph.D. dissertation, UCLA, 1991.

35. Mary Ware Dennett, letter to the California Campaign Committee, 20 September 1913, Park Collection, Box 3.

36. Alice Park, letter to Lavina Dock, 7 January 1913, Park Collection, Box 5; Alice B. Curtis, letter to Alice Park, 24 May 1916, Park Collection, Box 5; Alice Park, letter to Editor of the *American Suffragette* (n.d.), Park Collection, Box 2.

37. Michael Schudson, "Was There Ever a Public Sphere? If So, When? Reflections on the American Case." *Habermas and the Public Sphere*, 143–163.

38. Taylor, "The Evolution of Public Space in New York City," 291.

39. Ibid., 291–292.

40.   Stuart Ewen, *PR! A Social History of Spin* (New York: Basic Books, 1996).

41.   *Annual Report*, 52. The Empire State Campaign Committee was an umbrella organization containing almost all New York State suffrage groups. For more information on the Campaign and the Campaign Committee see DuBois, *Harriot Stanton Blatch*, 161.

42.   *Annual Report*, 53.

43.   Sara Hunter Graham, *Woman Suffrage and the New Democracy* (New Haven: Yale University Press, 1996), 73.

44.   *Annual Report*, 59–61.

45.   Carrie Chapman Catt, Draft, "Report Campaign and Survey Committee: A National Survey" (1916?), 8–9, NAWSA Papers/LOC.

46.   Taylor, "The Evolution of Public Space in New York City," 290–292, Ewen, *PR!*, 136–142.

47.   Social psychologist Gustave Le Bon's 1896 book *The Crowd: A Study of the Popular Mind* was one of the first social scientific works to legitimate these new concepts of the public. Ewen, *PR!*, 141, 142.

48.   Ibid., 134–138.

49.   Blatch and Lutz, *Challenging Years*, 129.

50.   Glenna Smith Tinnin, "Why the Pageant?," *The Woman's Journal*, 15 February 1913, 50.

51.   Michael R. Booth, *Victorian Spectacular Theatre, 1850–1910* (Boston: Routledge and Kegan Paul, 1981), 4.

52.   Anne Friedberg, *Window Shopping: Cinema and the Postmodern* (Berkeley: University of California Press, 1993), 3.

53.   Abelson, *When Ladies Go A-Thieving*, chapters 1 and 2; Leach, "Transformations in a Culture of Consumption," 322.

54.   For two notable critics of women's ability to possess a controlling gaze see Laura Mulvey, "Visual Pleasure and Narrative Cinema" in Brian Wallis, ed., *Art After Modernism* (Boston: New Museum of Contemporary Art), 361–373; and Janet Wolff, "The Invisible Flâneuse: Women and the Literature of Modernity," *Theory, Culture and Society* 2 (7) (1985).

55.   Friedberg, *Cinema and the Postmodern*, 29–37.

56.   Michael McGerr, *The Decline of Popular Politics: The American North, 1865–1928* (New York: Oxford University Press, 1986), 160.

57.   Anne Huber Tripp, *The IWW and the Paterson Silk Strike of 1913* (Urbana: University of Illinois Press, 1987), 145.

58.   Alice Park, unpublished remembrance, Park Collection.

59.   "A Peek at Organized Publicity," *Headquarters News Letter* 1 (April 15, 1915): 3, NAWSA Papers/LOC.

60.   *Annual Report*, 25, 60–68.

61.   Unidentified newspaper clipping, 1913?, Susan B. Anthony Ephemera Collection, Clippings 15, 57.

62.   Elisabeth Freeman, letter to Agnes Ryan, June 1913, NAWSA Papers/LOC.

63. Sara Algeo, unpublished speech, 1913?, 1–2, NAWSA Papers/LOC.

64. Ibid.

65. "Women in Grand Parade in New York," *San Francisco Examiner*, 9 November 1912, 86.

66. Eunice Dana Brannan, "Parade Stir Due to Advance of Suffrage," *New York Tribune*, 4 May 1912, 1.

67. F. F. Purdy, "Notes From New York," *Merchants Record and Show Window* 31 (December 1912): 40.

68. Ibid. For more on the art of early twentieth-century window dressing see Stuart Culver, "What Manikins Want," *Representations* 21 (Winter 1988): 97–116.

69. For more on suffrage stores see chapter 4. The Luna Park game was part of the elaborate Empire State Campaign. Called "The Hopperie," the game introduced players to the suffrage question by making them "hop on one leg up an incline over a map of non-suffrage states on to the suffrage states painted yellow, with the four . . . states [voting on suffrage amendments in 1915] featured at the top and painted blue." Despite high expectations, however, the Hopperie lost money. Vera Boraman, head of the state's press and publicity council, explained that it "was too much work, with no element of danger or excitement. As a suffrage sign and advertisement," however, she proclaimed it "a great success." Thirteen city newspapers featured it in twenty-nine stories. Rose Young, "Press Work," *Annual Report*, 60; Vera Boraman, "Report of the Press and Publicity Council," *Annual Report*, 66.

70. "Directions for Votes for Women Torchlight Procession, New Haven, Conn.," 1916, NAWSA Papers/LOC.

71. Grace A. Johnson, letter to Middlesex Suffragists, 1915, NAWSA Papers/LOC. Not all parade organizers demanded such rigid dress standards. Some suffragists went to great lengths to assure marchers that their participation, not their attire, counted. See, for example, the "Program and Information Flyer" for the 1916 NAWSA parade in St. Louis. After encouraging participants from non-woman-enfranchised states to wear a "white dress, yellow parasol, yellow sash, [and] small white hat if possible," and those from woman-enfranchised states to a "wear red, white and blue sash," the flyer made a special point of saying that all women were "invited to stand for suffrage whether she wears the regalia or not. It is women we want to show—not parasols." "Program and Information Flyer," 1916, NAWSA Papers/LOC.

72. "All Suffragists Ask is Fair Weather," *New York Tribune*, 4 May 1912, 4.

73. Nan Enstad, "Pretty Clothes and Picket Lines: Fashion and Female Heroism in the Uprising of the Twenty Thousand," paper in possession of the author.

74. "Incidents along the Way," *New York Tribune*, 5 May 1912, 3.

75. Maud Wood Park, "Campaigning State by State" in National American

Woman Suffrage Association, ed., *Victory: How Women Won It* (New York: H. W. Wilson, 1940), 78.

76.   Mary W. Dewson, "At Last Women Win the Vote," n.d., n.p., NAWSA Papers/LOC.

77.   McGerr, *The Decline of Popular Politics*, 146.

3. ON STAGE

1.   Tinnin, "Why the Pageant?," 50. Tinnin's obituary notes that she also helped organize the National Junior Theatre. See "Mrs. Glenna S. Tinnin," *New York Times*, 25 March 1945, 37.

2.   "Official Program, Woman Suffrage Procession" (National American Woman Suffrage Association, 1913), n.p. Participants included Florence Flemming (known as "the Greek dancer with the perfect arm"), Mary Shaw (the well-known Shakespearean actress), Fola La Follette (actress and daughter of Wisconsin senator Robert La Follette), and Lillian Nordica ("the prima dona"). See "Suffrage Tableau Will be Given on the Cold Steps of U.S. Treasury," 1913, unidentified newspaper clipping, Susan B. Anthony Ephemera Collection, Clippings 15, 43, Huntington Library; "Suffrage Pilgrims Will Pose in Classical Postures on the Steps of United States Treasury Building at Washington," 1 March 1913, unidentified newspaper clipping, Susan B. Anthony Ephemera Collection, Clippings 15, 41.

3.   MacKaye, "Art and the Woman's Movement," 683; Edwin Osgood Grover, ed., *Annals of an Era: Percy MacKaye and the MacKaye Family, 1862–1932* (Washington, D.C.: Pioneer Press, 1932), 41. For a record of works (including the 1913 suffrage pageant) by Hazel MacKaye, see pages 337–338.

4.   Kay Sloan, *The Loud Silents: Origins of the Social Problem Film* (Urbana: University of Illinois Press, 1988), 99–123. Other films, some for, but most against, woman suffrage, were produced independently by commercial filmmakers. Although a few looked at the movement seriously, most were comedies.

5.   Karen Blair, *The Torchbearers: Women and Their Amateur Arts Associations in America, 1890–1930* (Bloomington: Indiana University Press, 1994), 119; Martin S. Tackel, "Women and American Pageantry, 1908–1918," (Ph.D. dissertation, City University of New York, 1982).

6.   Mike Featherstone, "The Body in Consumer Culture," *Theory, Culture & Society* 1 (September 1982): 28. Warren Susman's pathbreaking essay " 'Personality' and the Making of Twentieth-Century Culture" in *Culture as History*, 271–285, helps illuminate this subject. Lears, "From Salvation to Self-Realization," 3–38, is also useful.

7.   May, *Screening Out the Past*, especially chapter 5; see also Kathy Peiss,

"Making Faces: The Cosmetics Industry and the Cultural Construction of Gender, 1890–1930," *Genders* 7 (Spring 1990): 142–169.

8.   Featherstone, "The Body in Consumer Culture," 27–30.

9.   Richard Sennett, *The Fall of Public Man* (New York: Knopf, 1977).

10.   Susman, *Culture as History;* Lears, "From Salvation to Self-Realization"; Featherstone, "The Body in Consumer Culture." The nineteenth-century idea of the body as a social map is explored in Sennett, *The Fall of Public Man*, chapter 8.

11.   Karen Halttunen, "From Parlor to Living Room: Domestic Space, Interior Decoration, and the Culture of Personality" in Simon J. Bronner, ed., *Consuming Visions*, 157–189.

12.   Nineteenth-century political parties also mixed entertainment and politics, but in different ways than suffragists. Both major parties sponsored parades, and, as Jean Baker has demonstrated, the antebellum Democratic party hosted minstrel shows. Baker, *Affairs of Party*, chapter 6.

13.   Mrs. J. W. Smith et al., "Dramatic Entertainment," *The Woman's Journal*, 8 November 1884, 360; Alice Stone Blackwell, "A Woman's Rights Play," *The Woman's Journal*, 23 May 1885, 161; Lucy Stone, "Let it Be Illustrated," *The Woman's Journal*, 16 January 1886, 20; Ella Cheever Thayer, "Lords of Creation: Woman Suffrage Drama" in Bettina Friedl, ed., *On to Victory: Propaganda Plays of the Woman Suffrage Movement* (Boston: Northeastern University Press, 1987), 83–115.

14.   "The Historical Pageant," *The Woman's Journal*, 18 May 1889, 156.

15.   "New England Annual Meeting," *The Woman's Journal*, 8 June 1889, 177; Lucy Stone, "Additional Pageants," *The Woman's Journal*, 15 June 1889, 188; Charlotte H. Allen, "Four Famous Pictures Seen in the History of Marriage," *The Woman's Journal*, 27 September 1890, 305.

16.   "The Historical Pageant."

17.   David Glassberg, *American Historical Pageantry: The Uses of Tradition in the Early Twentieth Century* (Chapel Hill: University of North Carolina Press, 1990).

18.   Tripp, *The IWW and the Paterson Silk Strike of 1913*, 145.

19.   Glassberg, *American Historical Pageantry*, 132.

20.   "New Work at Headquarters," *The Woman's Journal*, 2 December 1911, 380. For two existing catalogs see "Suffrage Plays" (New York: National American Woman Suffrage Association, n.d.), Helen Brewster Owens Papers, Schlesinger Library; "Suffrage Plays" (New York: National American Woman Suffrage Association, n.d.), Owens Papers. A number of suffrage plays are reprinted in Friedl, *On to Victory*.

21.   Gilman, "Something to Vote For," 143–153; Oreola Williams Haskell, "Put to the Test," *The Woman's Journal*, 6 January 1906, 1–2; 13 January 1906, 5–7; and 20 January 1906, 10–11.

22.   A synopsis of the play is given in "Program for the Afternoon," *The Suffragist*, 21 February 1914, 7.

23. "St. Louis–'The Big Third Act,' " *Headquarters Newsletter* (June 22, 1916): 10–12. For another example see the description of The Turn in "Suffragists Do Turn," *The Woman's Journal,* 7 September 1912, 281.

24. Joy Kasson, *Marble Queens and Captives: Women in Nineteenth-Century American Sculpture* (New Haven: Yale University Press, 1990), 78–79.

25. Alice Stone Blackwell, "A Campaign of Slander," *Flyer* (Boston: 1914?), NAWSA Papers, Library of Congress.

26. Sloan, *The Loud Silents,* 105.

27. Stanton, Anthony, and Gage, eds., *History of Woman Suffrage* 1:15.

28. Sloan also addresses this issue, as does Alice Sheppard, *Cartooning for Suffrage* (Albuquerque: University of New Mexico Press, 1994). Excellent work by Lisa Tickner demonstrates that English suffragists fought a similar battle over representation (*The Spectacle of Women*). However, none of these scholars recognize this battle's larger context within the consumer society.

29. "Has Initial Showing: Selig's Suffrage Film," *Motography* 12 (October 31, 1914): 589–590.

30. These themes were not confined to plays and pageants in the United States. Tickner finds similar archetypes in her study of English suffragists, *The Spectacle of Women*. And, as Sheppard (*Cartooning for Suffrage*) demonstrates, these themes also found expression in other forms of representation, including prosuffrage cartoons.

31. Selina Solomons, *The Girl from Colorado or The Conversion of Aunty Suffridge* (San Francisco: Votes-for-Women Publishing Company, 1911), NAWSA Papers/LOC.

32. "80 Million Want—? A Political Drama in 4 Reels," Pamphlet, NAWSA Papers/LOC.

33. Blatch and Lutz, *Challenging Years,* 138; May, *Screening Out the Past,* 119 notes Pickford's support for suffrage.

34. "State Correspondence: Massachusetts," *The Woman's Journal,* 16 April 1910, 62–63; see also Alice Stone Blackwell, "A Glimpse of Miss La Follette," *The Woman's Journal,* 9 April 1910, 58. Fola La Follette's stage career is described in Bernard A. Weisberger, *The La Follettes of Wisconsin: Love and Politics in Progressive America* (Madison: University of Wisconsin Press, 1994), chapter 4.

35. Gertrude Foster Brown, "Suffrage and Music—My First Eighty Years," unpublished manuscript, n.d., 147, Gertrude Foster Brown Papers, Schlesinger Library.

36. The one exception was Alice Paul, who, according to Ellen DuBois, felt "less comfortable with these working-class cultural forms." DuBois, *Harriot Stanton Blatch,* 316.

37. "80 Million Want—?"; Gertrude Foster Brown, letter to the President of the Suffrage Clubs and the Chairmen of the Campaign Committees,

2 October 1915, Brown Papers; "Votes for Women," *The Moving Picture World* 12 (June 1, 1912): 811.

38. Advertisement, "What Eighty Million Women Want," *The Moving Picture World* 18 (November 8, 1913): 627.

39. H. B. Laidlaw, *Organizing to Win by the Political District Plan* (New York: National Woman Suffrage Publishing Co., 1914), 9–10, NAWSA Papers/LOC. In some cases, the performing self could even be abstracted from the physical self and reduced to fit canned personality stories showing suffragists at their very best. The NAWSA had a publicity division devoted to "Personality, Interviews, [and] Biographies." Its sole purpose was to produce columns about leading suffragists that—like plastic—could be "shaped to the space and requirements" of the average county paper or the Sunday editions of larger papers. See Rose Young, "Leslie Woman Suffrage Commission Services: Suffrage Publicity by System," 29 March 1917?, NAWSA Papers/LOC. An advertisement for one such story on NAWSA president Carrie Chapman Catt stirringly promised to tell how a simple "farmer's daughter" became "one of the most prominent and powerful women in the world." Rose Young, letter to newspapers, 5 February 1917, NAWSA Papers/LOC.

40. See for instance Blatch and Lutz, *Challenging Years*, 182. For a later example see "The Woman's Parade," *The Woman Citizen*, 29 September 1917, 337.

41. Inez Haynes Gillmore, "The Women's March," *The Woman's Journal*, 4 May 1912, 141.

42. Davis, *Parades and Power*, 142–143.

43. Blatch and Lutz, *Challenging Years*, 132, 180.

44. Harriot Stanton Blatch, "Final Word to the Woman Marchers," *New York Tribune*, 4 May 1912, 1.

45. The NAWSA assumed the most blatantly racist position of any national suffrage organization. Fearing that recognition and inclusion of black women within their ranks would offend some whites, NAWSA leaders consistently deferred to the racist demands of its white southern members. For more on this subject—particularly on how black suffragists responded to racism within the movement—see Rosalyn Terborg-Penn, "African American Women and the Woman Suffrage Movement" and Wanda A. Hendricks, "Ida B. Wells-Barnett and the Alpha Suffrage Club of Chicago," in Wheeler, ed., *One Woman, One Vote*.

46. For the language of white republicanism's place in progressive-era thought, see Mink, "The Lady and the Tramp," 92–122.

47. "Politics," *The Crisis* 5 (April 1913): 267; "Suffrage Paraders," *The Crisis* 5 (April 1913): 297. For more on this incident see Hendricks, "Ida B. Wells-Barnett and the Alpha Suffrage Club," 268–270.

48. Although I have been unable to discover more information about Lin,

her willingness to march for woman suffrage stands in marked contrast to what ethnic studies scholar Judy Yung calls the "detachment Chinese women [in the United States] felt toward the women's suffrage movement in America." Most Chinese-American women felt a greater identification with the struggle for women's emancipation in China. Judy Yung, "The Social Awakening of Chinese American Women as Reported in Chung Sai Yat Po, 1900–1911," in DuBois and Ruiz, eds., *Unequal Sisters*, 201–204.

49. "NAWSA Catching Up With China," *The Woman's Journal*, 11 May 1912.

50. College students and college graduates proved the exception to this rule. They were urged to wear mortar boards and graduation gowns in order to symbolize the advancement of women's education.

51. Halttunen, *Confidence Men and Painted Women*, 181.

52. This is one case where gender, not racial, identity reigned supreme. Nonetheless, it is interesting to speculate about whether or not even white clothing could carry connotations about white racial identity and hegemony. Within the very different context of the Ku Klux Klan, white robes certainly suggested that a racial message was inextricably tied to all other ideological symbols.

53. For examples, see *Biographical Sketch of Gertrude Halliday Leonard*, n.d., NAWSA Papers/LOC; Kathleen McLaughlin, "What Women Have Done with the Vote," *New York Times Magazine*, 24 November 1940, 5; Laura Ellsworth Seiler, "In the Streets" in Sherna Gluck, ed., *From Parlor to Prison: Five American Suffragists Talk About Their Lives* (New York: Vintage, 1976), 190.

54. Florence E. Allen, speech honoring Maud Park, November 1960, n.p., NAWSA Papers/LOC.

55. Brown, "Suffrage and Music," 146.

56. Keeping Up With the Plow," *The Woman Citizen*, 2 June 1917, 10–11. See also "Advertisement for Sweet-Orr & Co. WOMANALLS," *The Woman Citizen*, 9 June 1917, back cover.

57. De Beck, "If he only knew how becoming it would be!," reprinted from *Pittsburgh Gazette Times*, n.d., NAWSA Papers/LOC.

58. For more on the embrace of publicity and male-oriented political tactics, see chapter 2.

59. See, for example, Seiler, "In the Streets," 200.

60. Graham, *Woman Suffrage and the New Democracy*, 60.

61. Susan W. Fitzgerald, "Rules for Open-Air Meetings," *The Woman's Journal*, 30 April 1910, 70.

62. L. E. Behymer, letter to Alice Park, 4 March 1911, Alice Park Collection, Huntington Library.

63. See, for example, Carrie Chapman Catt, letter to Mrs. Elizabeth Lowe Watson, 18 February 1911, Susan B. Anthony Ephemera Collection.

64. Rose Morgan French, letter to Alice Park, 10 October 1914, Park Collection.

65. Carrie Chapman Catt, letter to State Association Presidents, 13 November 1917, NAWSA Papers/LOC. Other examples of the NAWSA issuing public speaking directions include: "Headquarters Letter," *The Woman's Journal*, 29 April 1911, 132; "Program for Federal Amendment Days, enclosure 1 of Resolution Passed by the Board of the NAWSA on Wednesday November 8, 1916," NAWSA Papers/LOC.

66. Miriam Allen DeFord, "On the Soapbox" in *From Parlor to Prison: Five American Suffragists Talk About Their Lives*, 148.

67. Judge Jennie Loitman Barron, *The Women Who Won*, Radio Broadcast *Transcript*, Dick Horne, ed., 25 August 1960, 4, NAWSA Papers/LOC.

68. Unnamed correspondent, letter to Carrie Chapman Catt, 1911, NAWSA Papers/LOC.

69. For more on the exact nature of these social scientific theories and consumer capitalist arguments, see chapter 2.

70. Blatch and Lutz, *Challenging Years*, 129, 180.

71. Maud Wood Park, quoted in Blackwell, "A Glimpse of Miss La Follette." Blatch and Park's arguments parallel those of pioneering psychologist/advertising expert Walter Dill Scott. In an influential 1914 work Scott rejected Adam Smith's notion of rational men making rational economic choices. Scott argued that men and women made choices based on ease, comfort, whim, and suggestion. According to Scott, the best way for advertisers and business people to appeal to customers was to play upon their emotions, desires, and fears. Walter Dill Scott, *Influencing Men in Business: The Psychology of Argument and Suggestion* (New York: Ronald Press, 1914).

72. Kaja Silverman, *The Subject of Semiotics* (New York: Oxford University Press, 1983), 194–236.

73. Cognizant of the profitability and cultural legitimacy offered by middle-class family viewers, theater proprietors, filmmakers, and performers had begun refining and sanitizing their offerings in order to become more widely acceptable. Although working-class audiences still made up the bulk of motion picture audiences, middle-class men and women crowded into film theaters and actually attended them on a more regular basis than other customers. May, *Screening Out the Past*, chapter 6; Peiss, *Cheap Amusements*, especially pages 142–145; Kathy Peiss, "Commercial Leisure and the 'Woman Question' " in Richard Butsch, ed., *For Fun and Profit: The Transformation of Leisure into Consumption* (Philadelphia: Temple University Press, 1990), 105–117.

74. Sloan, *The Loud Silents*, introduction and pages 62, 86.

75. Good descriptions of color and abundance in pageants can be found in Virginia Clark Abbott, "The History of Woman Suffrage and the

League of Women Voters in Cuyahoga County, 1911–1945," unpublished manuscript (1949), 36, NAWSA Papers/LOC; MacKaye, "Art and the Woman's Movement"; "Official Program, Woman Suffrage Procession"; "Party Plans Big Bill at Vaudeville," *The Woman's Journal,* 31 August 1912, 274–275.

76.   "New York Has Big Suffrage Week," *The Woman's Journal,* 14 September 1912, 289.

77.   Tinnin, "Why the Pageant?," 60.

78.   "St. Louis—'The Big Third Act,'" 12.

79.   Glassberg, *American Historical Pageantry,* 115–117.

80.   *Biographical Sketch of Gertrude Halliday Leonard,* NAWSA Papers/LOC.

81.   James S. McQuade, "Chicago Letter," *The Moving Picture World* 21 (September 26, 1914): 1782.

82.   Sloan, *The Loud Silents,* 117.

83.   James S. McQuade, "Your Girl and Mine," *The Moving Picture World* 22 (November 7, 1914): 764, 765.

84.   "Your Girl and Mine," Pamphlet, NAWSA Papers/LOC.

85.   "Big Suffrage Week Opening Winter Season Victoria Theatre," Program, NAWSA Papers/LOC.

86.   See for example, Christine Galley, letter to Miss [Rosamond] Danielson, 28 July 1916, NAWSA Papers/LOC; Katherine Houghton Hepburn, letter to Rosamond Danielson, 1 July 1916, NAWSA Papers/LOC.

87.   Carrie Chapman Catt, "An Address to the Executive Council Including a Report on Campaigns and Surveys, Delivered at its Annual Pre-Convention Meeting," 10 December 1910, 11–13, NAWSA Papers/LOC.

88.   Solomons, *The Girl from Colorado,* n.p.

89.   Robert B. Westbrook, "Politics as Consumption: Managing the Modern American Election," *The Culture of Consumption: Critical Essays in American History, 1880–1980,* 145–173.

90.   For Hollywood's role in World War I jingoism see May, *Screening Out the Past,* chapter 5.

4. From Sunflower Badges to Kewpie Dolls

1.   Mary A. Livermore, "Show Your Colors!," *The Woman's Journal,* 5 May 1894, 137.

2.   I define woman suffrage commodities as objects produced for and by suffragists in order to support and advertise the movement. Despite their variety, these items can be divided into roughly two types: print matter (leaflets, newspapers, and books, for example) and nonprint matter (apparel, jewelry, food, decorative furnishings, and the like). Suffragists—like other reformers—viewed mass-produced literature as vitally important to their work. It brought the tenets of woman suffrage ideology to a

wide and diverse audience. Although seldom as directly edifying in character, nonprint matter also played a critical role in the movement. Badges, hats, and a plethora of other woman suffrage goods gave the movement a material expression that could be comprehended instantly and easily by supporters, detractors, and the perennially disinterested. With several notable exceptions, this chapter concentrates on these nonprint objects.

3. Hall, "Notes on Deconstructing the 'Popular,' " 227–240; Lipsitz, *Time Passages*; Janice Radway, *Reading the Romance: Women, Patriarchy, and Popular Culture* (Chapel Hill: University of North Carolina Press, 1984).

4. Mary Douglas and Baron Isherwood, *The World of Goods* (New York: Basic Books, 1979), 79.

5. John Brewer, "Commercialization and Politics" in McKendrick, Brewer, and Plumb, eds., *The Birth of a Consumer Society*, 238, 239.

6. Sean Wilentz, *Chants Democratic: New York City and the Rise of the American Working Class, 1788–1850* (New York: Oxford University Press, 1984), 88; Edith Mayo, "Campaign Appeals to Women," *Journal of American Culture* 3 (Winter 1980): 722–742; Roger A. Fischer, "1896 Campaign Artifacts: A Study in Inferential Reconstruction," *Journal of American Culture* 3 (Winter 1980): 706–721.

7. Ibid., 707.

8. For more on political party memorabilia directed at women see Mayo, "Campaign Appeals to Women," 722–729.

9. Bloomer, *Life and Writings of Amelia Bloomer*, 78.

10. Frances Willard, *Glimpses of Fifty Years: The Autobiography of an American Woman* (Chicago: Woman's Temperance Publication Association, H. J. Smith and Co., 1889), 430.

11. M.V.L., "The Lone Star of Suffrage," *The Woman's Journal*, 30 July 1892, 246. Suffrage commodities were not unusual in their ability to foster debate. Anthropologist Grant McCracken contends that "goods serve as an opportunity for a group to engage in an internal and external dialogue in which changes are contemplated, debated, and then announced." *Culture and Consumption: New Approaches to the Symbolic Character of Consumer Goods and Activities* (Bloomington: Indiana University Press, 1988), 136.

12. Michael Schudson, *Advertising, the Uneasy Persuasion: Its Dubious Impact on American Society* (New York: Basic Books, 1984), 232.

13. "Sunflower Badge for Suffrage," *The Woman's Journal*, 26 November 1887, 377. For more on the origins of the sunflower badge see Laura M. Johns, "The Origins of Our Badge," *The Woman's Tribune*, 1896, clipping, Susan B. Anthony Ephemera Collection, Clippings 14, 42, Huntington Library.

14. "Good Work in Iowa," *The Woman's Journal*, 28 September 1889, 311; Rachel Foster Avery, "From National American Suffrage Headquarters," *The Woman's Journal*, 6 June 1896, 180.

15. Carrie Chapman Catt, "Woman's Century Calendar" (New York: NAWSA, 1900), NAWSA Papers, Library of Congress.

16. Mary A. Livermore, "Mary Livermore on Fairs," *The Woman's Journal*, 13 January 1900, 16. For more on the importance of bazaars to women's voluntarism see Ginzberg, *Women and the Work of Benevolence*, 46.

17. For a good example of the exacting details that went into the planning of woman suffrage bazaars see Cora Scott Pond, "Bazaar Notes," *The Woman's Journal*, 23 October 1886, 340.

18. McCracken, *Culture and Consumption*, 133.

19. Ibid.

20. C.W., "The Country Store," *The Woman's Journal*, 26 April 1890, 132.

21. Livermore, "Mary Livermore on Fairs," 16.

22. E.D.C., "The Suffrage Bazaar," *The Woman's Journal*, 17 July 1886, 228.

23. "Bazaar Receipts and Expenses," *The Woman's Journal*, 22 January 1887, 29; Carrie Chapman Catt, "Mrs. Chapman Catt's Annual Address," *The Woman's Journal*, 8 June 1901, 175–178.

24. Harriet Taylor Upton and Elizabeth J. Hauser, National Column, *The Woman's Journal*, 16 July 1904, 232; "A Suffrage Exhibit," *The Woman's Journal*, 4 September 1909, 142.

25. Rachel Foster Avery, "From National American Suffrage Headquarters," *The Woman's Journal*, 6 June 1896, 180; "Report of Headquarters Work," *The Woman's Journal*, 6 February 1897, 43.

26. Such ties were not necessarily new to the woman suffrage movement. Even the earliest woman's rights journals, such as *The Lily* and *The Revolution*, included advertisements.

27. Mrs. May McHenry Keith, quoted in Rachel Foster Avery, "Bazar [sic] Notes," *The Woman's Journal*, 29 September 1900, 306.

28. Stanton, Anthony, and Gage, eds., *History of Woman Suffrage* 3:148.

29. Anthony and Harper, eds., *History of Woman Suffrage* 4:323. Interestingly, the owner of the carpet-sweeper factory was a woman, Mrs. M. R. Bissell, although no evidence links her to the suffrage movement.

30. Stanton, Anthony, and Gage, eds., *History of Woman Suffrage* 4:366.

31. Ibid., 436.

32. "Electricity Helps Women," *The Western Electrician*, reprinted in *The Woman's Journal*, 1 August 1908, 121.

33. Flyer, Massachusetts Woman Suffrage Association (November 1915), NAWSA Papers/LOC.

34. Alice Park, "Wear the Badge," *The Woman's Journal*, 27 September 1913, 306.

35. By the time the movement ended in 1920, Park's collection had grown to 178 badges and pins. Park, *Autobiography*. For Park's European travels see Park, letter to Mary McHenry Keith, 2 June 1913, Park Collection.

36. Agnes Ryan, "Suffrage and Style," *The Woman's Journal*, 4 February 1911, 33; Flyer (1911), NAWSA Papers/LOC; Mary Ware Dennett, letter to

Agnes Ryan, 26 May 1913, NAWSA Papers/LOC; "Summer Suffrage Novelties with 'Votes for Women' Slogan," *Headquarters News Letter* 2 (August 15, 1916): 6, NAWSA Papers/LOC; Rose Young, "Suffrage News Bulletin issued for the National American Woman Suffrage Association," 27 April 1917, NAWSA Papers/LOC; Edna Stantial, speech to the Emma Lazarus Clubs of Massachusetts, 1956, NAWSA Papers/LOC.

37.   "A Suffrage Exhibit," *The Woman's Journal*, 4 September 1909, 142.

38.   For an example of this sort of advertising see *The Woman's Journal*, 2 December 1911, 383. The first suffrage catalogs seem to have accompanied the movement's revitalization. Catalogs, however, were by no means a new way of selling goods. Thomas J. Schlereth notes that catalogs "came into their own during the gilded age," led most spectacularly by the Montgomery Ward catalog (1872). With the legislative creation of free parcel post delivery in 1913, consumption via catalog service became much more common. Thomas J. Schlereth, "Country Stores, County Fairs, and Mail-Order Catalogues: Consumption in Rural America," in Simon Bronner, ed., *Consuming Visions*, 364–365; for more on parcel post see Susan Strasser, *Satisfaction Guaranteed: The Making of the American Mass Market* (New York: Pantheon, 1989), 219–221. The NAWSA published its catalog monthly. See Anna DeBaun, letter to suffragists, 1916, NAWSA Papers/LOC. I have located a number of NAWSA catalogs, including those for January 1914, May 1916, and two that are undated. I have also found catalogs of woman suffrage supplies offered by the Illinois Equal Suffrage Association and the New York State Suffrage Association. The Illinois catalog sold printed matter and is included in the "17th Annual Announcement of the Chicago Political Equality League, Program of Convention," 1911–1912, NAWSA Papers/LOC. The New York Association sold a variety of objects; see "Supplies: New York State Suffrage Ass'n," n.d., Helen Brewster Owens Papers, Schlesinger Library.

39.   "The Suffrage Shop," *The Woman Voter and Newsletter*, May 1913, 11, NAWSA Papers/LOC; advertisement, *The Woman Citizen*, 15 September 1917, 296. Harriot Stanton Blatch's militant Women's Political Union also opened a suffrage store in 1913. In 1914, Blatch turned an old lunch wagon into "a roving shop." DuBois, *Harriot Stanton Blatch*, 154.

40.   "Suffrage Shop for Atlantic City," *Headquarters Newsletter* 2 (August 15, 1916): 4, NAWSA Papers/LOC.

41.   Alice Park, unpublished and undated note, Susan B. Anthony Ephemera Collection, Clippings 17.

42.   Park, *Autobiography*, 283.

43.   *Annual Report*, 25, NAWSA Papers/LOC.

44.   "Suffragettes furnish Homemade Food to Hungry Wall Street Brokers,"

clipping, *San Jose Mercury Herald*, 1915, Susan B. Anthony Ephemera Collection, Clippings 16. The Woman Suffrage Party of New York ran the "Votes for Women" restaurant and the Woman Suffrage Party Lunch Room. It is unclear whether the Lunch Room had moved and changed names or whether the restaurant existed in addition to the Lunch Room.

45.   *Big Suffrage Week*, Program, n.d., NAWSA Papers/LOC.

46.   "Suffragettes furnish Homemade Food to Hungry Wall Street Brokers."

47.   The history of mass-produced novelties, particularly those of a humorous character, is outlined in Michael-Jean Erard, "Novelties in Popular American Culture," *Journal of Popular Culture* 25 (Winter 1991): 1–16; see also Steven Heller and Steven Guarnaccia, "Novelties and Practical Jokes in America," *Print* 46 (Nov.–Dec. 1992): 80–86, 144–146. Both articles identity Daddy and Jake's of Boston, founded in 1915, as the first successful novelty store. They also associate the rise of the novelties industry with the birth of the Johnson Smith and Company catalog (1914), which sold a variety of humorous goods and one-of-a-kind items. Trade journals that covered the industry and provided it with a sense of professional identity began shortly before the 1910s. *Toys and Novelties* was established in 1909, and *Novelty News* in 1905.

48.   G. Holzapfel, letter to Rosamond Danielson, 11 May 1915, NAWSA Papers/LOC.

49.   American Specialty Company, letter to Helen B. Owens, 25 August 1915, Owens Papers. The New York State Woman Suffrage Association must have found this offer appealing. In September of that year the Association offered smaller suffrage clubs matchboxes labeled "The more light you get on Woman Suffrage the better it looks" on one side, and "Vote YES (X) on the Woman Suffrage Amendment Nov. 2nd" on the opposite side. Across the end the box read "1,000,000 New York State Women Want the Vote." The boxes sold for $2.80/1000. Ethan M. Cullen, letter to Helen B. Owens, 25 September 1915, Owens Papers.

50.   For more on the Cargill Company and the Butler Brothers Jewelry Company see their joint advertisements: *The Woman's Journal*, 15 October 1910, 171, 172 and *The Woman's Journal*, 22 October 1910, 177, 178.

51.   Purdy, "Notes from New York," 40.

52.   Advertisement, *The Woman Citizen*, 2 June 1917, 2.

53.   Miriam Formanek-Brunell, *Made to Play House: Dolls and the Commercialization of American Girlhood, 1830–1930* (New Haven: Yale University Press, 1993), 127–130.

54.   Advertisement for the Beacon Manufacturing Company, *The Woman's Journal* Papers, Schlesinger Library.

55.   Ibid.; Purdy, "Notes From New York"; and advertisement, *The Woman's Journal*, 15 October 1910, 171.

56. "A New Cracker for the Cause," *The Woman's Journal*, 8 November 1913, 259.

57. A number of newspapers allowed suffragists to publish special "suffrage editions." In these cases, suffragists took over most of the responsibilities of running the paper, including editorial work and advertisement soliciting. The NAWSA tried repeatedly to coordinate efforts so that suffrage editions could be printed simultaneously across the country. In order to ease the burden on local suffragists, the Association offered not only pattern advertisements, but also prewritten articles on a variety of subjects.

58. Mrs. Sara M. Algeo, letter to Mrs. Miller, 30 January 1917, NAWSA Papers/LOC.

59. Mary Ware Dennett, "National Headquarters Letter," *The Woman's Journal*, 20 May 1911, 156.

60. Joe B. Hosmer, "The Ad' Women and Suffrage," *The Woman's Journal*, 5 August 1916, 251.

61. Cott, *The Grounding of Modern Feminism*, especially chapter 5.

62. Dennett, "National Headquarters Letter," 156.

63. Agnes Ryan, "Valentines for Votes," *The Woman's Journal*, 18 February 1911, 56.

64. Ibid.

65. "Women's Rights at Bay Shore," *San Francisco Examiner*, 29 January 1909, Susan B. Anthony Ephemera Collection, Leaflets 2, 62, Huntington Library.

66. Advertisement, *Good Housekeeping* (November 1920):69; see also advertisement for the American Laundry Machinery Company, *Good Housekeeping* (October 1920):187 and advertisements for the Republican Party in *Good Housekeeping* (November 1920):185 and the *Saturday Evening Post* (October 30, 1920):124.

67. Advertisement, *American Magazine*, October 1932, inside front cover.

68. Suffragists were not the only Americans to feel the influence of this aesthetic. Important works by William Leach, Jean-Christophe Agnew, and Richard Wightman Fox indicate that men and women from a variety of perspectives both promoted this mode of perception and found themselves trapped by its confines. See Leach, *Land of Desire*; Jean-Christophe Agnew, " 'A House of Fiction': Domestic Interiors and the Commodity Aesthetic" in Simon J. Bronner, ed., *Consuming Visions*, 133–155; Richard Wightman Fox, "Epitaph for Middletown: Robert S. Lynd and the Analysis of Consumer Culture" in Fox and Lears, eds., *The Culture of Consumption*, 101–141.

69. For a general critique and definition of kitsch see Matei Calenescu, *Five Faces of Modernity: Modernism, Avant-Garde, Decadence, Kitsch, Postmodernism* (Durham: Duke University Press, 1987), 225–262.

70. Andreas Huyssen makes a similar argument about the feminized connotations of mass culture in his important essay "Mass Culture as

Woman: Modernism's Other" in *After the Great Divide: Modernism, Mass Culture, Postmodernism* (Bloomington: Indiana University Press, 1986), 44–62.

71.   Ibid.

72.   For more on this unique candy see Antoinette Funk, letter to Helen Brewster Owens, 27 July 1914, Owens Papers.

73.   Ryan, "Valentines for Votes," 56.

74.   In making kitsch a defining characteristic of suffrage commodities, suffragists may have succeeded in at least re-gendering political memorabilia. According to Edith Mayo, political parties produced an unusually small number of campaign souvenirs between 1916 and 1932. This probably stemmed from a number of factors, including the decline of the party system and new forms of campaigning—many of which reflected the general commercialization of politics. It is interesting to note, however, that the decline in partisan commodities coincided with the steady escalation in the production of suffrage goods. Does a correlation exist? We can only speculate, but perhaps the widespread distribution of sentimentalized suffrage goods so successfully feminized/kitschified the concept of political commodities that male-run political parties minimized their use, fearing that too much campaign paraphernalia might pollute and emasculate their images. Even when it became certain that the national enfranchisement of women would take place, the parties did not return to the large-scale production of campaign souvenirs until the 1930s, after it was clear that women presented no threat to the political status quo, either through voting en masse or through actively joining the electioneering fray.

5. Selling Suffrage News

1.   Agnes E. Ryan, *The Torchbearer: A Look Forward and Back at* The Woman's Journal, *the Organ of the Woman's Movement* (Boston: The Woman's Journal and Suffrage News, 1916).

2.   Sally Stein, "The Graphic Ordering of Desire: Modernization of a Middle-Class Women's Magazine, 1914–1939," *Heresies* 18 (1985): 8.

3.   Flexner, *Century of Struggle*, 82.

4.   Blackwell, *Lucy Stone*, 236.

5.   For a detailed analysis of the paper's early content see Susan Schultz Huxman, "*The Woman's Journal*, 1870–1890: The Torchbearer for Suffrage" in Martha M. Solomon, ed., *A Voice of Their Own: The Woman Suffrage Press, 1840–1910* (Tuscaloosa: University of Alabama Press, 1991), 88.

6.   Flexner, *Century of Struggle*, 156.

7.   Henry Blackwell, "What's in a Name!," *The Woman's Journal*, 22 January 1870, 1.

8. Flexner, *Century of Struggle*, 156.

9. Gerald Baldasty, *The Commercialization of News in the Nineteenth Century* (Madison: University of Wisconsin Press, 1992), chapters 1–4.

10. "Premiums! Premiums!," *The Woman's Journal*, 3 June 1871, 172.

11. Blackwell, *Lucy Stone*, 239–240.

12. Lydia Maria Child, "Handsome and Useful Gifts," *The Woman's Journal*, 7 December 1878, 385; "Farmer Brown's Wash-Day," *The Woman's Journal*, 2 July 1870, 202–203.

13. "Seven Reasons for Advertising," *The Woman's Journal*, 23 December 1899, 405.

14. For more on these reformers see chapter 1.

15. Ryan, 17. *The Torchbearer* gives circulation figures for the years 1908–1915. As noted later, a drop in prices in 1904 led to an increase in circulation. By 1908, circulation was 2,400. Considering the *Journal's* history, and the exuberance with which the editor noted this increase, it is unlikely that circulation had ever before exceeded this figure.

16. Frank Luther Mott, *American Journalism: A History of Newspapers in the United States Through 260 Years: 1690–1950*, rev. ed. (New York: Macmillan, 1950), 507.

17. Frank Luther Mott, *A History of American Magazines, 1885–1905* (Cambridge: Belknap Press, 1957), 17.

18. Huxman, "*The Woman's Journal*, 1870–1890," 91.

19. Agnes E. Ryan, "A Woman's Journal Story," *The Woman's Journal*, 27 March 1915, 97.

20. Neither circulation nor income figures are available for this period. Like most small and mid-size periodicals, the *Journal* probably preferred to reveal as little of this information as possible, especially since advertisers largely based their spending decisions on circulation figures. But editorials and letters make it clear that the *Journal* was consistently losing money. According to one editorial, by 1906 the *Journal* had been losing "thousands" of dollars annually. Alice Stone Blackwell, "Woman's Journal Prospering," *The Woman's Journal*, 27 January 1906, 14.

21. Henry Blackwell, "Another Year," *The Woman's Journal*, 3 January 1874, 4.

22. "Our Twenty-Fifth Birth-Day," *The Woman's Journal*, 5 January 1895, 4.

23. Charlotte Perkins Gilman, "To My Readers in Especial," *The Woman's Journal*, 3 December 1904, 386.

24. Baldasty, *The Commercialization of News in the Nineteenth Century*; see also Mott, *American Journalism*, chapters 36–43.

25. Gilman, "To My Readers in Especial."

26. Alice Stone Blackwell, "A New Departure," *The Woman's Journal*, 10 December 1904, 396.

27. Remarkably, no biography of this fascinating woman exists. The bits and pieces of her life can be pieced together from a number of sources, however, including Lynne Masel-Waters, *American Women Writers* 1, ed.

Lina Mainiero (New York: Ungar, 1979), 164–165; Geoffrey Blodgett, _Notable American Women 1607–1950_, ed. Edward T. James (Cambridge: Belknap Press, 1971), 156–158; _Who Was Who in America 2_ (Chicago: A. N. Marquis, 1963), 2.

28. Ibid.

29. Blackwell, "Woman's Journal Prospering."

30. Since this is the first year for which actual circulation figures are available, it is unclear how significant an increase this represented. As noted earlier, Blackwell specified that subscriptions increased once the price was reduced. Likewise, the exact amount by which deficits fell is unknown. For more specifics about the period immediately following this change see figures 5.1–5.3.

31. Gilman, 153.

32. Susan B. Anthony, quoted in Anthony and Harper, eds., _History of Woman Suffrage_ 4:216.

33. Alice Stone Blackwell and Agnes E. Ryan, "Advantages of Merger," _The Woman's Journal_, 9 July 1910, 110.

34. Ibid.; Alice Stone Blackwell, letter to Mrs. McCulloch, 8 June 1911, Catherine Waugh McCulloch Papers, Schlesinger Library.

35. Ryan, The Torchbearer, 17. The data in figure 5.1 is derived from this source.

36. Theodore Peterson, _Magazines in the Twentieth Century_ (Urbana: University of Illinois Press, 1964), 60.

37. The women who read and worked for the newspaper did not always follow the now standard practice of either underlining or italicizing _The Woman's Journal_ as a title. In recording their words, I have followed their example.

38. Agnes E. Ryan, "Selling _The Woman's Journal_," (Boston: n.d.), n.p., Helen Brewster Owens Papers, Schlesinger Library.

39. Sally Levinson, letter to _The Woman's Journal_, 6 September 1913, NAWSA Papers/LOC.

40. Alice Stone Blackwell, "Push _The Woman's Journal_," 1912?, _Woman's Journal_ Papers, Schlesinger Library.

41. Ryan, "A Woman's Journal Story" in _The Torchbearer_, 17. The data in figures 5.2 and 5.3 is derived from these sources.

42. Ibid.; Blackwell, "Push _The Woman's Journal_."

43. Ibid.

44. Mary Ware Dennett, quoted in "Minutes of the Official Board Meeting, 5 June 1912," NAWSA Papers/LOC.

45. Blackwell, "Push _The Woman's Journal_."

46. Ibid.

47. William R. Taylor, _In Pursuit of Gotham: Culture and Commerce in New York_ (New York and Oxford: Oxford University Press, 1992), 81, 82.

48. Ewen, _PR!_, 54.

49. Stein, "The Graphic Ordering of Desire," 8.

50. Blackwell, "Push *The Woman's Journal.*"

51. Taylor, *In Pursuit of Gotham*, 124, 131.

52. For the battle over the *Journal's* paper stock see Alice Stone Blackwell to Catherine Waugh McCulloch, 9 November 1912, McCulloch Papers; The fight over moving the paper to New York is recalled in Blackwell, "Push *The Woman's Journal.*"

53. Ibid.

54. Sofia M. Loebinger, letter to Alice Park, 3 September 1910, Alice Park Papers, Box 2, Correspondence File, Huntington Library.

55. Agnes E. Ryan, "To Whom it May Concern," *The Woman's Journal*, 19 October 1912, 331. At this time, the paper was officially renamed *The Woman's Journal and Suffrage News.*

56. Blackwell, "Push *The Woman's Journal.*"

57. Ibid.

58. Ryan, *The Torchbearer*, 16–17.

59. Ibid., 44.

60. Ibid., 42–44. For the increase in monthly magazines during this period see Peterson, *Magazines in the Twentieth Century*, 58.

61. Ryan, "A Woman's Journal Story."

62. Agnes Ryan, letter to Anonymous, 31 July 1915, NAWSA Papers/LOC.

63. Agnes Ryan, letter to Suffragists, 24 July 1916, NAWSA Papers/LOC.

64. Agnes Ryan, letter to Elisabeth Freeman, 31 July 1913 (b), NAWSA Papers/LOC.

65. Agnes Ryan, letter to Elisabeth Freeman, 31 July 1913 (a), NAWSA Papers/LOC.

66. Ryan, *The Torchbearer*, 17. See figure 5.1.

67. Harriet J. Roworth, letter to Agnes E. Ryan, 26 January 1913, NAWSA Papers/LOC. Another reader sent a similarly critical letter about the *Journal's* advertisement for the "Roxroy 'fortune-teller.' " "We ought not to go into partnership with a faker," argued the woman. "I believe you can afford to get on without this man's advertising money better than you can with it. I hope you will pardon me for 'presuming to presume' but this sort of advertising seems to me to be too small, too insincere, too uncertain to be associated with the fine, lofty, truthful, splendid purposes of *The Journal.*" Nixon Waterman, letter to Agnes Ryan, 12 September 1913, NAWSA Papers/LOC.

68. Agnes E. Ryan, letter to Harriet J. Roworth, 29 January 1913, NAWSA Papers/LOC. The presence of the *Ladies Home Journal* advertisement in the *Journal* raises its own set of questions. Mainly, why would a magazine that opposed suffrage advertise in the leading prosuffrage newspaper? Although the answer remains a mystery, it does suggest some sort of sea change in public perceptions of suffragists.

69. Ryan, "A Woman's Journal Story."

70.   Ryan, *The Torchbearer*, 52.

71.   Ibid., 59. My calculation of *Journal* expenses covered by contributions includes stock purchases, since it is clear stockholders could expect nothing back from their investment.

72.   Unpublished press release, 16 December 1916, Park Collection, Box 3.

73.   "Announcement," *The Woman's Journal*, 6 January 1917, 1.

74.   Alice Stone Blackwell, "A Happy New Year," *The Woman's Journal*, 6 January 1917, 4.

75.   Blackwell, "Push *The Woman's Journal*."

76.   For the details of the Leslie bequest and the legal battles it provoked see Rose Young, *The Record of the Leslie Woman Suffrage Commission, Inc., 1917–1929* (New York: The Leslie Woman Suffrage Commission, Inc., 1929). In addition to publishing a suffrage magazine, the bureau financed various news, feature stories, and publicity projects.

77.   The terms of the sale are detailed in *Alternative Propositions of the Leslie Woman Suffrage Commission to Alice Stone Blackwell*, 31 March 1917, NAWSA Papers/LOC. Notice of Blackwell's acceptance of the plan is mentioned in *Minutes of the Special Meeting of the Executive Committee of the Leslie Woman Suffrage Committee*, 3 May 1917, NAWSA Papers/LOC.

78.   Clara Hyde, letter to Mary Gray Peck, 16 April 1917, NAWSA Papers/LOC; Young's life is briefly traced in "The Story of Miss Rose Young," *The Woman's Journal*, 17 March 1917, 65, and *Who Was Who in America (Chicago: Marques Who's Who, 1962), 1392*.

79.   "Help Wanted," *The Woman Citizen*, 16 June 1917, 45.

80.   Hyde, letter to Peck.

81.   Rose Young, quoted in the *Annual Meeting of Stockholders of the Woman Citizen Corporation*, 5 March 1920, n.p., NAWSA Papers/LOC.

82.   Young, *Record of the Leslie Woman Suffrage Commission*, 77.

83.   Brown, "Suffrage and Music," 205.

84.   *Minutes of the Special Meeting of the Leslie Woman Suffrage Commission*, 26 June 1924, 225, NAWSA Papers/LOC.

85.   Brown, "Suffrage and Music," 204. The commission chose Brown largely because of her husband's expertise. When Catt told Brown that the commission wanted her to take charge of the magazine, Brown expressed reservations, noting that she knew nothing about publishing a periodical. " 'Oh, but your husband knows all about running a magazine, and he will help you,' " encouraged Catt.

86.   Ibid., 208. Exact circulation figures remain unclear for this period.

87.   Before the depression, the average circulation of the 365 magazines was even higher; in 1929 it was almost 95,000. Peterson, *Magazines in the Twentieth Century*, 59–60.

88.   Carrie Chapman Catt, quoted in the "Minutes of the Annual Suffrage Meeting of the Leslie Woman Suffrage Commission," 29 July 1929, 6–7, NAWSA Papers/LOC.

89.   Ibid.

90.   Ibid.

91.   Caroline Slade, letter to Carrie Chapman Catt, 19 July 1929, NAWSA Papers/LOC.

92.   Brown, "Suffrage and Music," 209.

93.   Ibid.

94.   Mrs. Edna S. Blair, letter to Agnes Ryan, 28 September 1913, NAWSA Papers/LOC.

95.   Jennifer Scanlon, *Inarticulate Longings: The* Ladies' Home Journal, *Gender, and the Promises of Consumer Culture* (New York: Routledge, 1995), 183–188.

96.   Jessie Anthony, "The Diary of a Newsy: On Selling Suffrage Papers on a London Street Corner," unpublished manuscript, 1911, Anthony Family Papers: Jessie Anthony Papers, Huntington Library.

6. RINGING IN A NEW DAY

1.   "Joy Bells from Cape Cod to Seattle," *The Woman Citizen*, 18 September 1920, 436.

2.   Untitled, unpublished description of Suffrage Victory, 1920, NAWSA Papers, Library of Congress.

3.   DuBois, *Harriot Stanton Blatch*, chapter 6 is a recent exception.

4.   Genevieve Gardner McBride, "No 'Season of Silence': Uses of 'Public Relations' in Nineteenth- and Early Twentieth-Century Reform Movements in Wisconsin," (Ph.D. dissertation, University of Wisconsin-Madison, 1989), 301.

5.   Michael McGerr, "Political Style and Women's Power, 1830–1930," *Journal of American History* 77 (December 1990): 864–885.

6.   Harriet Taylor Upton, "Women Demand Lower Prices," *The Woman Citizen*, 6 September 1919, 345.

7.   McGerr, "Political Style and Women's Power"; Cott, *The Grounding of Modern Feminism*; Sara M. Evans, *Born for Liberty: A History of Women in America* (New York: The Free Press, 1989).

8.   McGerr, "Political Style and Women's Power"; Cott, *The Grounding of Modern Feminism*; Theda Skocpol, *Protecting Soldiers and Mothers: The Political Origins of Social Policy in the United States* (Cambridge, Mass.: Belknap Press, 1992).

9.   See especially Cott's analysis of the failure of the Equal Rights Amendment in the 1920s, *The Grounding of Modern Feminism*, chapter 4.

10.   "National League of Women Voters General Plan of Work for 1922–23," (1922), n.p., NAWSA Papers/LOC.

11.   "Minutes, Special Meeting Leslie Commission," 20 September 1922, NAWSA Papers/LOC.

12. Liette Gitlow, "The Culture of Politics: The Get-Out-the-Vote Campaigns and the Commodification of Political Culture, 1920–1929," Paper delivered at the American Historical Association Annual Meeting, Atlanta, Georgia, 1996.

13. Marjorie Shuler, "Questioning Candidates," magazine clipping, 1921, NAWSA Papers/LOC.

14. McGerr, *The Decline of Popular Politics*, chapter 6.

15. See, for example, Westbrook, "Politics as Consumption," 143–173, and Greg Mitchell, *The Campaign of the Century: Upton Sinclair's Race for Governor of California and the Birth of Media Politics* (New York: Random House, 1992).

16. Scanlon, *Inarticulate Longings*, 183–188.

Index